Created and Directed by Hans Höfer

INSIGHT GUIDES

Madeira

Edited by Ute York
Main photography: G.P. Reichelt, Gerhard Oberzill
Translated by Graham Fulton Smith, Sarah Byrt and
Rodney Shaw

APA PUBLICATIONS

MADEIRA

First Edition (2nd Reprint)
© 1993 APA PUBLICATIONS (HK) LTD
All Rights Reserved
Printed in Singapore by Höfer Press Pte. Ltd

Distributed in the United States by:	Distributed in Canada by:	Distributed in the UK & Ireland by:	Worldwide distribution enquiries:
Houghton Mifflin Company	**Thomas Allen & Son**	**GeoCenter International UK Ltd**	**Höfer Communications Pte Ltd**
2 Park Street	390 Steelcase Road East	The Viables Center, Harrow Way	38 Joo Koon Road
Boston, Massachusetts 02108	Markham, Ontario L3R 1G2	Basingstoke, Hampshire RG22 4BJ	Singapore 2262
ISBN: 0-395-66434-9	ISBN: 0-395-66434-9	ISBN: 9-62421-154-X	ISBN: 9-62421-154-X

ABOUT THIS BOOK

The relatively small amount of literature published on Madeira does not really reflect the appeal of this island paradise stuck out in the middle of the Atlantic. But Madeira has been the destination of discerning voyagers for centuries. Elisabeth, Empress of Austria, found solace from her woes on Madeira and Sir Winston Churchill came here to find peace and quiet and to paint its beautiful scenery. Packed with superb photography and authoritative texts, *Insight Guide: Madeira* reveals the magic of the island to a broader public, rolling all its fascinating aspects – its history, its culture, its flowers, its wine and its breathtaking scenery – into one complete volume.

The Authors

The task of bringing all the diversity of Madeira under one roof was entrusted by Apa Publications to project editor **Ute York**, a travel journalist and author from Munich. She had three good reasons for creating a book on Madeira: firstly she loves islands, secondly she is fascinated by their history, and finally she is passionately fond of flowers. Her own contributions to the book include the essay on the origins of the island, the chapters "Columbus and Madeira", "Early travellers – Distinguished Visitors" and a description of the wonderful contraptions the Madeirans once used for getting about their steep and rugged island.

All the authors involved in the project are experts in one or another or a combination of many Madeiran topics. Although Dieter Clarius spends much of his time working on a Rhenish newspaper, his chief interest is Madeira. Every spare moment is spent on the island, discovering all the latest information for his tourist pamphlet for Germans, *Madeira Aktuell*. In *Insight Guide: Madeira* he guides us along his favourite hiking trails, writes about the parts played by piracy and slavery in the island's history, and documents the conditions of poverty in which a fair number of the islanders now have to live.

Journalist **Martina Emonts** has gone a step further. She gave up her job with a German newspaper to settle on Madeira, although it must be said that the pangs of love also played a part in this decision. She has now lived there for five years as the wife of a Madeiran ship captain in Funchal. She speaks Portuguese as if she had been born on the island and her job of teaching German to students and tour guides helps her to keep right up to date on all the island news. She compiled the Travel Tips section of the book as well as writing "Excursions and Tours", "Porto Santo" and the articles describing important local crafts – embroidery and wickerwork and those distinctive blue tiles that adorn so many house and church walls on the island.

Petra Deimer is a marine biologist and lives as a journalist and author in Hamburg. She chairs the Society for the Protection of Sea Mammals and participated in the establishment of Madeira's marine national park. Here she gives a personal account of how one-time whalers have now converted to become whale protectors.

The Munich journalist **Cornelia von Schelling** feels at home on Madeira because it is one of the places in which her mother tongue is spoken: she grew up in Brazil. She was responsible for describing the role of women on Madeira, a piece which could not

York

Emonts

C. v. Schelling

Clarius

Deimer

have been written in such depth without her knowledge of the language, as well as the article "Melting Pot Madeira" about the island's rich racial mix. She also wrote about Madeira's historically tense relationship with Portugal, its traditionally good relationship with England and the famous Reid's Hotel.

Christa Eder worked for many years in the editorial department of a popular German women's magazine. Today she combines her love of cooking with her unquenchable passion for travel. Few secrets of Madeiran cooking have eluded her article on the island's cuisine.

For the Munich botanist **Dr Günther Hebel**, there is no more worthwhile trip than to the plant world of Madeira. He knows the name of every single plant and feels a sense of euphoria whenever the subject of Madeira is mentioned.

The Viennese writer and photographer **Gerhard H. Oberzill**, author of the chapter on Funchal, says he feels at home anywhere in the world, a fact to which many travel books and articles bearing his name are testimony. He could, he says, have written about Funchal from memory, because he knows every inch of Madeira. Quite a number of the photographs in this book come from his archives.

To research the history of the discovery and settlement of Madeira, **Paul Otto Schultz** burrowed deep into the archives of the national library. The fascinating snippets of information he stumbled upon are contained in his "Tales of Discovery".

The Photographers

Most of the photographs in the book were submitted by the Hamburg photographer and **G.P. Reichelt**. According to Reichelt, the island is "almost as nice as Bali".

Other photographers who made a substantial contributions include **Leonore Ander** and **Thomas Grimm** from Hamburg.

Thanks are due to all the many others who with their knowledge and assistance have contributed to the creation of this book. On Madeira itself, special thanks go to **Dona Maria Luisa**, **Dona Fátima** and **Antonio** from Tourismo in Funchal, **Dr Freitas** from the Museu Dr Frederico Freitas, **Augustios Vasconzelos**, **Doris Abrantes**, **Augustinho** and **Leandro** from the Institute of Handicrafts and **Costa Neves** from the national park authority.

The translation into English was overseen by **Tony Halliday** and the English edition was supervised in Apa's London editorial office by **Dorothy Stannard**.

Heubl   *Oberzill*   *Reichelt*   *Ander*   *Grimm*

History and Culture

TRAVEL TIPS

The "Island of Eternal Springtime", "Lovers' Isle" or the "Pearl of the Atlantic" are just a few of the epithets awarded to Madeira by visitors from all over the world. The natural charm and beauty of the island hasn't changed since it was first settled by the Portuguese in the 15th century.

In the beginning it was sugar, the island's "white gold", which drew foreign visitors to the island. It was followed by the legendary Madeira wine – already familiar to connoisseurs in Shakespeare's time. Today, it is the unique character of the island's landscape, the splendour and variety of its exotic vegetation and the mild climate which makes Madeira a favourite choice among nature lovers, hikers and holiday-makers who simply want to relax in comfort – and do so at any time of the year.

Few islands in the world can offer such a varied and spectacular landscape over a small area of only 286 sq. miles (741 sq. km). The southern mountain slopes, once carpeted with laurel woods, are now covered in picturesque terraces growing local produce. The relatively inaccessible mountain region of the interior offers hikers and intrepid drivers ever-changing views of misty gorges, green valleys and deserted plateaux. Along the coast, the eye is caught by bizarre formations of lava, towering cliffs splashed by foaming surf and the offshore islands of Porto Santo and the Desertas – sanctuaries for seals, fish and birds.

In addition, Madeira offers a lively history enhanced by romantic legends about its discovery, controversy regarding its historical relations with Portugal – the mother country – and an intriguing "British connection".

But it is not just the picaresque and picturesque that are explored in *Insight Guide: Madeira*; the book also focuses on the island's problems, in particular its appalling poverty and low average income, which at £120 a month per head of population is one of the lowest in Europe.

Now Madeira is pinning its hopes on membership of the European Community, with its markets for wine and tropical fruit. Above all, it is the growth of tourism which offers most economic promise for the island. Madeirans like to distinguish between two types of visitors: those who return again and again, and those who visit just the once. We trust you will join that group of travellers which returns regularly to the island. But to regulars and newcomers alike, Bemvido a Madeira! – Welcome to Madeira!

Preceding pages: dolphins off Madeira; a detail of the choir stalls in Funchal's cathedral; basking in the sun; breaktime for fishermen. **Left,** the view from Cabo Girão.

ORIGINS IN MYTHOLOGY

We know most facts about this small island paradise set in the middle of the Atlantic, including the height of its tallest mountain (Pico Ruivo: 6,107 ft/1,861 metres), the exact number of plants growing there (112 species comprising 760 varieties, of which 16 originally grew only on Madeira), and the average rainfall in Funchal during April (1.37 inches/35.3 mm).

We also know that the "Atlantic's floating flower pot", as it is frequently dubbed, is a massive chunk of rock rising about 20,000 ft (6,000 metres) above the sea bed. Only the top 6,107 ft (1,861 metres) tower above the waves. It boasts a length of 38 miles (61 km) and a breadth of just 16 miles (25 km), though the fact that it is so heavily piled with mountains makes distances appear much longer to the walker or motorist.

However, what scientists cannot agree upon are the more fundamental questions about the island – how the rocky mass really came into being. Myths and theories abound about the origins of Madeira, including the speculation that it is the remains of Atlantis – the last remnant of the fabled civilisation engulfed by the great ocean floods 80,000 years ago and said to have sunk west of the Straits of Gibraltar.

More serious theories believe that Madeira is of volcanic origin, but scientists are still unable to agree on whether the vast underwater eruptions which produced it occurred some 30 million years ago or 5 million years later, or whether the cauldron encircled by steep rocky walls at Curral das Freiras is an extinct volcano or merely a product of erosion.

More interesting for most visitors to Madeira, however, is the speculation that, together with the Canary Islands, the Azores, the Cape Verde Islands, the Caribbean Islands and Iceland, Madeira could be a remnant of the mysterious Lemurian mainland, thought to have once been located between America, Africa and Europe. Unlikely though it may sound, this theory is not without some foundation, most notably in finds of fossilised plants which have been extinct since time immemorial. Einstein himself once pondered on this possibility.

DO DI CASTEL VIMIOSO

LA MADERA

E CASTEL MELHOR

Villa do Machico

Punta de Laurentio

*Isola di Madera, ò due Bois
la più settentrionale delle Canarie
scoperta nel 1420
da Gion Consalues, e Tristano Varca per nome
dell'Infante Henrico di Portogallo*

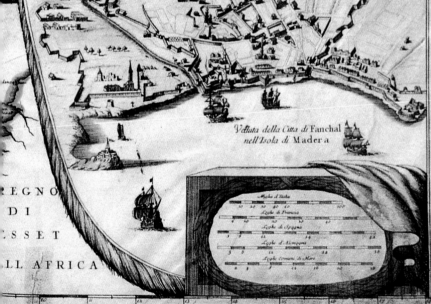

Oriente

*Veduta della Città di Fanchal
nell'Isola di Madera*

REGNO
DI
FESSET

NELL AFRICA

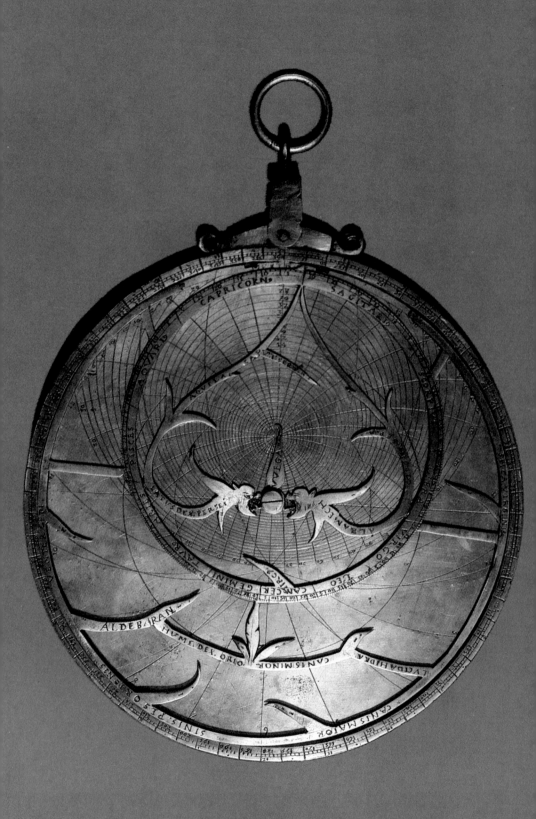

There are numerous theories relating to the discovery of Madeira; most are based on legend rather than historical evidence, though the fact that they have elements in common suggests that they may contain some grains of truth. The first concerns a tragic love story of an English nobleman written by the medieval chronicler Valentine Ferdinand (alias Fernandes), a printer from Bohemia who lived in Lisbon from 1495 to 1561. The tale he wrote includes what is thought to be the oldest accounts (in Latin) of the islands of Madeira and Porto Santo.

Where he found his sources for this tale is a matter of speculation. It seems likely that since the industrious Fernandes also worked as an interpreter and agent for European trading companies, he heard about the fate of the exiled English nobleman and his beloved in a Funchal harbour inn, where he would have consorted with captains, shipowners and merchants. In that era, vessels would sail into port with crews of cabin-fevered adventurers who could scarcely wait to share their experiences – and wildest fantasies – with an astonished world.

Fernandes, like Shakespeare, was well aware that the common folk of his time – 15th-century Portugal – enjoyed nothing more than hearing about the deeds of their betters and so incorporated the yarn of the nobleman and the discovery of Madeira into one of his stories. The facts, as far as we know them, therefore, are mixed with a generous portion of fiction, but they seem to indicate that the originator and the tellers of the love story – who would have added their own embellishments of course – were Christian seafarers.

The legend: According to the story, the nobleman, Sir Robert Machin (or Machyn), was exiled from England for unknown reasons. He purchased a small ship and had his goods and chattels taken on board together with several goats to provide milk and meat for the journey. He was accompanied by his

crew and his concubine – a mistress of lower social standing. The object of his voyage was Portugal, but the travellers were caught in a storm near the island of Berlenga, and this swept them southwards until they suddenly sighted land. Machin and his crew went ashore, taking the goats with them.

The land is thought to have been Porto Santo, because when visibility improved "they saw more land across the sea and sailed over there to see what sort of a country it was." The ship anchored in a bay, which they

called "Machin". (Later, the theory goes, the Castilians "Iberianised" the name of the bay, calling it Machico; a port on the east coast of Madeira still bears this name today.)

Machin, assuming control of their misfortune, instructed his crew to set up camp on the shores of the bay and went off alone to explore the island. On returning from his foray three days later he found that the crew had mutinied and disappeared with his ship, leaving only his page and mistress behind. The treacherous crew had tried to talk them into going with them, but, loyal to the last, they refused, saying: "God would not want us to desert our master."

Preceding pages: the history of Madeira's origins is unclear; a 17th-century chart of the islands. **Left,** nautical aids of bygone days. **Right,** Henry the Navigator, the king of discoverers.

Life on the desert island could not have been sweet, even for the lovers. Distressed by the hopelessness of their situation, Machin's mistress gave up hope and died "of grief". According to the tale, Sir Robert built a small chapel to serve as her last resting place and called it Santa Cruz.

But the tale doesn't end there. As in all good stories, the evil crew were punished for their treachery. Their plans for escape were thwarted when another violent storm blew up and drove their ship on to Morocco's Barbary Coast. There they were captured by the Moors and thrown into prison.

Machin and his page were determined to return to civilisation. Managing to build a

raft, they put out to sea but they, too, ran into a savage storm and were tossed on to the very same beach where the disloyal crew had been captured.

The two castaways were duly captured by the Moors and imprisoned with the traitors. It was Sir Robert's opportunity to avenge the treachery which he believed had ruined their best chance of escape from the island. In fury, he jumped on the first seaman he could lay his hands on, ready to kill him.

It was this which, according to the tale, led to the wider discovery of Madeira. The Moors were so surprised at such violence among countrymen and co-religionists that they reported it to the King of Fez. He summoned them to appear before him. The King thus came to learn of the existence of Madeira, but "since he could gain no profit from the island", he dispatched Sir Robert Machin to King John I of Castile to report on the island's existence and ask the Castilian monarch if *he* would like to benefit from its discovery. King John, however, was far too busy waging war to be much interested in taking Madeira.

Variations on a common theme: There are many different versions of this story; some are very elaborate, others straight to the point. Most of them are based on a version produced about 150 years after the one by Fernandes: *Epanáfora Amorosa*, written by Francisco Manuel de Melo in 1654. The charm of this version is enhanced by its lavish baroque setting: Sir Robert Machin's martyrdom in the dungeons of the infidels is a motif El Greco would have been proud to immortalise on canvas. Melo calls Machin *o Machino*.

As in the Fernandes version, the hero is a member of the lower nobility, and a rather earnest type of person with no time for Edward III's courtiers, whose favourite pastimes are jousting and carousing with wine and women. Sir Robert operates on an altogether higher plane and in this version – unlike Fernandes', in which the heroine is low-born – Sir Robert breaks the rules of etiquette by falling in love with Ana de Erfert, a "most exquisite" young lady and the toast of Edward III's court. Ana, pledged by her father to a nobleman of much higher rank, falls "hopelessly" in love with Robert. To prevent a misalliance between Ana and a simple knight, Ana's father has the wedding date brought forward and Robert is thrown into prison. Miraculously, he manages to escape. The young lovers flee and board a ship for France.

As in the other version, their plans are disrupted by a tempest. After 13 days drifting hopelessly at sea, they sight a densely wooded island. The couple, accompanied by their friends and servants, spend three tranquil and presumably happy days on the uninhabited island. Then, just as they return to ship, another storm blows up and propels the ship and its crew to the Moroccan coast, where the crew are captured and imprisoned. Ana, who, like Fernandes' heroine, seems to have had a frail constitution, dies three days later of a broken heart. A grief-stricken Robert o Machino buries his beloved Ana and lays wreaths of flowers on her grave. (A later version written by Canon Dias Leite even tells of a moving epitaph in Latin.) Robert's subsequent sea voyage on a makeshift raft naturally has a stormy ending, and he, too, is captured by the Moors and left to waste away in a dungeon.

Before the incarcerated Robert o Machino dies, however, he tells the story of his lamentable odyssey to a Castilian cellmate. He is made of sterner stuff than the grief-stricken Robert. After the payment of ransom money, the Castilian returns to his home country with the news of the discovery of Madeira.

(Wood Island), but it is known that the neighbouring Canary Islands were visited long before the days of the Italian, Aragonese and Mallorcan seafarers. From there, Madeira is clearly visible and reachable (especially with a little help from one of the Atlantic's frequent storms), and there was considerable shipping traffic in these waters during the first half of the 14th century.

The facts are few but undiputed. At the beginning of the century – and some historians set the date at 1312 – a Genoese called Lancelotto Malocelo, tried to establish a colony on the island he named after himself, Lanzarote. But the occupying forces of Lancelotto Malocelo failed to consolidate

The historical version: Fantasy isn't left out of the historians' version of the discovery of Madeira either. They attribute its discovery to the ancient seafarers, the Phoenicians, who plied the Mediterranean coast on their trading ventures for centuries, frequently stopping off at such islands as Madeira for shelter and water. They believe that after the Phoenicians the island fell into oblivion.

Exactly when it was rediscovered is uncertain. A Florentine map dating back to 1351 shows Madeira as the "Isola di Legnane"

Left, Portugal has a long tradition of discoverers. **Above**, an exact replica of an old caravel.

their hold on the island due to the fierce resistance of the local Guanche tribe, who still appeared to be living in the Ice Age. The tribesmen beat back the invaders with their primitive weapons and killed Malocelus.

In 1342, the Castilians also took part in expeditions to the Canary Islands, and in 1344, Luis de la Cerda, a descendant of King Alfonso X of Castile, drew up a bold plan to conquer a large group of legendary islands, among them the Canary Islands.The Pope gave his blessing to this project, appealing to the kings and princes of Christianity to join de la Cerda in a crusade against the heathen islanders. But, with more tangible affairs of state to attend to, they left Luis de la Cerda to day-dream on his own.

Alfonso IV of Portugal (1325–57) called upon the Pope to validate him as ruler of the Canary Islands. He claimed that he had been sending sailing ships to the Canaries for many years, and that Portugal was the European kingdom closest to these islands. Madeira was only a short distance away from the direct Canary Islands route, and on this wooded island his vassals were able to obtain timber and fresh water, as well as fresh meat – presumably from the descendants of poor Robert Machin's goats.

Famous seaman: In 1415, Portugal managed to establish a foothold on the African

wind, and commissioned seafarers to discover new routes to India and China. His main aim was to exploit the rich resources of these countries.

But the lands he "discovered" were not all desolate or even unknown to others. "There is some misunderstanding over the two words 'discover' and 'discovery'," writes Salvador de Madariaga, the Spanish biographer of Christopher Columbus. "They are interpreted far too narrowly, as though a seafarer or cosmographer speaking of discovering a certain country necessarily means wild and unexplored territory. That is not the case. For people in the 15th and 16th centuries 'discovery' meant nothing less than 'integration

continent: Morocco's seaport of Ceuta was besieged and taken, an event marking the beginning of an era of Portugal's worldwide expansion. It was at Ceuta that a young Portuguese prince soon started to make a name for himself: Infante Dom Henrique, known in our history books as Henry the Navigator (1394–1460). He collected all the latest information concerning navigation, cosmography, sea maps, shipping, newly discovered countries and coastal regions, all of which he had evaluated at his "documentation centre" in Sagres in the western Algarve. He designed a brand-new type of ship, the caravel, which could sail against the

in the Christian community'."

Nonetheless Henry the Navigator was a driving force in the discovery of the world beyond the established trade routes. Seafarers cautiously nosed their vessels southwards along the West African coast. Cape Juby (Cape Bojador) was not navigated until 1434. Even the most seasoned seafarers had not dared to venture beyond the cape, believing that behind it lurked the bottomless depths of the "Dark Sea" and preferring to stay put on the latitude of the Canary Islands. Time and time again, an impatient Henry the Navigator tried to dispel their fears by producing hard facts. He finally managed to cajole them into sailing farther south with bribes and promises of land.

Reports of the new exploration gradually aroused interest in Africa – or rather in the exploitation of Africa's riches. Trade relations were established, with forts and trading companies springing up all along the African coast. The most coveted commodities were gold, ivory, pepper, sugar cane – and slaves.

Henry the Navigator was one of the first to bring black Africans back to Ceuta. His purpose was to have them made into good Christians, but others had less worthy ideas about the black Africans' fate. In 1441, Antão Gonçalves took the first slaves to Madrid. Henry could not prevail against the general

and the other islands were settled" of two veteran knights who asked the Infante for permission to lead a "fleet against the Moors". Instead, he employed them to go off to Guinea, an exploration he had been planning for some time. Their sailing ship never reached Guinea, for they, too, ran into one of the region's ferocious storms and were swept away to Porto Santo. They landed safely and after exploring the island decided it was suitable for settlement. The chronicle does not actually assert that the knights discovered Porto Santo but does say that they were the first Portuguese to carry out any climatic, geological and hydrographic studies there, albeit of a rather rudimentary nature.

view that there was nothing morally wrong with slave traffic, which was growing into a lucrative business.

The fall of the Moorish port of Ceuta created a new thirst for action and adventure in Portugal. Two knights in particular, who had fought boldly in the siege of Ceuta, were eager to reap more glory. In his *Crónica dos Feitos da Guiné,* one Gomes Eanes de Azurara tells in the chapter "How Madeira

Left, the Chapel of Machico. Above, the discoverers are thought to have landed in the Bay of Machico. Following page: remnants of Manueline art.

According to Valentine Ferdinand, the chronicler with whom this chapter begins, one of the Portuguese knights, João Gonçalves Zarco, had been told about the existence of Madeira by a Castilian. Ferdinand also mentions two companions with whom Zarco had arranged to organise the island settlement project: Tristão Vaz Teixeira and Bartolomeu Perestrelo.

History constantly spotlights successful men of action, figures like these three dauntless Portuguese knights, who in the best traditions of their times and station, set out in search of fame and fortune, never sure where their journey would take them.

ARCHITECTURE OF
THE DISCOVERERS

Visitors to Madeira encounter not only the famous art periods of Gothic and baroque, but also the local Manueline style, the "architecture of the discoverers". It is named after Don Manuel, a member of the Portuguese ruling house of Aviz, who in 1484 succeeded his murdered brother Diego as Grand Master of the Knight Templars and Regent of the Archipelago. He was crowned King of Portugal 11 years later. Historians named him *O Venturoso*, "The Fortunate", because it was under Manuel I that the country's golden age of discovery, world trade and cultural refinement began.

The foundation stone for this era was laid three-quarters of a century earlier by Henry the Navigator (who, incidentally, ventured to sea only once, and that was on the crossing to Ceuta to conquer the Moorish "infidels"). Henry founded a nautical academy at Sagres on the southwest tip of Portugal, where, with remarkable military precision, he drew up a strategy to conquer the world.

To help him, he recruited the services of geographers, astronomers, shipbuilding engineers and naval captains who hailed from every European seafaring nation. Equipped with the knowledge that the earth was round (decades before Columbus), and with the Arab astrolabe and various other navigation aids at their disposal, the intrepid and treasure-hungry adventurers set sail in their three-masted caravel vessels.

In 1419, they reached Madeira, in 1430 the Azores, in 1470 the equator; in 1488, Bartolomeu Diaz rounded the southern tip of Africa and named it the "Cape of Storms" (only later were seafarers confident enough to rename it the Cape of Good Hope). One year later, Vasco da Gama discovered the sea route to India's Malabar Coast; in 1500, Pedro Cabral set foot on Brazilian soil; and in 1521, Fernão Magalhães – albeit under the Spanish flag – embarked on the first attempt to sail round the world.

The successful sea voyages and the discovery of far-away countries were reflected in the art of the period. The basic architectural style did not alter; on Madeira it was late Gothic, in the mother country, a transition to Renaissance could be observed. But when the stonemasons went to work on the buildings, they gave them an elaborate baroque flair and portals and façades were predominantly enhanced with nautical motifs: looped ropes, anchors, fishing nets, astronomical instruments, coats of arms, marine animals, and exotic themes all brought back by the discoverers of the "New World".

The finest examples of the Manueline style originated on the mainland: in the Monastery of the Hieronymites and the Tower of Lisbon's Belém suburb, in the Batalha Monastery and the Castle of the Knights Templar at Tomar.

On Madeira, however, stone embellishments were less prolific. Firstly, the island was still provincial, despite its strategic importance and economic prosperity, and secondly, the artists – in particular the cathedral's master builder, Pedro Eanes – came from Alentejo, the barren flatlands and the hills "beyond the Tejo", which flows through the city of Lisbon. Instead of importing European trends they tended to look to the Moorish influences in Spain for inspiration, in particular, the *azulejos* – the famous blue tiles – and their fine geometrical patterns.

The best examples of the Madeiran version of Manueline style are to be found in the park of Funchal's Quinta das Cruzes, the one-time estate of Madeira's discoverer Gonçalves Zarco. It has now been turned into an "archaeological garden" containing a display of relics from all over the island, including two fine window cases which were rescued from the demolition of an old town house dating from 1507.

The Oriental ornamentation already referred to can be seen at its best on the superb Moorish-style ceilings of the parish church at Calheta on the southwest coast of the island and in the capital's cathedral. Other notable remains of the Manueline architectural style include the ornaments on the apse of the cathedral and on Funchal's Old Customs House, the interiors of the Church of Our Lady at Estreito da Calheta and the parish church at Santa Cruz.

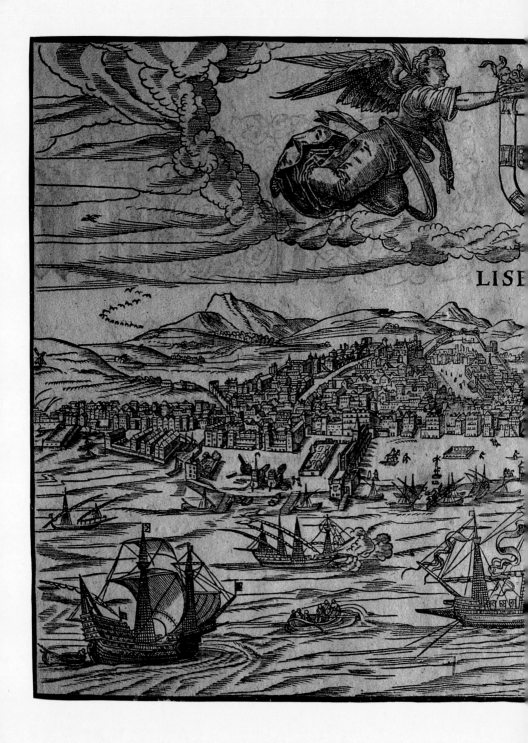

LISE

The beginning of settlement on Madeira is dated at 1425. Considerable progress must have already been made by the time Henry the Navigator transferred areas of land to three *capitanos*, naval captains, on behalf of King João I. It was a transfer which was not quite legal because Henry was only the king's youngest son. Nevertheless, the measure was officially approved, and the *capitanos* received their land as *donatàrias*, i.e. in the form of donations or hereditary fiefs. In return, they assumed responsibility for the

economic development and the maintenance of law and order in their respective fiefdoms. The monarch retained his feudal rights, in particular his supreme authority of command. This arrangement is confirmed by a document signed by King João I in 1433.

Donatores and capitanos: The land was allotted as follows: Machico was given to Teixeira (1440), Porto Santo to Perestrelo (1444), and Funchal to Zarco (1450). The *capitanos* then set about investing trustworthy subordinates or other applicants with special rights – for instance the right to operate sugar mills, to bake bread or produce salt – for which charges were naturally made.

Part of these payments flowed back into the coffers of the donor, which Henry used to finance his expeditions and support the Order of the Knight Templars, of which he was Grand Master. Naturally, the king also imposed taxes. Trustworthy settlers were given land to cultivate, which after five years became their own property, assuming that the *capitanos* were satisfied with the state of the plantations. Alfonso V "The African" (1432–82) ultimately confirmed the legal situation in the archipelago, much to the delight of the *capitanos*.

Funchal and Machico soon developed into flourishing towns, the former becoming the major trading centre in the Atlantic. When Prince Henry the Navigator died in 1460, he was succeeded in office by his adopted son, the Infante Fernando, and then by his widow as guardian of Duke Diogo, her younger son. Diogo was executed some years later for allegedly conspiring against King João II (1455–95), and the office passed to the young Duke of Beja. Following his accession to the throne as Manuel I in 1495, patronage of the island of Madeira passed once and for all to the Portuguese Crown. This put an end to the frequent outbreaks of open resistance to the Crown by the island's noble families whose loyalty to the donor had been stronger than to the king.

Early boom: Manuel's commitment to the cultural development of the arts in the archipelago is manifested by the numerous edifices constructed in Manueline style. But the settlers also erected their own monuments: the *poios*, the cultivated terraces with their unique irrigation channels, and the *levadas*, which fringe the steep flanks of the mountains like a covering of fine lace.

Wine, grain and sugar cane were grown on the island from the very beginning. A document from the year 1461 already emphasises the importance of these products as export commodities. Mention is also made of "dragon's blood", the sap of the *dracaena* tree, and *orseille*, a red plant dye. But in those early days, it was grain that proved to be vital for colonisation. The early settlers brought useful plants, farming know-how and implements from the Iberian peninsula to the archipelago. In 1452, the first consignment of slaves – negroes from Africa and Guanches from the Canaries – was shipped over to work in the lucrative sugar-cane plantations. One can well imagine what status these natives enjoyed in the islands' wealthy society.

Indeed, economic prosperity on the islands was astonishing. The basis of the boom was the highly fertile soil. According to the historians Francisco Alcoforade and Diego Gomes, 650 bushels of grain were grown from one bushel of seed, compared with a maximum of 40 bushels in Europe. Nevertheless, by 1466 the islands were already importing grain; in 1478, there was only enough grain for two months, and in 1485 famine broke out.

The reason for this was that it was far more profitable to grow sugar, and the cornfields gradually gave way to the prolific sugar plantations, But profitable as it was, the cultivation of sugar cane rapidly impoverished the soil. As a result, the Azores grew into the granary of the archipelago, and of Madeira. The market in the Mediterranean region and in northern Europe developed an almost insatiable appetite for the "white gold" from Madeira. The production curve soared to 205 percent between 1450 and 1506 before rapidly plunging to the 60 percent mark. The soil was exhausted and from 1530 onwards sugar cane was replaced by vines from Cyprus and Crete.

Merchants and noblemen: Initially, Madeira's upper class consisted solely of the aristocratic landowners, predominantly the families of the *capitanos* and the minor landowners dependent on them. From 1480 onwards, various contingents of settlers arrived from Castile, Italy, Flanders and France. Many of them were merchants, who invested in the sugar plantations and the extensive irrigation systems. They maintained connections with the world of high finance and the commercial centres of Europe. The newcomers often performed the triple role of

landowner-merchant-financier. It was hardly surprising, therefore, that these enterprising gentlemen soon attracted the attention of the island aristocracy and upper middle class. In other words, a well-arranged marriage with a substantial dowry was a reliable way of increasing your land and improving your social standing into the bargain. A resourceful merchant might even manage to capture the heart of a wealthy *capitano's* daughter.

Grand Capitano Zarco, however, paled at the thought of his daughter falling prey to

such a misalliance, and requested appropriately aristocratic suitors to be sent from the royal court at Lisbon. King Manuel responded graciously and dispatched a trio of young noblemen for inspection.

The population grew rapidly, with wave after wave of emigrants from Europe flooding the quays. The small group of settlers which had accompanied the three founding fathers – Teixeira, Zarco and Perestrelo – in the 1420s had already grown into 150 leading families by the 1440s and had multiplied to no less than 800 families by 1450. According to the population census of 1514, the island already had 5,000 inhabitants.

COLUMBUS AND MADEIRA

"The great Christopher Columbus also lived on the island for several years after marrying Doña Filipa, the daughter of Bartolomeu Perestrelo. He received navigational documents from his father-in-law and other Portuguese seafarers, from which he obtained important information for the discovery of the New World – an achievement which has made him immortal."

This declaration, in 1892, marking the 400-year celebrations of the discovery of America, pays official tribute to the connections between the famous explorer and the small island of Madeira, at least in Chicago and Seville where such celebrations are staged in grand style. Reference is even made in the document to the houses at Funchal and Porto Santo in which Columbus is supposed to have lived – their names inscribed in gold for emphasis.

Despite these claims by the Spanish and the Americans, the Madeirans themselves refused to substantiate them, saying that it had not been proved that Columbus had lived on Madeira. It was only with reluctance that they eventually condescended to send a good-will telegram congratulating the US government on the 400th anniversary of the discovery of America. For many years, right up until the age when money and fame might be gained out of such a connection, the Madeirans were wary about accepting any credit for having assisted the great seafarer in his preparations for the momentous discovery of the New World.

The facts: Indeed, it is not easy to assemble convincing proof that Columbus lived on the island in the years before he set off to discover America; no reference can be found in any of the relevant archives. Before 1492, the year of the discovery of America, it is known that Columbus was nothing more than one of the numerous Genoese soldiers of fortune trading in Portugal and intent on becoming rich overnight. This motley band of adventurers was hardly popular among the Portuguese, and little notice was taken of

them on Madeira. On the other hand, the archives relating to later years contain so many references to Columbus that we can assume he did live on the island after discovering America.

The official version now runs as follows: Columbus came to Portugal in 1476 and sought access to Lisbon society, primarily to the Genoese emigrants from his native city. He soon succeeded, and a wealthy merchant sent him to Madeira to buy sugar cane. His first trip in 1478 was only moderately suc-

cessful because the money for the first shipload he had purchased failed to arrive on time. But by 1484, six years later, he was already an expert in the sugar-cane sector; at least, that is what he claimed to be in a letter to the queen of Portugal.

In the letter, he outlined a plan for an expedition, hoping to arouse enough of the queen's interest to raise the necessary funds for his project. He told her that Madeira sugar would be an ideal source of nourishment for the crew, describing its nutritional value, prices and the best time to buy it – facts that could only be known to someone working in the sugar trade.

Left, Columbus was a young man when he lived on Porto Santo. **Right**, stepping ashore on American soil.

We also know that Columbus married a young woman from Madeira: Dona Filipa Moniz, the daughter of the legendary Capitano Perestrelo, the first hereditary feudal lord of Porto Santo. Columbus experts are still scratching their heads over how this obscure seaman of humble birth achieved this considerable marital feat. Had Filipa indulged in an affair and been banished from court to Porto Santo, where she was viewed as a "hand-me-down" on the local marriage market? Did Columbus marry her merely to gain access to influential circles?

Speculation is still rife among Columbus biographers. But one thing is certain: Perestrelo and Columbus both had ancestors

from Piacenza in Italy, which might have accounted for some common bonds. It is not known, however, whether Columbus's marriage to Filipa was a happy one nor where their one and only son was born.

It is now widely believed that for several years Columbus lived partly in Funchal and partly on the island of Porto Santo. Sceptics dispute the veracity of the latter claim, pointing out that an ambitious explorer wasn't likely to install himself on a desert island. But there is one good reason why Columbus should: his wife's brother was the Capitano on Porto Santo, a fact that endowed Columbus with some prestige and opened the doors to those circles involved in navigation, geography and exploration of the world's oceans. Moreover, the island was also the home of the *dracaena* palm whose "dragon's blood" was a costly dyestuff, a valuable trading commodity and a ready source of money on the international market.

Through his constant dealings with the seasoned mariners of Porto Santo, Columbus acquired important information on the large land mass across the ocean. He learned how to sail in the Atlantic, and it is thought to be here that his dream of discovering the New World began to take concrete shape. He studied the tides, carefully examined the flotsam and wreckage washed up on the island's shores by the western tides, and scrutinised the ancient maps and records from Perestrelo's library, given to him by his mother-in-law.

Another theory has it that the existence of America was revealed to Columbus by a shipwrecked seafarer who, caught in one of the Atlantic's violent storms, had been swept westwards and discovered new land there. Sailing back home he was struck by another storm and washed up on Madeira, where he confided his discovery to Columbus. That story, however, probably belongs in the realm of legend.

Even the sound historical evidence regarding Columbus and Madeira failed to stir the Madeirans. When an English tourist guide arrived on the island and stoutly insisted that there was an historical connection between Madeira and Columbus the islanders showed their disdain by promptly demolishing the house in Funchal where the famous explorer was supposed to have lived.

The Madeirans have recently undergone a change of heart. Interest in Christopher Columbus has resurfaced on the island lately in anticipation of the 500th anniversary of the discovery of America in 1992. The house in which he is supposed to have lived in Porto Santo has now been renovated and made into a museum devoted to the discoverer. This time there is no intention of playing down his links with the island. Madeirans everywhere are proudly celebrating it.

Left, Columbus is thought to have lived in this house on Porto Santo, and nobody can prove anything to the contrary. **Right**, a very special breed: the fishermen from Câmara de Lobos.

SLAVERY

Slavery is a dark chapter in the history of many countries. It is an aspect of the past which is difficult to come to terms with and in many cases it is simply ignored. Slaves were already being shipped to Madeira by the middle of the 15th century. Today, the only thing that reminds visitors of this sad episode in the island's history are a few streets with names like Rua das Pretas (Street of the Negresses), Rua da Mouraria (Street of the Moorish Quarter), or Lombo do Mouro (Hill of the Moors).

Without slavery, Madeira would certainly not have flourished as the supplier of sugar to Europe as it did in the late Middle Ages. The very first settlers were quick to recognise that it would be impossible to make the land arable on their own. Help was found in the form of slave labour. In 1552, there were 3,000 slaves on Madeira.

During the early centuries of the colonial era, they worked in the fields and sugar plantations, where their main task was to build the famous *levadas*, the island's vast network of artificial irrigation channels. The slaves often had to hew the channels out of precipitous walls of rock while suspended in baskets above an abyss. Slave labour created the basis of the island's present vast network of over 1,300 miles (2,100 km) of *levada* channels and 25 miles (40 km) of underground tunnels.

The majority of the slaves on Madeira were captive Moors and Berbers, but there were also black Africans, natives of the Canary Islands and even Indians. They have all left their own mark on the island, on its music and dances, costumes and folk tales, and on local ways of cooking food.

According to the historical records of that time, the black slaves were mainly imported from North Africa. Slaves from Guinea were prized most for their strength and robust constitution, and were generally assigned to work in the fields.

The trade in captive natives was regulated by a contract drawn up by the island's leading families and the governors of the African colonial regions. A letter written by an African chieftain, D. Manuel, condemning the abduction of helpless human beings, describes this practice. The natives of the Canary Islands, the Guanches, were also hunted down, and imported mainly from the island of Gomera. Around 1582, Tristão Vaz de Veiga, the governor of the archipelago, had 12 Indian servants in his residence.

Slaves were often auctioned. In many cases a contract was made guaranteeing them free-

dom on the death of their master. A certain Dona Branca d'Atouguia, for instance, gave instructions in her will for two of her slaves to be admitted to the convent of São Bernadino after her death.

The business of buying a slave was treated with great seriousness by the landowners. Conde Guilio Landi who paid a visit to the island at that time reports as follows: "Trading with slaves calls for great care because it is by no means sufficient to merely parade the slave back and forth. A careful physical examination must be carried out to establish if the body has any flaws, such as missing teeth, which would make the slave physi-

Left, slave drivers thought nothing of using such gruesome instruments of torture. **Right**, slaves were sold by weight.

cally weaker than a healthy one still in possession of all his teeth."

A law passed on Madeira in 1470 decreed that any slave seen on the streets after the evening curfew would be treated as a fugitive; that rule applied even if they were carrying messages or running errands for their masters. The curfew bell was still rung regularly in Machico until 1906, and traces of the corresponding law can still be found in Ponta do Sol, where street-doors are inscribed with instructions forbidding slaves to cross the mountain ridge after the bell had been tolled.

If a slave fled, he could be sold by any person who managed to catch him if his own houses; only after they had been set free could they do so.

Slaves were sometimes used as confidential agents by the island's gentry. One such agent, named Damião, belonged to Dona Branca de Atouguia, the owner of Campanário. She came to rely on his intelligence and discretion, and upon the death of her first husband, she made Damião manager of her estate. Dona Branca made his appointment official by having it recorded in the public notary's office.

Naturally, the clergy also had their say on the slavery issue, anxious as they were to salvage the souls of the island's heathen slave population. And so it happened that

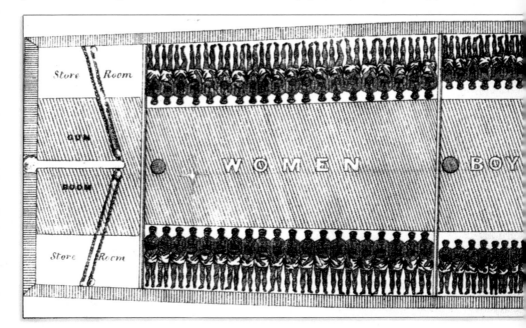

master had failed to find the fugitive within four months of his escape. According to a decree issued by King Manuel, the owner of a disobedient slave was allowed to cut off one of his ears. Later, in 1481, slaves had to bear a visible mark on their breast or arm as a public symbol of their bondage.

Apparently, the slaves were not treated as badly on Madeira as in other parts of the world. According to the records, "People were kind to them. Some of them were allowed to learn a handicraft, many were treated like children of the family and were often set free to marry farm labourers." As early as 1473, a law was passed forbidding slaves to

Bishop D. Luis de Figueiredo, the official representative of the Catholic Church on Madeira, ordered all local slave-owners to ensure that slaves of both sexes were given proper religious instruction. In 1505, the Bishopric of Funchal had already ordained that every male and female slave who were "living in sin" must get married. All the clergy in the Bishopric of Funchal were forbidden to keep slaves, in particular female slaves who were under the age of 50. The Bishop was evidently quite concerned about the virtue of his professedly celibate clergymen.

It was not until 1537 that Pope Paul III

criticised the conditions under which slaves were kept in those days. And a further 200 years were to expire before slavery was abolished once and for all on Madeira, with a ban on the purchase of slaves in Africa in the year 1761. When a slave-ship anchored off Madeira in that year, the sale of its human cargo was prohibited by an injunction issued by the district court. The total abolition of slavery in Portugal, however, was not achieved until 1858, when a ban was introduced on the initiative of the Marquis Sá da Bandeira which prohibited the selling and keeping of slaves.

Marriages between liberated slaves and farm labourers had been common for centuries, and once slave ownership was abolished entirely the former slaves were soon assimilated in the population. Today, the observant visitor to the island will detect in the Madeiran population many handsome faces, with the dark complexion and full lips characteristic of their forbears.

gral culture. For instance, the tradition of dancing in a circle is reminiscent of the African round dance; and the custom of bowing the head while dancing is another African influence. The movements of many dances reflect the harsh living conditions endured by the black slaves. One dance is called the *obaile pesado* (the strenuous dance); it comes from Ponta do Sol and Canhas, where many of the slaves once lived. Other dances symbolise the laborious work they carried out on the land and in the sugar plantations, some of them even depicting complete work sequences graphically mimed in dance form.

The Moors instilled songs with a vibrant

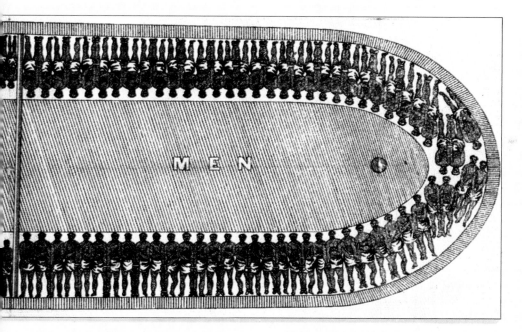

undertone of sentimentality and melancholy. *Do Berço*, an old lullaby passed down from those early days of slavery on Madeira, goes thus: *Imbala, preta, imbala / menino do teu Senhor / canta-lhe bem amoroso / aninalo com Amor* (Rock your master's son in your arms, slave woman / Sing him a song that is sweet / Embrace him with your love.) And this old song — full of romantic sexuality — is still popular among Madeirans today: *Dei um beijo numa preta / cheirou-me a café torrado / Nunca na minha Vida dei um beijo tao bem dado*: (I gave a black girl a kiss / It tasted of black coffee / The most wonderful kiss of my life.)

Traces of foreign influences are also evident in the music and dances of the island people. Many such traces, however, have become so typically Madeiran in the course of time that one needs to be an expert ethnologist to sift them from the island's inte-

<u>Above</u>, packed for shipment like sardines.

Pirates spread fear and terror all over the world's oceans well into the 19th century. They invaded the coastal settlements, sailed up the rivers, plundering and pillaging the villages and leaving behind them a path of death and destruction.

Madeira and Porto Santo constantly suffered attacks by pirates, who, seeming to appear from nowhere, landed on the beaches and ravaged the towns and settlements. Their ships were generally manned by motley crews of sailors from many different countries:

recognise the approaching vessels, with the dreaded Jolly Roger flying from their masts, earlier than the inhabitants of the main island of Madeira.

Huge bonfires were then lit to warn the people of Machico of an advancing pirate fleet. On a clear day, Pico do Facho affords a magnificent view of Porto Santo from its peak 1,080 ft (329 metres) above the sea. The mountain owes its name to the fires and torches lit to warn the inhabitants of the valley of approaching corsairs. Sentinels,

Morocco, Algeria, England and France. It was not easy for the coastal and island inhabitants to protect themselves against these ocean brigands. The pirates were skilled in handling their ship's cannons and, fearing nothing and no one, they attacked with a reckless and fearsome brutality. For centuries, the Madeirans lived in permanent fear of pirate forays.

Between the 15th and 17th centuries, the inhabitants of Madeira and Porto Santo succeeded in building up an efficient early-warning system. Since the pirates almost invariably sailed in from the north or west, the fishermen of Porto Santo were able to

posted on its peak round the clock, kept a close watch on Porto Santo in case imminent danger was signalled. When it was, the inhabitants of Porto Santo could only rescue themselves from pirates by fleeing into the interior of the island. They took as much of their belongings as they could carry. When they returned, they invariably found their houses destroyed by fire.

Machico still has two fortresses which testify to the determination of the inhabitants to defend themselves against the pirate fleets. The fortress of S. João Baptista was built on the eastern side of Zarco Bay in 1708. Two years previous to this, the triangular Forte do

Ampore was constructed on the coast of Machico.

Two fortresses were also built in Funchal to defend the town's inhabitants against attacks from the sea. But these, too, were unable to protect the townspeople against raids by the pirates. It was not without good reason that in 1566 the nuns from the Santa Clara Convent in Funchal chose to seek refuge in the remote Curral das Freiras (Valley of the Nuns). That was the year when Madeira was hit by the worst catastrophe in

horse and, brandishing his mighty sword, rode down to the beach with a handful of faithful comrades. There, he struck an awe-inspiring pose, threatening the would-be intruders with his sword. News of Zarco's bravery and legendary skill in combat must have spread through the entire pirate community, because the three vessels promptly weighed anchor and speedily turned tail for the open sea.

In 1566, however, the island had no Zarco and no heroic figure whose mere appearance

its history. The pirate invasion of the year 1566 is considered to have had more fatal consequences than any subsequent natural disaster that has befallen the island.

In the days of João Gonçalves Zarco, when our local hero's reputation was at its zenith, pirates had been only a minor problem. People on the island still proudly tell the tale of the day when three pirate ships anchored in the bay at Funchal, and Zarco, already somewhat advanced in years, boldly saddled his

Preceding pages: repelling the pirates. Left, Captain Kidd is said to have visited Madeira. Above, a vanquished town surrenders.

on the scene would have been enough to strike fear into the hearts of a fierce band of brigands. Nor was the early-warning system at Porto Santo and Machico of any help either. This time, the pirates had assembled a huge armada that was too powerful for the island defences. Madeiran chronicles and several Portuguese historical records describe this tragedy in sad detail.

They report that the protector of the island, the 5th Commander of Funchal, Simão Gonçalves da Camara, happened to be on furlough at the royal court in Lisbon at the time, but had appointed his uncle Francisco Gonçalves da Camara to act as his deputy during his absence. Knowledge of this fact reached a certain Gaspar Caldeira, a Portuguese intent on wreaking revenge on the Madeirans.

Caldeira had been one of the biggest timber merchants on the African Gold Coast, but he had abused his rights, and his property was confiscated by the Portuguese government. He fled to France to ponder on how to avenge himself, no matter how or on whom. He knew of course that there were very wealthy merchants on Madeira, and he had just learned that in the absence of the 5th Commander the island's defences against an attack from the sea were even more vulnerable. The Madeirans would be easy prey for

aristocrat could hardly resist the temptation to take a share of those riches.

At all events, Montluc managed under false pretences to obtain the support of King Charles IX for this "expedition", without divulging the real aims of the voyage. Following the king's example, other high-ranking French families were also inspired by the nobleman's venture and unwittingly assigned their strongest and bravest men to man his pirate fleet.

In early September 1566, Montluc and Caldeira were able to put to sea with a formidable armada of 11 ships manned by a crew of 1,300 buccaneers. Propelled by powerful autumn winds, the pirate fleet landed

ships bristling with cannon and brigands armed to the teeth.

So Caldeira hatched an evil plot and in Bertrand de Montluc he found a shady accomplice to sponsor him. A nobleman at the court of King Charles IX, Montluc bore what was a prestigious name in those days, for the Marshall de Montluc, his father, had made history for France on the battlefield. Why Bertrand de Montluc got involved in what was to be a risky and brutal act of piracy is unclear. Probably Caldeira had beguiled him with tales of the rich booty waiting on Madeira for the taking and, with the cost of court living as high as it was, the young French

on Funchal's Formosa Beach at nine o'clock on the morning of 3 October. The corsairs attempted to invade the town from two different directions. Despite desperate resistance by the townspeople at the gates of São Paulo, they were finally overrun, leaving the way free for the pirate horde to storm the fortress of São Laurenço, where the acting governor of Funchal had retreated with his troops. The fortress fell, and although there were still brave pockets of resistance throughout the town, Funchal finally succumbed to the ferocious attacks of the invaders.

Madeiran troops had assembled at various points on the island, but as the old chronicles tell us, their commanders decided not to march to the rescue of Funchal because they considered their own forces to be too weak and were afraid of provoking the blood-thirsty pirates to commit even greater atrocities against the population. Because of this, the only possible chance of rescuing Funchal was wasted.

Bertrand de Montluc was mortally wounded during the attack on São Lourenço and was succeeded by the Viconte de Jas. The onslaught lasted 16 days, and what the pirates could not stow away on board ship they simply destroyed. Thousands of wine casks were split open and left to run dry, and the entire sugar stocks destroyed. The ships'

prevent the pirates from entering the house of God, but they forced the door open, killed the stalwart priest in cold blood and stole the church silver.

When help finally arrived from Lisbon, it was too late. The pirates had already weighed anchor and set sail for the Canaries.

This well-chronicled invasion is just one of the many suffered by the islanders in the course of their history which are today remembered in schools all over the island. A more recent instance of invasion, which many islanders still remember vividly, has little to do with pirates who have long ceased to rove the seas, but the story is still worth telling. During the World War I, German submarines

holds were crammed with costly furnishings plundered from the homes of the wealthy islanders, together with silver stolen from Madeira's monasteries and convents and the stocks of the big mercantile houses. Worse still, more than 300 people were massacred by the invaders.

Today, when you cross the threshold of Funchal's imposing Sé Cathedral, you are at the exact spot where the priest was slain in those fateful autumn days. He had tried to

Left, death by hanging was the usual end for a pirate. **Above**, the fortress of São Lorenço was stormed by pirates in 1566.

attacked and sank several French vessels anchored in the harbour of Funchal. Submarine guns also bombarded the town and destroyed a number of houses.

During the attack, the townspeople of Funchal solemnly vowed to erect a statue in honour of Nossa Senhora da Paz, Our Lady of Peace, once the ordeal was over. They kept their vow, erecting a marble statue and a chapel above Monte. At the foot of the statue of Nossa Senhora da Paz, fishermen from Câmara de Lobos built a symbolic rosary out of large rocks next to the anchor chain of the sunken ship *Surprise,* as a symbol of lasting peace.

LOVE, HATE AND PORTUGAL

João Gonçalves Zarco is revered in Portugal as the discoverer of Madeira and Porto Santo. He resided as governor in Funchal for over 40 years. Since those early days, the people of Madeira have only rarely been a source of political trouble to the mother country. One of the very few uprisings, the "hunger revolt" of 1931 in protest against an extremely harsh decree passed by the Salazar regime, was crushed within just four weeks.

And there was only one serious attempt to break away from Portugal, staged after the revolution of 1974 by the wealthy classes who feared that they would forfeit all their worldly possessions under a "communist" government. Support for them quickly died down and this separatist movement has no political significance today.

The majority of the islanders were and continue to be loyal Portuguese citizens. Taught at an early age to respect the far-off state of Portugal and to observe their duty to the nation as a whole, they learned that it was important to be politically obedient. On every classroom wall, the obligatory crucifix was flanked by a portrait of the ruling dictator, under which was inscribed these words of warning: *A nação é tudo; tudo pela nação* – the nation is everything, everything for the nation! At no time in the course of history, however, was the mother country of Portugal much concerned about the welfare of the population of the *ilhas adjacentes*, the adjacent islands.

Portuguese domains: During the period of royal rule, Portugal was mainly interested in utilising additional land for its system of feudal tenure. Between 1460 and 1910, the kings of Portugal were in constant need of land for distribution to their close and even distant relations. These so-called *donatórios* were obviously happy with the proceeds from the crops grown on their newly acquired estates, but that did not mean that they felt obliged to leave the mainland and personally run their island estates.

During the entire 450 years of the Portuguese monarchy, only one royal couple deigned to visit the island of Madeira, and they never bothered to return to their exotic overseas territory. Madeira's island estates were generally run by a *capitano do donatório*, the landowner's factor, or by a *colono*, a tenant. In most cases, the *capitano* was a *fidalgo*, an aristocrat or officer who, generally without private means, was intent on preserving the island's feudal system.

Families lived very well off their newly-acquired estates and were able to employ a multitude of servants. They spent one part of the year on the large country estates and the other in their *quintas* – splendid villas, set in lush gardens and screened off from the outside world by high walls. Many of these properties can still be admired today, most of them nestling on the western mountain slopes of Funchal. Several of the villas were and still are used only as holiday homes, enabling their owners to retreat to the cool highlands and escape the summer heat.

Far worse off, of course, were the lower classes which formed the greater part of Madeira's population. Before the Revolution staged on the mainland in 1974, a rigid two-class system existed on the island, as it did in the rest of Portugal, which only a rising middle class could change.

Independent economy: Fortunately, Madeirans ensured from the very beginning that their agricultural sector could adequately supply the population and exist without help from Portugal. And while production was geared solely to the economic needs of the mother country, the island did not make the mistake of relying on a monoculture, as Portugal's Latin American colonies did. The Madeirans were forced to engage in diversified farming, if only to meet the massive payments in kind that were demanded by their feudal masters.

This factor also rescued the island from economic disaster in the 16th century. For years, the island had given top priority to the cultivation of sugar cane, with considerable success. But the boom came to an abrupt end when Brazil suddenly appeared on the world market as Madeira's strongest competitor. In response, Madeiran growers began to concentrate on the cultivation of the island's traditional products, and greater priority to wine-growing.

Madeira could now consider itself lucky

that it was not a colony but a part of Portugal: A decree was passed in the year 1643, for example, stipulating that every ship on its way to Brazil had to stop at Funchal and take wine and provisions on board. That made Funchal an obligatory port of call not only for Portuguese vessels sailing from the mainland to the southern and south west parts of their empire, but also for international shipping. In their flourishing centre of trade and commerce, which today is almost as cosmopolitan as Lisbon, the people of

open market; on the other hand, they are still dependent on close economic cooperation with mainland Portugal, for the island is faced with competition from far more efficient producers in every sector of the big European market.

Of course, the EC granted the island favourable start-up conditions: Madeira can continue supplying its bananas to Lisbon until 1996; wine-growers can still claim subsidies for cultivating the grapes for fine Madeira wines; and large export quotas are

Funchal developed a keen sense of pride vis-à-vis the mother country; they in no way shared the inferiority complex of many modern Madeirans, who feel that they are not considered to be full citizens by the mainland Portuguese.

The EC – a new challenge: Portugal's entry to the European Community in 1986 has also created a new basis for Madeira's relations with the mother country. On the one hand, the Madeirans hope that a new economic impetus will increase their chances on the

Salazar, Portugal's prime minister, decided the fate of Madeira between 1932 and 1968.

in effect to help guarantee sufficient marketing scope. But will Europeans develop enough of a a taste for the sweet Madeira wine to justify such high quotas? Or will Madeirans eventually have to import table wines from the mainland because they no longer have enough decent land on which they can grow vines? That would in all likelihood undermine the islanders' pride and lead to possible dissension with the mother country.

So the ambivalent relationship which has existed for centuries between the island and the mother country seems destined to persist, even in this new economic context.

Relations between England and Portugal, and between England and Madeira in particular, have always been especially close and cordial. A 14th-century legend relates that the island was discovered by a handsome young Englishman, Robert Machin, and his lady love, Anne d'Arfet, who, fleeing from her tyrannical father, had been shipwrecked on the island shores.

An English mother: Romantic as the legend is, however, recorded facts tell us that the person really responsible for the discovery

of Madeira was none other than Henry the Navigator. We say responsible because despite his "Navigator" title the Portuguese prince never undertook the voyages of exploration himself. His contribution was to plan each one to the last meticulous detail, dispatching his sea captains on a series of long journeys of discovery along the African coast and into the Atlantic. One such expedition succeeded in discovering the island of Madeira.

This historical event marked the beginning of an unbroken chain of close links between England and Madeira. Henry's mother was Philippa of Lancaster, the English wife of Portugal's King João (John) I, whose marriage forged the alliance signed between the two countries in 1373. Exactly 600 years later (in 1973) the British consul on Madeira commissioned the well-known sculptor Mestre Texeira to carve a bust of Queen Philippa. It now stands in the garden of the English church in Madeira.

In the 17th century relations between the two islands were bolstered by another royal alliance – the marriage of England's Charles II to the Portuguese noblewoman Catherine of Braganza. At that time, England was already represented on Madeira by its first consul; the island's English community started to grow and so did their substantial economic interests.

In fact, at this time Madeira was very close to becoming an English possession entirely, for the monarch's marriage contract provided for the surrender of important Portuguese territories to the Crown as part of Catherine's dowry. Had Charles II not agreed to accept the dowry as it stood, the Portuguese would undoubtedly have thrown in Madeira as well.

British trade privileges: Madeira therefore remained a Portuguese overseas territory. Nevertheless, the alliance of the two nations created various trade privileges for the English merchants on Madeira. One important clause in the marriage contract between Charles and Catherine concerned trade with the American colonies: While America otherwise only imported goods shipped from English ports, under this arrangement Madeira was permitted to export its wine to the New World, providing it was shipped directly by English merchant firms. These firms transported Madeiran wine to all their branches in the western hemisphere.

The privileges granted by King Charles II to the Englishmen on Madeira also attracted more and more English settlers to the island. In 1768, the English seafarer and discoverer, Captain James Cook, anchored his ship *En-*

Left, Isabel dela França, the English lady who wrote a book about Madeira's customs. **Right**, Philippa of Lancaster, the English wife of King João I.

deavour off the coast of Madeira. He was actually on the beginning of his famous trip around the world and had only stopped off at the island to take provisions on board, notably wine – 200 bottles per man! With a crew of 94 thirsty seamen to supply, good business was done by Madeirans and Englishmen alike.

Many of the English who chose to make a living on Madeira quickly became extremely wealthy. They settled down quickly and joined the island's social élite. It was not unusual for them to adopt Portuguese versions of their names, even in the first generation. For example, Sir John Drummond, Master of Stobhall, was proud to assume the

the dramatic decline of sugar exports the island experienced a renewed surge of economic prosperity. Madeira wine was renowned the world over for its high quality; even vodka-drinking Russian czars developed a taste for the full-bodied ruby wine, and legend has it that while awaiting execution in the Tower of London in 1478 the Duke of Clarence, pondering on the best way to die, decided he would like to be drowned in a cask of "malmsey" – the old name for Madeira wine.

Madeira wine was most popular in England. Catherine of Braganza ordered that the wine should be imported for consumption by the population as a whole and not just by the

name João Escorcio – John the Scot. Today, there are two Portuguese branches of the family he founded on Madeira: the Drummonds and the Escorcios.

When wine production reached its zenith at the end of the 18th century, Portuguese-British relations were also at their best. More and more British merchants and exporters settled on the island, because Funchal was also an important port of call on the long sea route to Africa and India.

The British made colossal profits from the wine trade; in 1800, wine exports were estimated to have reached an incredible 9 million bottles a year. And for the first time since

royal court as it had been until then. From then on, it was drunk in considerable quantities by all sections of the British population. It is recorded that in 1622 during the celebrations held to mark the birth of Shakespeare (six years after the bard's death) a cask containing over 100 gallons (500 litres) of malmsey was driven through the streets of London. The procession halted at the George Inn, where the contents of the cask were dispensed to the merry crowd.

Shakespeare himself referred to the wine from Madeira in *Henry IV*. Poins, one of Sir John Falstaff's comrades, accuses him of having sold his soul to the devil on Good

Friday in exchange for a glass of Madeira and a piece of chicken.

Blandy, Leacock & Co: The family who really ruled the roost in Funchal were the Blandys, who ran the leading merchant firm. It was at the Blandy estate that King Carlos and his queen resided in appropriate style on their visit to the island in 1901.

The first Blandy arrived on Madeira at the end of the 18th century. The family made their name as shipping agents and wine exporters. Charles Blandy and his partner, Thomas Slap Leacock, who handled the wine export business, were the people responsible for getting the island's economy back on its feet after the collapse of the sugar trade. The

Numerous fellow countrymen of the Blandys, Leacocks and other British emigrants followed in the footsteps of the successful merchant families, if only to spend the mild winters on Madeira. After all, living costs and travel expenses on Madeira were far lower than the cost of running a house in England. Moreover, the island was much easier to reach than the Algarve, Gibraltar or the Riviera, because travellers could board any of the numerous ships sailing to and from the southern Atlantic, the Caribbean and the USA.

British tourism: In the middle of the 19th century, tourism began to grow into one of Madeira's major sources of income. Wealthy

Leacocks founded a commercial firm which still operates under the name of Leacock & Co. Ltd.

It was also these two families who in 1852 and 1873 rescued the island's wine industry after it had been devastated by the *phylloxera* virus. They replanted the island's vineyards with vines from the USA and Mauritius. Thanks to them, Madeira's wine-growing industry recovered and was able to produce bumper harvests again by 1900.

<u>Left</u>, still very British: the Savoy in Funchal. <u>Above</u>, Winston Churchill came to paint on the island.

English people and affluent travellers from other European countries came to discover Madeira: sun-worshippers, business people eager to profit from industrialisation on the island, tuberculosis patients in search of relief in Madeira's subtropical climate, famous writers, politicians and other people of note travelled to the island to enjoy a life of luxury in the hotels on the bay of Funchal.

Winston Churchill paid a lengthy visit to Madeira in 1949, and enjoyed it so much that he later returned to the island. He spent his visits painting local scenes and landscapes, particularly the little fishing village of Câmara do Lobos.

In 1922, a seaplane made the first direct flight from Lisbon to Funchal, establishing the basis for regular flights between England, Lisbon and Madeira the journey to the island became much smoother and quicker. After World War II, the British transport line Aquila Airways, operated a flying-boat service, transporting passengers between Southampton and Funchal and back. However, a disastrous air crash in 1958 interrupted air traffic to and from the island. It was not resumed until 1964 on the completion of Madeira airport.

Support in times of trouble: An important historical date in the history of the British connection is the year 1801, in the midst of flown on the mast of Madeira's fortress, and in Funchal a formal document of capitulation was signed to symbolise the island's solidarity with Britain's King George III.

Several months later, the British officially handed back the island to the Madeirans, but their troops remained there until the signing of the peace treaty with France in 1814. While the British were considered to be allies, they were also regarded as an occupying force with the task of defending the island against a possible invasion by the French – and of protecting the commercial interests of both the English and the Madeirans.

Many of the 4,000 British soldiers stayed

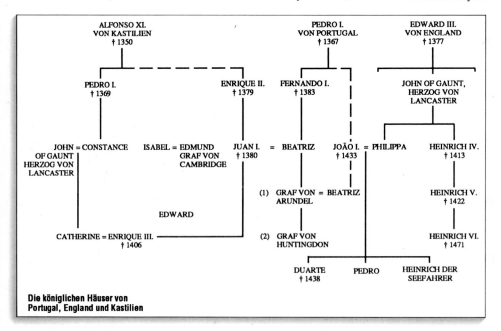

Die königlichen Häuser von Portugal, England und Kastilien

the Napoleonic Wars. The British government, allied with Portugal, dispatched troops to Funchal to prevent Madeira from being invaded by France. Their task was to help the Portuguese garrison defend the island. One year later, after the Treaty of Amiens had been signed, the English troops departed; they had not only helped to preserve peace, but had also won the friendship of the Madeirans.

In 1807, when Napoleon invaded Portugal, England's Admiral Hood returned to Funchal with his troops and the English once again assumed responsibility for the defence of the island. The admiral had the British flag on the island, marrying local women and building up a new livelihood. The old water fountain at Santo da Serra is inscribed with the names of members of that British expedition: Taylor, Hardy, Turner, etc. And the unusually large number of blue-eyed, fair-haired inhabitants of the villages there and in the regions of Monte and Camacha, where sections of the British garrison were stationed, would suggest that they are the descendants of British soldiers and their Portuguese wives.

Napoleon's souvenir: The British and the Madeirans had their final encounter with Napoleon on 23 August 1815, albeit from a safe distance. That was the day on which Admiral Sir George Cockburn arrived in Funchal on his ship *Northumberland*. He anchored well out to sea, however, and the only islander allowed to board the vessel was Henry Veitch, the British Consul. He was rowed over to "welcome" the ship's prominent passenger, Napoleon Bonaparte, who was en route to exile on St Helena.

Henry Veitch paid his respects to the former French emperor and handed him books, fruit and bottles of the best Madeira wine to cheer him up on his gloomy voyage. Napoleon returned this favour with a gift of gold coins, which the consul saved until 1822 when building work began on the neo-classical

famous export article besides its wine, its world-famous embroidery. In 1860, Miss Elizabeth Phelps, an Englishwoman, began to encourage the export of Madeira's embroidered tablecloths, pillowcases, bedspreads and other items to Victorian England. Miss Phelps also got the Madeiran women to adapt their embroidery to English tastes, without spoiling the unique character of their needlework. Women of all ages still sit in front of their houses, bent over embroidery destined to grace the the dining table of an English household.

Madeira's good relations with Britain also proved their worth in World War II: fearing a Spanish-German attack on Gibraltar, the

British evacuated about 2,000 families from the strategic military base at the tip of Spain to Madeira, where they were cordially received by the islanders.

Holy Trinity Church of Madeira's Anglican community. Then the consul had the cache of gold coins buried under the foundation wall of the church.

The consul was an enthusiastic amateur architect, and his former country residence, Jardim da Serra, set in the hills behind Estreito de Câmara dos Lobos, is well worth visiting.

Madeira without its English heritage is hard to imagine, not least because of another

Left, blood ties: the royal houses of England, Portugal and Castile. **Above**, King João I holds a banquet for his father-in-law John of Gaunt, the Duke of Lancaster.

British evacuated about 2,000 families from the strategic military base at the tip of Spain to Madeira, where they were cordially received by the islanders.

The English have been able to cultivate and enjoy their special English way of life on Madeira. Luxury hotels like Reid's and the Savoy have long been enclaves of the traditionally-minded English upper classes and preserve the elegant ambience of their counterparts in London. The Madeirans accept this readily, and for the English it is especially pleasurable to be able to be themselves and enjoy life in a climate that is warm but never unbearably hot.

THE VIGIA, MADEIRA, THE WINTER RESIDENCE OF HER

L MAJESTY THE EMPRESS OF AUSTRIA.—SEE NEXT PAGE.

DISTINGUISHED VISITORS

The first visitors to risk the Atlantic sea trip, which was long, dangerous and full of privation, did so largely for commercial reasons. Tales of the prosperity already prevailing on the once uninhabited island 50 years after its discovery attracted adventurers and soldiers of fortune from all over the globe. One of the first visitors was Christopher Columbus, who at that time was only interested in making money from the cultivation of sugar cane, not on voyages of discovery.

He was followed by other seafarers, among them Captain Kidd, one of the most notorious buccaneers of all time. We are told that he did no harm to the Madeirans, however, and even that he buried his legendary treasure off the islands of the Desertas.

Another famous seafarer to visit Madeira was Captain James Cook, who was of course an explorer and navigator rather than a pirate. Nevertheless, there is a small drawing on the outside wall of the Ole Monte Tavern up in Monte, where tickets can be purchased for the Quinta "Nossa Senhora da Conceição": Though it looks for all the world like a piece of graffiti, it is said by the islanders to be a depiction of a pirate looking suspiciously like James Cook.

The historical background to this unique piece of mural decoration is probably altogether different from what is claimed: pirates and smugglers used to store and trade their contraband the most remote places they could find. Monte used to be one of them – until it became the launching pad for one of the island's most popular tourist attractions: the exhilarating toboggan trip down the cobbled streets to Funchal.

Many of the travellers who stopped off at Madeira en route to Africa or South America – Italians, French, but mostly English – were captivated by the beauty of the island and gave glowing accounts of its attractions on returning home. The English in particular praised the wonderfully mild climate and by

the middle of the 19th century Madeira was a fashionable holiday destination. Emperors and kings, aristocrats and politicians, painters and writers, in short everybody who could afford it, came to the island in search of rest and relaxation, preferably for the whole winter, a practice which in those days was considered very chic indeed.

The small island was anything but prepared for this sudden invasion of sophisticated travellers. In 1840, Funchal had just two hotels, and even 45 years later there were only six. But the distinguished travellers and their entourages generally preferred to take a *quinta*, one of Funchal's idyllic villas which were let complete with servants. The owners of most of these *quintas* were wealthy English and Madeiran merchants. In 1835, the island boasted a hundred such *quintas*, each one more beautiful, more romantic and more luxurious than the next.

Sorrowful Sissi: One of the first and most celebrated visitors to the island was Empress Elisabeth of Austria and Hungary, more popularly known as Sissi. Her striking beauty is documented by a portrait in the Vicente museum of photography in Funchal. It was

Preceding pages: the Quinta Vigia in the middle of the 19th century. **Left**, the Empress Elisabeth of Austria, one of the most beautiful women of her time. **Right**, Captain Cook also called in at Madeira.

on Madeira that the consumptive Austrian empress at last managed to recuperate from her grave illness – at least, according to official accounts.

But Sissi's biographer, Brigitte Hamann, offers a different version of the story. She claims that Sissi's illness was a mere pretext and that the true source of her anguish was her marriage crisis and the crushing boredom of life at the imperial court in Vienna, aggravated by constant disputes with her mother-in-law, who acted as the real confidante of Emperor Franz Josef.

As a result of these and other problems, the unhappy empress was stricken by constant "nervous crises", from which she sought

MaDeira Pirate was Here Nov. 11, 1887

relief by going on various stringent crash diets. At all events, her personal physician feared she would not survive a further winter in Vienna and prescribed his despondent royal patient a cure on Madeira.

Dutifully, Sissi embarked for Madeira on the royal yacht, *Victoria and Albert*, placed at her disposal by England's Queen Victoria. It was followed at a respectful distance by a support vessel carrying a substantial portion of the Viennese court and Sissi's personal staff. According to the ships' log-books, all the members of the illustrious party were struck down by seasickness on the rough Atlantic voyage – that is all except for the

Austrian Empress, who managed to survive the ordeal unscathed, despite her apparently frail constitution.

But once installed on Madeira in the splendid seaside villa of Quinta Vigia in Funchal, she was soon bored to death. Sissi was homesick; she pined for her children, locked herself in her suite, weeping endlessly and eating listlessly – much to the dicomfort of her retinue who, according to the strict dictates of court protocol, had to down their own cutlery as soon as the empress herself had finished eating.

Apart from her daily outing on horseback, she rarely left the villa, and her entire retinue complained bitterly about the royal lethargy and the excruciating boredom at court. Nothing could console Europe's most beautiful crowned head. "Just imagine", wrote a courier arriving from Vienna with letters and gifts from Emperor Franz Joseph, "an ornamental grove of camellias, rising 30 metres high with thousands of buds and blossoms, and only 25 metres away from the villa the rocky ocean cliffs – with a cactus growing in every crevice!"

But to the empress and her jaded retinue it was sheer monotony. To quote another courier: "The town is dirty and the streets are paved with sharp little cobble stones, making it quite impossible to take a leisurely stroll." He also complained that social life on the island was non-existent: "The Empress spends most of her time with her pets and card games."

Sissi's stay on Madeira certainly improved her health and also enhanced her legendary beauty, which she herself had now come to recognise and accept for the first time in her life. Nevertheless: "If I had known what it was going to be like here," she wrote, "I would have chosen somewhere else to spend such a long visit. For even if the air is invigorating, one needs more than that to lead a pleasant life."

A tragic visit: Unlike the unhappy empress of Austria, Empress Amelia of Brazil, who had stayed at the Quinta Vigia several years previously, developed a deep affection for the small island, although her visit was marred by family tragedy. Amelia was the widow of

Left, graffiti on the Ole Monte Tavern. **Right**, Emperor Charles I of Austria died while in exile on Madeira.

King Pedro IV of Portugal, an enlightened monarch and one highly respected by the Madeirans. On arriving on the island, Amelia and her daughter, Princess Marie Amelia, were welcomed by enthusiastic crowds of islanders. The people were especially enchanted by the beautiful young princess, who, like many others, had come to Madeira to be cured of tuberculosis.

Empress Amelia and her ailing daughter stayed at the Quinta Vigia for five months before the Princess suddenly died, a mere 22 years old. During her visit, she had made herself so loved by the population that weeping crowds assembled at the harbour to see off the ship carrying Empress Amelia and

her daughter's coffin back to Brazil.

Empress Amelia never forgot the island, and although she never returned to Madeira she had a hospital built for tuberculosis patients which still bears the name of Princess Marie Amelia.

Emperor Charles I of Austria: The visit paid to the island by the last Austrian Emperor, Charles I, also ended in tragedy. After the end of World War I, the monarch was sent into exile. He chose the island of Madeira – his mother Zita was of royal Portuguese blood – and moved into a suite at Reid's Hotel. But in his reduced circumstances he was unable to afford what were fairly sizeable hotel bills even in those days and readily accepted the offer of accommodation in the Quinta Gordon in Monte.

He lived in the *quinta* for several months and soon gained the respect of the local population for his frequent kindnesses and humility. But the quiet peace that he had found on Madeira was to last longer than he would have hoped. He suddenly died of pneumonia. His wife buried Charles I in the church at Monte and then left the island with her seven children.

A Russian count: Count Lambert, *aide de camp* to the Russian empress, is the central figure in another tragic story told on Madeira. The count was plagued by chronic and mysterious attacks of melancholia. It was rumoured that "for private reasons" – a phrase used in aristocratic circles to denote a love affair – he had incurred the wrath of a Russian general. According to the rules of the day, it was agreed to solve the problem by casting lots, the loser being doomed to take his own life.

The unfortunate general lost and committed an honourable suicide. But the count did not get away scot-free: the event caused him to lose his peace of mind for all time. He left Russia for Madeira, and moved into the ill-fated Quinta Vigia. There he spent years restlessly making his retreat more beautiful, more magnificent and more idyllic – and becoming increasingly melancholic in the process. He tried to seek refuge in travel, but returned time and time again to his villa, where he would spend his days staring despondently out to sea. When he eventually died, the count's wife sold the Quinta Vigia and left Madeira, which is quite understandable under the circumstances.

The splendid old *quintas* are no longer leased to guests today, but some of them can be visited for an entrance fee. Today's visitors stay in the island's greatly expanded number of hotels. Some 10,000 hotel beds await visitors to the island, and a further 10,000 will be added in the next few years. Madeira, therefore, has ceased to be the island of aristocrats, adventurers – and convalescents. Fortunately, it has avoided instead becoming a target of mass tourism.

Left, this is how the Quinta Vigia looks today. **Right**, Sissi was here! A feature in the *Illustrated London News* on 5 January 1861.

THE EMPRESS OF AUSTRIA IN MADEIRA.

THE British Royal yacht Victoria and Albert, having on board her Imperial Majesty the Empress of Austria and suite (some thirty-six in number), anchored in Funchal roads at eight o'clock on Thursday morning, the 29th of November. Considering the time of year, the Victoria and Albert had an exceedingly quick run of four days and a half from Plymouth to Madeira. The Osborne was also in attendance on her Majesty. At ten o'clock her Majesty left the yacht under a Royal salute from the shore. On landing her Majesty was attended by the civil and military Governors and all the principal authorities, amidst the enthusiastic cheers of an immense concourse of people, to the residence—named the Vigia—which had been prepared for her reception.

The Vigia, honoured as her Majesty's "sunny home" for the winter months, is one of the most enchanting, picturesque spots in the world. The mansion is most luxuriously furnished. The lower saloons, which lead into each other by large folding-doors, are 100 feet in length, and present a truly palatial appearance. The building, situated on an eminence about 150 feet above the level of the sea, overlooking the town of Funchal, is in the villa style, low, and surrounded by a deep verandah, having for a background a splendid range of mountains some 4000 to 5000 feet high. In front, the garden walks lead to a broad terrace, forming a delightful promenade along the border of a rocky cliff commanding a magnificent and extensive sea view. The whole is in the midst of a beautiful garden, bright with flowers and luxuriant with the most splendid specimens of tropical plants and trees from all parts of the world. Amongst them are some old friends of the West—the mango, avocado pear, guava, banana, and tamarind, all in rich bearing ; as well as many acquaintances of the East—the camphor, cinnamon, clove, and others.

Let us hope that the Royal visitor may soon be able to add her attestation to thousands of others to the beneficial effects of that delicious clime. The latest accounts from Madeira state that the health of the Empress was quite satisfactory. —————

For Madeira, the 19th century ended in a string of disasters: a spate of famines and epidemics, the destruction of its vines, and constant political friction between the island's conservative and liberal factions. A succession of governors had in each of their brief three-year terms of office managed to change little in Madeira's rigid feudal structures. One admirable exception to this damning generalisation was José Silvestre Ribeiro, a governor with progressive ideas who greatly improved the educational system and social facilities, and modernised the infrastructure.

Ups and downs: After the dissolution of the Portuguese monarchy, and the proclamation of the republic on 5 October 1910, the government made determined efforts to establish democracy on the island and to grant the "District of Madeira" considerable autonomy. Nevertheless, the mills of change continued to grind slowly on the island; the republic, which led a precarious political existence from 1910 to 1932, altered neither the conservative attitudes ingrained in most of the inhabitants nor their deferential behaviour towards their betters. The traditional passivity of the Madeirans helped to cement dictatorial power over the island.

In 1932, the then Minister of Finance, Antonio de Oliveira Salazar, staged a military coup, which marked the end of the Portuguese republic. The ultra-conservative dictator was still in power after World War II, when Portugal was plunged into economic and political crisis.

During the 36 years of dictatorial rule, the Madeirans did little publicly to oppose the authoritarian regime of Salazar, nor did they benefit very much from his liberal successor, Prime Minister Marcello Caetano, who was ousted by the military coup of 1974. By a curious quirk of history, the ousted politician and Portugal's President Américo Tomàs stopped at Madeira on their way into exile in Brazil. Unlike Napoleon Bonaparte before them, they were allowed to set foot on the island, but they got no more than a chilly welcome from the Madeiran authorities, who made them spend the night imprisoned in the ancient fortress of São Laurenço overlooking the harbour.

But apart from this isolated incident, the aftermath of centuries of authoritarian rule was sufficient to stifle the liberal tendencies which had started to emerge at the beginning of the 20th century. Any attempts by the Madeirans to oppose the military dictatorship by force would naturally have been

futile, and the islanders were anyway encumbered by backward and fatalistic attitudes deriving from a series of historical and social factors.

The Madeiran character: The English author and Madeira expert, Francis Rogers, has investigated the main features of the Madeiran character which gave rise to this mentality and attempted to explain them historically in his book: *Atlantic Islanders of the Azores and Madeira.*

He points to a feeling of solitariness and isolation among the inhabitants, caused by Madeira's insular location in the Atlantic hundreds of miles from the mother country.

Left, Funchal's street cafés are well-frequented all the year round. **Right**, Madeira's famous export: the strong, sweet wine.

In his opinion, a strongly fatalistic attitude to life is typical among the inhabitants of all small islands, especially when exposed to unpredictable storms, severe earthquakes and other natural catastrophes (not to mention the tragedies inflicted by invading pirates and punitive military expeditions). The side-effect of all this is manifested in an innate fatalism and resignation, in particular towards directives from the mainland government. There is a strong feeling, especially among the poorest islanders, that they are being governed by a remote assembly on the mainland and are unable to take life into their own hands.

There were other factors which contrib-

Even these days, with the exception of the inhabitants of the capital and port of Funchal, the islanders tend to be shy and extremely withdrawn, or at least reserved, feeling themselves to be unaffected by worldly matters. This feeling is also compounded by a deep religiousness, strong family ties – people tend to socialise with family members rather than friends – and a strict observance of traditional values.

Traditionally any underlying dissatisfaction with social circumstances or Madeira's isolation from the mainland tends to find an outlet in the urge to escape and emigrate rather than to engage in active political opposition to the government.

uted to their sense of helplessness. The division of the 11 inhabited Portuguese islands into four completely separate administrative districts governed from Lisbon made the islands incapable of cooperating with one another from the very beginning and prevented them from developing a feeling of joint identity, strength and mutual responsibility. This lack of regional identity was compensated for by a pronounced patriotism and deep respect for the state and nation, linked with a readiness to be loyal, submissive and obedient to authority – characteristics already instilled into the first settlers by the Portuguese monarchy.

End of dictatorial rule: That said, the military coup instigated by General Antonio de Spinola, which ousted President Caetano on 24 April 1974, and the take-over by the new military regime were celebrated as much on Madeira as on the mainland. But scarcely a year later, opposition against the provisional government was already growing. It was widely feared that communist influence would increase throughout the country.

Such fears were especially prevalent in rural areas both on the mainland and on Madeira itself; to the small-holders, dependent as they were on the local oligarchy and the conservative clergy, communism represented a threat to their traditional existence on the land. The principles to which they felt bound – the Catholic faith, the right to own land, the rural way of life, their traditional attitudes and moral values – all seemed to be endangered by the growing force of communist ideology on the mainland. For the first time since the settlement of Madeira, a growing number of conservative elements on the island began to agitate against the government in Lisbon.

In summer 1975, they founded the right-wing separatist movement, *Frente de Libertação Madeirense* (FLAMA), which fought for total secession from the mother country. Various acts of sabotage, like the

the islands and the mainland drew to a close. In contrast to their compatriots on the mainland, landowners, hoteliers and entrepreneurs on Madeira lost none of their properties in the tumultuous times that characterised the end of the 1970s and beginning of the 1980s, before Marxist doctrines were finally abandoned for capitalism.

New autonomy: So what did Madeira actually gain from the 1974 revolution and the democratic constitution given to the island in 1976? Compared to before, quite a lot. Both the Azores and Madeira have become largely autonomous regions with their own regional government, which itself is answerable to the regional parliament. In addition, the is-

destruction of the radio station in Funchal, were ascribed to FLAMA. But the organisation's activities were of short duration only, because by the end of the same year the communist danger had already been averted on the island. In Madeira's regional elections, the governing Social Democrats won an impressive 65 percent of the poll – the widely feared communists managed to muster a mere 0.6 percent.

Soon after that, the confrontation between

Left, tourism has begun to boom since the airport was opened. **Above**, terraced fields are typical of the landscape in the south of the island.

land groups send deputies to parliament in the Portuguese capital. This means that the islanders have their own say in important issues of foreign and defence policy. They have been able to impose their own taxes and excise duties since 1976.

Today, relations between Madeira and Portugal are much more convivial. Since 1974, tourists from the Portuguese mainland, realising how little their Portuguese escudos were worth abroad, have started to discover Madeira, which they had virtually ignored until then. Needless to say, this is also helping to improve relations between the mother country and Madeira.

Once word of the settlement of the Atlantic islands in 1420 had spread throughout the Portuguese empire, the first large-scale wave of emigrants embarked for Madeira. It wasn't only adventurers who flocked there; entire family clans from northern Portugal also braved the hazardous sea voyage to start a new life on the island. They were followed later by Spaniards, Italians and Dutch families, who saw no future for themselves in the densely-populated and unhygienic cities of their home countries.

atically driven out of Spain. These Moors or *moriscos* were descendants of North African Arab populations. Over the centuries, they had become no less Spanish than they were Arab. Their families had lived in Spain for generations, but they were driven out in the wake of the *reconquista*. The Moors were accepted on the island with the same equanimity as the Jewish refugees from Spain, who, following the recapture of the Iberian Peninsula by the Christian armies, were forced to live the life of social outcasts there

With sugar cane being produced in ever-increasing quantities, the local inhabitants were soon unable to handle the work on their own. To help them, black slaves were imported from Africa and the Cape Verde Islands, together with Berber tribesmen from North Africa and Guanches from the Canaries. As in the other Portuguese colonies, the black and white sections of the population on Madeira mixed and intermarried; marriages between the island's white men and black slave women were quite common, and they produced abundant offspring.

During the 16th and 17th centuries, Moors also arrived on the scene after being system-

and then ultimately expelled from the entire Spanish region.

Several street and place names testify to the historical presence of these minorities: for example, Funchal's Rua da Mouraria – the street of the Moorish quarter, where the Museo Municipal is located – or the Rua das Pretas, "Street of the Negresses", in the same quarter. In the course of one of the numerous *levada* tours, walkers also pass the Lombo do Mouro, the ridge of the Moors. And if you make an excursion to the Azores, you would find a Porto de Judeos and an Igreja de Mouros – a Jewish port and a Moorish church.

For the sake of completeness, reference

must also be made to the French corsairs, who invaded Madeira in 1566 and not only plundered the island but also fathered numerous children. Spanish troops arrived in 1580 to occupy and integrate Madeira and Porto Santo into a Spanish-Portuguese union. They stayed there for 30 years and many of the soldiers – taking the union more literally than the Spanish government had actually intended – fathered numerous Spanish-Portuguese children.

Linguistically, neither the Spanish, the

ish troops stationed on Madeira during the Napoleonic Wars between 1807 and 1814 gradually realised that life would be much easier if they learned the lingo. In the course of time their efforts were recognised and they were accepted by the islanders and became upright Madeirans. Their blue eyes and fair hair naturally puzzle visitors, who wonder how blond people like these could have come to inhabit a sub-tropical island, not knowing that they are the descendants of the 4,000 British soldiers who saved the

Italians nor the Dutch could keep their hold on Madeira. In fact, the Portuguese spoken on the island contains very few words adopted or derived from any of the languages spoken by the immigrant groups. Today, all the population groups which have emigrated from the Continent or from Africa speak the local Portuguese, with the exception of the British, who never give up speaking English.

But here, too, there is an exception that proves the rule: The descendants of the Brit-

Preceding pages: friendly locals. Left and above, from very blond to very dark. The Madeirans' ancestors came from all over the world.

island from the iron grip of Napoleon.

The Madeiran archipelago was discovered and settled relatively late in time, and considering it had existed in the Atlantic undiscovered and unspoiled for thousands of years, its own history is correspondingly short. In the course of its rapid civilisation, Madeira has become home to a collection of people of the most varied origins.

Of course, the Portuguese contribution is prevalent. But when we take a closer look at the faces of the Madeirans, we can also recognise striking northern European, Arab and black African influences, all blending with the predominant Portuguese features.

Day after day, Avó, a Madeiran grandmother, sits on the ground in front of her small cottage, working on her embroidery and keeping a watchful eye on her youngest grandchildren.

Their mother, Celina, must go out to work for a living. With a group of other young women, Celina travels every day in an open truck to Funchal, where she works long hours as a hotel maid. In the evening, she is driven back home, where she immediately starts cooking and cleaning for her family.

Her husband also works hard, but at least he has time for relaxation. After leaving work, he heads for his local bar. At that time of day only men are to be found in these island institutions. They spend a couple of hours drinking with their friends and then head home for supper.

That is not to say that progress in sexual relations and female emancipation has not been made in Madeira. Avó is illiterate. When she used to travel with her husband, he would ride on his donkey and she would walk behind him. Celina, on the other hand, attended primary school and her husband runs a car. Maria, Celina's 19-year-old daughter, is the first female member of the family who has been able to take vocational training after finishing school. She is training to become a beautician, and has no intention of getting married until she has obtained her diploma. Maria's fiancé fully supports her vocational aspirations.

Madeiran society is changing, but it is still unquestionably dominated by men, and it is likely to stay that way for at least the forseeable future. Portuguese women – and especially those on the remote Atlantic islands – are faced with quite different obstacles from those confronting women in other European countries. From childhood, they find themselves under the constant supervision of males – father, brothers, husband, sons – all of whom are intent on seeing that their womenfolk do not stray from the path of virtue. Family supervision becomes more

Preceding pages and **left**: the young and the not so young are often worlds apart. **Right**, she comes from a very different world.

rigorous still for girls at the onset of puberty, the very time when their youthful male counterparts are bent on having fun – if possible with girls.

Until well into the 1970s, no so-called decent girl would dare be seen unaccompanied on the streets after dark and no girl was allowed to leave the house in male company, apart from that of her brother, uncle or cousin. Nor was a girl allowed to date a boy of her own choice. Friends of the family or relations were constantly on chaperon duty to ensure

that young couples did not succumb to "carnal desire". Until just a few years ago, it was still common for parents to choose marriage partners for their daughters.

Naturally, the bride was expected to have preserved her virginity before marriage. This still applies in country villages and even in Funchal itself among the most poorly educated members of the lower classes. The power of the Catholic church, with its rigid strictures on sexuality and marriage, is still immense on Madeira.

On the whole, so far it is only the educated that are questioning these traditional precepts. Female students and employed women are becoming increasingly independent and are beginning to rebel, albeit cautiously. Even for these women, an engagement ring is usually regarded as being necessary before they enter into sexual relations with a man. The big problem, of course, is when an engagement is broken off, and the next man on the scene has to come to terms with the fact that he was not the first.

Engaging habits: A fiancée "*está pedida*" – has been "booked" – and is therefore no longer available. Though many engaged couples have to wait years before they can finally get married – the groom-to-be may have to do military service or be earning too little to support a family – couples still insist

enter marriage virtually ignorant of the facts of life. Their parents are embarrassed to discuss sexuality in anything but the vaguest terms, and the subject is still absolutely taboo in Madeiran schools.

Such ignorance of sexual matters may not apply to the young city women who are making increasing efforts to live their own lives, but it is still remarkable how willingly they slip into the role played by their own mothers when they marry. Most female children are brought up to help in the house and look after their younger brothers and sisters and they cling to the role which earned them the recognition and approval of their parents when they get married. As *donas de*

on getting engaged. It serves to reassure a man that his future wife remains absolutely faithful, and a woman knows where she stands, especially when no firm marriage date can be set.

An engagement is generally celebrated at a big family party, when the family and relations begin to fill up her "*baú de felicidade*", a heavy chest containing the bride's trousseau and dowry.

Generally the ideas that engaged couples have about marriage are limited, and very much based on the marriages of their parents. In the poorer sections of the island population some unfortunate young women even

casa – quite literally "mistresses of the house" – most of these housewives live according to the strict rules of their own traditional family upbringing.

Family ties play an important role for Madeirans, far greater than is the case in many other European countries. They are not confined to a narrow mother-father-child relationship, but embrace what can be a huge family clan. The extended family even includes second and third cousins – all of them *primos* and *primas*. And considerable influence in family matters is also wielded by the *padrinhos*, the godparents, who foster a close relationship with the parents of their godchildren, the *compadres*, and take their role extremely seriously.

Such strong family affiliations naturally tie down Madeira's womenfolk, but they also offer some important advantages: they offer security and ensure that no one becomes lonely and neglected. Unmarried women, widowed aunts, grandparents – they all enjoy the guardianship of the extended family. Single people, living alone in flats, are virtually non-existent on Madeira. When girls leave home before marriage, perhaps to study or take a job, they generally live with relations. Aunts and uncles feel duty bound to keep a sharp eye on the comings and goings of their young charges. If a girl comes

structure than to risk provoking the very people with which they share their personal worries and all the joys of family festivities.

All the big celebrations are real family occasions. That even applies to the religious festivities, which are attended by relations from every generation. It is quite normal for Madeiran families to get together several times a year to dance and celebrate. Since the family is more important than anything else and few islanders choose to go their own way, conflict of the generations is far less pronounced than in Northern Europe. Emigrants, too, remain closely attached to their families and many send their parents money year after year.

from a village background, their parents are especially apprehensive about the risks of urban living.

Few women dare to question the numerous unwritten rules that govern their lives, even though the new constitution in 1976 proclaimed the equality of men and women a basic right. Madeiran women appear to lack the strength and will really to challenge the roles ascribed by tradition. Used to submitting themselves to parental control, women find it far easier to fit into the family

Left, young and in love in the park. Above, washing day at the mountain stream.

Apart from its two-class system, Madeira also has a "two-sex" system. Until 1976, boys and girls were taught in separate classes in school. Mothers are still largely responsible for looking after the children and running the house – even when they go out to work – while their husbands are responsible for everything that takes place outside the home. The fact that this also applies to the upper class is most evident when couples are invited out: the men tend to talk animatedly about business, sport and good food, while their womenfolk sit in separate groups and discuss everyday housekeeping problems.

Foreign women married to Madeirans often

find it difficult to accept the invisible but impenetrable barrier separating their world from the world of their menfolk. The dominant position of men in Madeiran society is no longer anchored in law, but daily life does not always keep step with legislative reform.

Nor is it all that long since equality didn't even exist in law in Portugal. Before the introduction of the Civil Code in 1966, no woman could leave the country without the written permission of her husband. She was not allowed to purchase, sell or manage her own property, nor to incur debts. If she went out to work, she could not dispose of her own earnings, for her husband was "the head of the family, who officially represents his kin

women than most other countries in Europe, but the number is now increasing year by year. It is no longer a stigma when a women boosts her husband's earnings; in many cases, the poor state of the family finances and the spiralling cost of living leave no alternative. This is enabling more women to penetrate sectors of employment which were once strictly male domains.

Rural/urban divide: Madeiran women are also restricted by larger domestic responsibilities, due to larger numbers of children, than are usual in the rest of Europe. In rural families, it is not unusual to find ten or even more children. In general, rural Madeirans are either ignorant about methods of birth

outside the family and makes all decisions connected with married life."

In consequence, most Portuguese men, especially those of the middle and upper classes, refused to allow their wives to go out to work, because that was incompatible with their status as the master of the house and suggested to outsiders that they were not earning enough to support their families. It was also thought to entail different risks: other men might make advances to a married woman, who might be tempted to return them, or she might come to take more interest in her job than in her family.

Portugal still has fewer gainfully employed

control or do not practise it for religious reasons. Such parents still tend to rejoice more over the birth of a son than a daughter. And a boy is still likely to be given a better education than a girl.

In the city, more and more girls are insisting on obtaining further education and qualifications before they settle down to marriage. Family planning is also widely practised, and the divorce rate is increasing. Men on Madeira may still have the last word, but lengthy and heated discussion with the womenfolk will usually precede it.

Above, the look of emancipation.

DIARY OF AN ENGLISHWOMAN

"The first walk I took in Funchal was up the street immediately opposite our door, bearing the very appropriate name of Break-back Street," wrote Isabella de França in her *Journal of a Visit to Madeira and Portugal 1853–1854*.

Isabella, the new (but, at 57, not young) English bride of a Madeiran *morgado* (owner of substantial ancestral lands), was one of several Victorian ladies to record their visits in journals that were later published. Others included Lady Emmeline Stuart Wortley (1854), and Emily Shore, a young invalid who died of tuberculosis on the island in 1839. It is Isabella de França's journal, though, that most vividly captures Madeira's *belle époque*.

As the wife of a Madeiran nobleman, albeit one brought up in London's Covent Garden, she penetrates all stratas of the island's small society. Her observations are both lively and knowledgeable. Humour underlies the whole, surfacing with perfect delivery every few paragraphs or so. Though frequently at the Madeirans' expense, it extends to the numerous foreign visitors, including invalids. Describing a Madeiran ball, she says: "The most remarkable thing at these balls is to see invalids, who in England would be confined to their beds, polking as if they went by steam, and that not once, but at a succession of balls throughout the winter."

Her journal includes plenty on scenery, flora and fauna, but she realised, before most, that people are the most interesting aspect of a place. Isabella is especially good on prevailing social relations and etiquette. When it came to death, she notes, the Madeiran practice was to bury the corpse within hours. "The first intimation of a friend's death is an invitation to his funeral."

Invitations, whether for funerals, weddings or balls, entailed a plethora of social pitfalls, mostly due to the Madeirans' propensity for accumulating names and titles (Isabella and her husband officially had nine). These, she said, were usually substituted by a nickname: "A young friend of

ours was married on 12th October, and in due course we received the cards in the English style, but the Bridegroom had so many names that he could not get them all into his card, yet nobody calls him anything but Codfish."

Listing the nicknames she has come across, she notes that even ladies do not escape the custom: "A Lady who was here two years ago was first called Flora, from her head dress containing more flowers than were then generally worn; but afterwards she was known as the Boiled Chicken, on account of the whiteness of her skin... An English lady, of great beauty but large proportions, is called The Great Britain."

Isabella gives a detailed account of the domestic customs of the time. Calling on a Portuguese acquaintance, she is astonished when the lady's maid, in her delight at seeing a visitor, lifts her high in the air, a misplaced familiarity which Isabella puts down to Moorish origins. Many female servants, she tells us, performed the function of companions, the heavy chores being seen as men's work.

Washday, Isabella records, was spent on the riverbank, where the vigorous mode of washing compensated for lack of detergent. Not that the maids didn't improvise: "Sometimes they put [the washing] in baskets, with alternate layers of cow dung, which they say is a great detergent, and allow the water to flow through it." This produced excellent results: "The linen when dry is as white as snow, and the getting up is admirable," Isabella enthuses.

Though believed to have been intended for a wider audience than her husband, Isabella de França's *Journal* remained unpublished for over a century. In 1939 a private collector of Madeiriana purchased the "three hundred and forty-two pages, of bluish linen paper, written in a graceful feminine hand", and in 1969 his son, Dr Frederico Augusto de Freitas, undertook its publication.

The manuscript was illustrated by 24 watercolours, also thought to be the work of Isabella. Though not of high artistic merit, they are competent and very charming. She, after all, was a stern art critic. Of the paintings she saw in Funchal's castle, she said, "they are all painted in a style that would disgrace a signpost."

A FIGHT AGAINST POVERTY

Poverty has always been widespread on Madeira. Over the past 200 years, it has driven hundreds of thousands of Madeiran farmers and city dwellers overseas to South Africa, Latin America (in particular Venezuela), the USA and Europe. These amiable islanders – like all Portuguese – are respected the world over for being hard workers.

They are called "emigrants" by the people who have remained on the island. Many of them, having made their fortunes abroad, have returned in recent years and are now investing considerable sums of money in the island, building hotels and restaurants, creating employment and livelihoods, thereby saving their fellow Madeirans from having to emigrate themselves. Even so, poverty still prevails.

Originally, Madeira was a very wealthy island, with sugar and wine providing a healthy livelihood for its inhabitants. The legendary fertility of the island's soil made it possible to cultivate anything. But natural resources must be managed carefully if they are to continue providing wealth; sadly, this wasn't the case in Madeira.

The road to poverty was signposted by policies forged on the mainland of Portugal as long ago as the 17th century. When Catherine of Braganza married England's Charles II in 1660, she brought important trade privileges as part of her dowry. Many English companies availed themselves of these privileges and settled on Madeira. As a result, for centuries there was a considerable outflow of capital from important sectors of the Madeiran economy to Britain. To some extent there still is.

Poverty really set in during the middle of the last century, however, when the bulk of the island's vineyards were destroyed by mildew. Many vintners went bankrupt, and even the island's most prosperous families were on the verge of starvation. Considering that 12–16 children were not uncommon for a Madeiran family in those days, it is easy to envisage the scope of the catastrophe. To make things worse, two years later the island

was infested by a cholera epidemic, which claimed 10,000 victims.

As documented elsewhere in this book, the other source of Madeira's former wealth, sugar, was also fated to decline. Until the middle of the 17th century, Madeiran sugar dominated the European market virtually without foreign competition and was sold as a costly delicacy. But once the large plantations in South America and Cuba began to produce on a bigger and more economical scale, Madeira was driven out of the market.

The final blow came with the discovery of sugar beet as a source of the coveted crystals by the Berlin pharmacist, Markgraf, in the year 1747. Within a century, sugar beet had replaced sugar cane as the major source of the world's sugar.

Today, only one sugar-cane press is operating on Madeira – in Porto da Cruz – producing the raw material for the distillation of *aguardente de cana*, the popular and potent local schnapps.

With the decline of the sugar trade, numerous workers' families also lost their source of income. Plantations, laid out specially for the growing of sugar cane on ter-

Left and **right**, visitors do not tend to see much of the extreme poverty on the island.

races, were simply abandoned and allowed to fall into neglect.

Help came from the private and government sectors which stepped in to support various cottage industries based on traditional island handicrafts. By the end of the last century, these had grown into viable export-orientated branches of the island's economy. One pillar of private support was Elizabeth Phelps from England. Popularly known as "Bella", she taught the island womenfolk a style of embroidery tuned to the taste of Victorian England and organised sales in England. In doing so, she managed to save many a Madeiran family from becoming destitute. Now famous, Madeiran em-important source of income. It still remains a cottage industry, with entire families working at home to produce over 1,200 different wicker models.

The hidden poor: Despite these cottage industries and a steadily growing tourist sector, there are still very many islanders living in poverty. This may not be obvious to visitors, since by and large the poorest islanders live well away from the normal tourist paths. These destitute families live in makeshift shelters made from wooden crates, protected against rain and wind by plastic sheets, or in containers that have fallen off lorries and been abandoned by the drivers. There are still some Madeirans who have set

broidery is still largely done by women working at home. "Embroidery factories" purchase the decorative linen, wash and iron each article and pack them ready for sale. Nowhere in the world is piecework calculated so carefully as here: the outworkers are still paid per stitch.

Another island industry is carpet embroidery, which first began to produce marketable goods in the 1930s, when a factory was set up. Basket-making also grew out of necessity. While baskets had been traditionally used in the vineyards and for transporting goods along the island's steep paths, it was not until 1880 that basket-making became an up home in caves and cook their frugal meals of watery soup on open fires.

Such poverty is inevitably accompanied by other social problems. There are numerous families impoverished by the widespread alcoholism on the island. Among the lower classes in particular, it is not unusual for the head of the family to spend all the little money he earns at the harbour drinking and playing cards at his local bar.

Government authorities have recently been cooperating with relief organisations in

Some Madeirans live in shanty conditions on the outskirts of Funchal.

tackling poverty on Madeira. The fishermen's families of Câmara de Lobos are just one example of the poor families to benefit from slum clearance projects. The authorities moved them into public assistance dwellings, and cleared up the slum area. Direct aid takes many different forms, ranging from the consignment of containers packed with clothing to simple sewing machines and toys for the children of the island's poor families.

What is most crucial in the long term, however, are the self-help projects financed and run by the government in association with charitable organisations. They show poor Madeirans how to help themselves – for example by setting up cottage industries – and not rely on inadequate government handouts. In addition, the relief organisations have been successful in organising overseas sponsorships for children; these have enabled them to obtain schooling or vocational training and given them a real chance in life.

In researching this article, we accompanied a *padre*, a priest attached to one of the local charitable organisations, on his visit to a destitute family living in the country – a stiff 20-minute walk from the nearest road. In a small clearing surrounded by dense vegetation, we finally found their home, a makeshift hut built from old crates, scraps of wood and rotting boards. This provided shelter for a family of 12.

The padre is a regular and welcome visitor to the family, a fact which helped to dispel their initial distrust of the strangers accompanying him. Like all poor islanders, they were ashamed of their poverty. Embarrassed, the mother quickly tried to clear away the garbage in front of the hut with her bare foot. She had been cooking the family's frugal "lunch" – a thin, pale vegetable soup, bubbling in a big pot standing on three bricks over an open fire.

The degree of their poverty is staggering for a European country. The padre asked to see one of the daughters, who had torn open her calf the week before. The wound looked bad, and the padre promised her mother to have the girl collected for treatment the following day. One of the other children is unable to speak at the age of four; nobody knows why. The older children don't go to school, although school attendance is now compulsory on Madeira. The reason is that they are ashamed of their ragged clothes.

After inspecting the family's scanty food supplies, the padre pulled a glass of powdered milk and two loaves of bread out of his bag and gave them to the mother, who thanked him profusely. She never knows when her husband, on whom the family must depend, is going to return; sometimes, she told us, weeks go by before he turns up at the family home again.

Spiralling costs: For poor Madeiran families, life is a sheer struggle for survival. Tourism, a vital source of income for many other families, has had devastating consequences for the poor sections of the population. Like everywhere else in the world, by bringing foreign exchange to the island the wealthy tourists have caused living costs to spiral, and, because the small island has to import most of the commodities it needs, prices on Madeira are now comparable with those in European industrial countries like Britain, France or Germany. If you think restaurants are inexpensive, bear in mind that this is only due to low staff costs. Several staple foods and services – bread and public transport, for example – are subsidised by the government.

In general, wages and salaries are low; the legal minimum wage per month in industry and trade is only about £130 net. A young Madeiran bank clerk who can speak English, French or German earns about £200 a month, a primary school teacher with 10 years' professional experience will take home about £250, and a secondary school teacher with 29 years of teaching behind him, £400 a month after the deduction of tax and social contributions.

No one earning such incomes can afford any luxury, especially since the lack of housing has caused rents to climb to an astronomical height. Many Madeirans therefore try to boost their incomes by taking on second or even third jobs.

It is hardly surprising that in such circumstances it is the poor that suffer most. Many are forced to rely on public welfare. The underlying causes of this situation were created by monoculture farming introduced centuries ago. Whether the European Community will bring relief in the future, and whether aid – should it actually arrive – will reach the most remote makeshift homes on Madeira, is more than questionable.

The human preference for festivals over work is perhaps nowhere so pronounced as on Madeira. The islanders' tight schedule of public holidays and traditional festivities testifies to that. When, as sometimes happens, a workday is sandwiched between two public holidays, Madeirans, like other peoples with a zest for life, tend to build a *ponte* – a bridge – and celebrate a three-day festival, day and night.

This determination to celebrate stems from traditional hardship and the attendant need to cast off the burdens of life's daily grind. It is compounded by the much-quoted phenomenon of insularity: the possibilities of breaking the rules of social life are limited, so the islanders cultivate the illusion of doing so by abandoning themselves to private and public festivities.

Public and private festivals are celebrated with great gusto and expense. No-one who sends out invitations need worry about refusals, providing there is the prospect of lots to eat and plenty to drink, the responsibility for which falls to the housewives – *donas da casa*. The women of Madeira spend weeks preparing for an important festival, cleaning their homes in readiness for the expected guests, cooking their best dishes and baking special cakes.

Promessa: One of the most important festivals on the island is the feast of Our Lady of Monte. Every year on Assumption Day, 15 August, pilgrims pour into Monte from every corner of the island, on foot, in small overloaded trucks or by bus, singing and praying on their way. Down on their knees and praying unceasingly, pilgrims slowly and painfully make their way up the 68 grey, basalt-stone steps to the church to fulfill the *promessa*, the solemn oath which their forbears swore in times of trouble.

Originally, the *romarias*, or pilgrimages, were typically Portuguese in character, but in the course of time the Madeirans created their own *Fatima*, as it were, by proclaiming Monte as their very own place of pilgrimage.

Left, the festival of Corpus Christi, as witnessed by Isabella de França. **Right**, the *fado* has been revived for the tourists.

Legend has it that this was the place where, in the 18th century during the early years of Portuguese settlement, the Virgin Mary appeared to a poor shepherd girl.

It was Pope Pius VII who proclaimed Nossa Senhora do Monte the patron saint of Madeira. Since then, a lot of wax has been burned, not only in the form of candles but also in models representing parts of the human body, for the devout pilgrims, firmly believing that Our Lady will hear and graciously answer their prayers, hope that physi-

cal disability and ill health will be cured on their visit. Monte is the Lourdes of Madeira, where faith and superstition blend.

After fulfilling their religious obligations, the pilgrims then indulge in the profane part of the festival, the *arraial*. This is when they relax from the exertion of their pilgrimage and partake in the traditional feast.Makeshift stalls, built from bundles of laurel branches, are hastily set up along the route. They offer *espetada*, meat on laurel-twig skewers, grilled over charcoal fires; *pesticos*, and tasty hors d'oeuvres. Local wine flows copiously on such occasions. Special treats for the children include *bonecos*, tiny edible dolls, made from flour, water and yeast, decorated with blue and red silk paper, though nowadays the custom of baking these sweets is unfortunately waning.

Streets and paths are festooned with coloured flags and garlands of flowers – myrtle, laurel and hortensia – to provide the proper festive background for the procession proudly bearing the statue of Madeira's patron saint through Monte.

If you decide to take part in this festival – the largest and probably the most typical of all Madeira's festive occasions – you will need to have at least a couple of days to spare; from midday of 14 August, when the festival commences with a firework display and music, to the night of 15 August when it ends, there is virtually no way out of the small township above Funchal.

If you don't care to get involved in all the commotion up on the hill, then at least one aspect of the festivities can be viewed in comfort from the terrace of a Funchal café: the church and streets of Monte are lit by a myriad of lights and lamps.

All of the island's pilgrim festivities have two things in common: their religious motivation and their strong secular character. What distinguishes them, however, are the special "attractions" each village offers its pilgrims. Monte's special feature is the *promessa*, to fulfil which some pilgrims even indulge in self-flagellation; at Machico's Festival of the Sacred Sacrament, which is held on the last Sunday in August, there is the lighting of a huge bonfire in the valley on the previous evening, followed by a series of torch-lit processions.

On St Peter's Day, celebrated in Ribeira Brava on 29 June, the *charolas* are inundated with gifts of harvest produce. Caniçal celebrates the festival of Nossa Senhora da Piedade with a procession of fishing vessels: one boat takes the statue of Our Lady from the chapel to the village and back. Sometimes, it is quite simply the picturesque setting and the unique features of the pilgrimage itself which give each festival its own special charm.

One such feature is the mysterious and untranslatable *desafio* or *despique* – a form of singing – an improvised vocal report of village news, which can contain all sorts of embarrassing bits of gossip, rendered in rhyme form for hours on end. The verses of the inventive vocalists are accompanied by the strains of simple string instruments, such as the *braguinha*, which resembles the Hawaiian ukelele. This traditional form of singing competition is not originally Madeiran, but indigenous to the Portuguese mainland. The islanders, however, have elaborated the musical genre to such a degree that today they can justifiably describe it as being typically Madeiran.

The pagan aspects of these religious festivals display many characteristics which show Madeira to be a melting pot of diverse cultural influences.

Popular festivals and folklore: Entirely secular, even though they are always blessed by the local priest, are the village festivals sponsored by the agricultural board; for instance, the Apple Festivals at Camacha and Ponta do Pargo, the Chestnut Festival in Curral das Freiras, the Sheep-Shearing Festival at Santana – one of Madeira's oldest festivities – and the Agricultural Exhibition in Porto Moniz, to mention just a few.

These and other such occasions are popular festivals in the true sense of the word, and they are accompanied by typical regional fare, from local cider to chestnut soup. The festivities are accompanied by the obligatory music and dances performed by local folklore groups.

Much of Madeira's rich folklore tradition, with its diverse traditional dress, music and dance, remains unexplored terrain for the average tourist. Most of these, alas, are content to watch the young mini-skirted Madeiran girls performing folklore evenings staged by the big hotels and don't imagine that they are being undersold.

Visitors wishing to experience authentic Madeiran folklore should not miss the "24-hour-dance session" at Santana's folk dance festival held every July. The village explodes into a festival of colours, melodies, and rhythms. A popular local instrument is the *brinquinho*, a quaint type of percussion device of north Portuguese origin, which features wooden dolls in traditional dress sliding up and down a pole to the rhythm of the music. Bells and *castanholas*, which closely resemble castanets, are mounted on the dolls' backs and produce a fascinating percussion sound.

Traditional dress is worn everywhere on the island. As you will notice, Madeiran costume is very popular in Funchal, especially among flower-girls and waitresses in the folkloristic restaurants and hotels. It is a gaudy, artificial creation, however, dating back to the 1930s and has very little in common with the traditional dress still worn by the island's villagers.

Characteristic features of the island's traditional dress are the women's cap, whose stalk used not to be quite as long as it is today; the men's woollen cap, the *carapuça*, a type of balaclava with ear-flaps which you will notice worn even on the warmest summer days; the *capa*, a cape thrown over the left shoulder to leave the right one free for carrying loads; and the *botas*, half-length goatskin

the days of Madeiran slavery, when the unfortunate slaves were forbidden to look their masters in the eyes, and had to jump up and dance the *bailado* at the snap of their fingers.

Official events: Beside the village festivities, there are various official events organised by the local authorities, notably the numerous sporting occasions. Anyone who has attended a Madeiran football match can understand why they are called popular festivals. They are also said to testify to the effectiveness of the three "F" formula reputed to have been devised by the Portuguese dictator, Salazar, to keep his people content and amenable: Fatima, football, and *fado* – the traditional folklore music of con-

boots with a characteristic red stripe on the turned down uppers.

The folk dances have certain features in common with the dances of the Minho in northern Portugal, while their melodies are reminiscent of the melancholy strains of the southern region. But in all of them, the dancers move in a circle, their bodies bent at the waist, their heads bowed in gestures of humble submission, their arms outstretched and their feet scarcely lifted off the ground. The style of this dancing is said to have originated in

Schoolchildren celebrate the Day of the Tree in Funchal.

tinental Portugal.

In fact, Salazar, nationalist and populist as he was, banned the *fado*, with its melancholic Arab strains, in Portugal. This did not worry the Madeirans, however, because they had their own island folklore music.

International sporting competitions, rallies and games keep the island's sports fans happy throughout the summer months. More money is being spent on extending sporting opportunities. Tennis champions savour the splendid isolation of the chic Quinta Magnólia club. A great deal of public money is now being invested in this sport, frequently in collaboration with the big hotels, which sponsor attractive tennis tournaments for publicity purposes.

The islanders spend a great deal of time and money on their festivals, whether it be the Flower Festival in June or the Wine Festival in September. Madeirans relish their festivities and celebrate them *para o inglês ver* – for the eyes of the Englishman – as an old Portuguese saying goes.

In fact this is more than just a saying where the big festivals are concerned. The Tourist Office funds the bulk of the island's festival and recreation budget and every year organises an extensive programme of extravagant and costly events. They are designed specifically to attract the tourists and are often wrongly publicised as being "typically Madeiran". Admittedly, some of these events can claim to be based on certain elements of island folklore, but they were only devised in their present form in recent years, and it is not by accident that the festival schedule coincides with the main tourist season.

Nevertheless, all of these festivals are colourful and exciting spectacles, especially Carnival. The Madeirans celebrate it in Brazilian style, much to the delight of visitors who are encouraged by local revellers to join in. In Funchal it is an extravagant affair with dancing in the streets to pulsating samba music. Carnival in the villages is celebrated in a rather different way and is sometimes accompanied by outbreaks of ugly violence (be warned).

The festival of festivals: The great festival on Madeira, and the one which combines official policy and a popular desire for ritual and celebration, is Christmas. Celebrations get off to an early start on the island, with Madeirans already being *em festa* on 8 December and remaining in a state of elation until Epiphany. A meditative and melancholy Advent is unheard of among the people of Madeira.

Hundreds of thousands of coloured lights illuminate Funchal, enabling the electricity industry to earn a small fortune, and bands and folklore groups perform for free in the streets. In the countryside, villagers attend the nine special masses celebrated at dawn before Christmas Day, and they slaughter a pig – an impressive ritual that has been performed for centuries.

Each year huge nativity figures are lovingly unpacked and set up in the home of every Madeiran family. The market becomes a hive of activity, with cheerful shoppers thronging the busy stalls. The market caters for everybody – rich and poor, young and old – and the bright sunshine makes sure that the joyful mood is not spoiled by North European winter melancholy.

The culmination of the island's annual festivities is the famous New Year's Eve firework display, presenting another opportunity for the Madeirans to demonstrate their pyrotechnical prowess. In Funchal harbour cruise liners, tugs and cargo boats sound their sirens in a fierce competition for top decibel ratings. Then at 11 p.m., the town flares up in a great blaze of light. Tradition demands that every householder turns on all

the lights and opens every window.

Epiphany is the occasion for yet another impressive festival, celebrated in the countryside with traditional Epiphany singing. Some villages celebrate Santo Amaro Day on 15 January, the day on which the old year traditionally ends. It does so with a radical sweep-out of the household's cupboards and drawers to make room for the New Year, which is certain to feature an exciting replay of Madeira's festivals. In fact, Carnival is just around the corner.

Above, Christmas is celebrated for a whole month on Madeira. **Right**, the Easter procession.

Many epithets have been bestowed on Madeira in the course of its history, most of them paying tribute to its fabulous vegetation. "Flower of the Ocean", "Island of Eternal Spring" and "Floating Garden of the Atlantic" are just a few of the glowing tributes that have been heaped on this sub-tropical island. The variety of flora has not only captivated botanists; its plants, flowers and trees also make a lasting impression on amateur gardeners and lay visitors to the island.

Isabella de França's description of her first

Although visitors are naturally attracted first to the stunning-looking tropical plants, botanical interest tends to concentrate on Madeira's unique laurel woods, which are home to a rich variety of endemic plant species. Madeira has 92 of these species, representing about 8 percent of all of the island's wild flora. This is due to the stable climatic conditions prevailing on the island – northeast trade winds and Canary ocean currents are the decisive factors – which have enabled Madeira to preserve a floral world

impression of the island as she tripped off the boat in 1853 is full of the gardens "...now flowering with oleander, heliotrope, blue hydrangea, the white blossom of the coffee tree, and a thousand other flowers new to an English eye, and more brilliant in colour than can be described."

The indigenous plant varieties blend with exotic varieties to create a varied but harmonious floral display. Above all, it is the unique wealth of exotic tropical and sub-tropical species, introduced and cultivated in the parks and gardens over the past two centuries, that give the island its particularly lush character.

which was common throughout Central and Southern Europe during the Tertiary period. Due to a deterioration of the climate, in most places these plants could no longer flourish, but they did manage to survive on a few Atlantic islands: namely Madeira, the Azores and the Canary Islands.

Old maps and prints depict Madeira carpeted with woods, a former characteristic which accounts for its name – *madeira* is the Portuguese word for wood. But in the wake of settlement and the steady encroachment of agricultural development, the area of dense woodland gradually dwindled.

Pine forestry replaced much of the original

woodland: W. H. Koebel, in his study of the island published in 1909, reported that pine forestry had become a profitable industry, the trees being "employed to make the pergolas and trellis-work upon which the vines are trained" and being an important source of fuel for the islanders.

Today, we can distinguish between three stages of vegetation on Madeira: the intensively cultivated lowland and coastal region, also called sub-tropical bush region, rising to a height of 2,300 ft (700 metres) above sea

ing mainly of maritime pine *(Pinus pinaster)* and Tasmanian blue gum *(Eucalyptus globulus)*. In addition to these, small groups of Douglas fir *(Pseudotsuga taxifolia)*, Lawson cypress *(Chamaecyparis lawsoniana)*, Japanese red cedar *(Cryptomeria japonica)* and Indian silver fir *(Abies spectabilis)* were planted.

Coastal and lowland vegetation: The vegetation which used to dominate the lowland is now limited to a few rocky sections of the island's coast. Many varieties can be found

level; the warm, temperate zone of the laurel woodlands at 2,300–3,900 ft (700–1,200 metres), and the cool, temperate moor and bush region in the highlands above 3,900 ft (1,200 metres).

Between the lowland zone and the laurel wood zone, a transitional zone at 2,300–3,300 ft (700–1,000 metres) was created by the planting of alien monocultures consist-

Preceding pages: Madeira – flower island in the Atlantic. **Far left**, the *cattleya*, a species of orchid. **Left**, an aloe. **Above**, the blossom of an agave. **Above right**, one of the countless species of lily on the island.

there which are well adapted to their dry and stony habitat. The most striking flora in this zone are the colonies of tuna *(Opuntia tuna)*, a cactus introduced from Central America in 1826 for the cultivation of the cochineal insect. Prickly pears *(Opuntia ficus-indica)*, with their edible fruit, also flourish near island settlements.

In the midst of the many different grasses and annual herbs, introduced from the Mediterranean region, grow species like jimson weed datura *(Euphorbia piscatioria)*, a bush with gnarled branches and a poisonous milky sap, which used to be employed for catching sea-fish. Other varieties include the *Aeonium*

arboreum with its yellow blossoms, the bushy globe daisy *(Globularia salicina)*, with its small, white flowers and the splendid "Pride of Madeira" *(Echium nervosum)*, with its imposing steel-blue blossoms.

The fissures of the basalt cliffs and the lava rocks are a home for the *Mesembryanthemum crystallinum,* whose leaves glisten like ice crystal, the Kaffir fig *(Carpobrotus edulis)*, with its fleshy leaves, and Madeira stock *(Matthiola maderensis)*, which has striking lilac-coloured flowers.

Of special floral interest are the moist areas flanking the *levadas*, where the soil contains a wealth of nutritional substances. Particularly rich in plant life on the southern

sisting of honeysuckle *(Lonicera etrusca)*, the elm-leaved blackberry *(Rubus ulmifolius)* and the *Senecio mikanioides,* the *Ipomoea acuminata*, and the *Semele androgyna.* Places where land cultivation has been neglected for many years form a refuge for many plant species, which compete keenly with one another for control of the ground at their disposal.

Relatively uninteresting for plant lovers due to their lack of flora are the eucalyptus and pinewoods, which have supplanted the laurel woods at a height of 1,900–3,000 ft (600–900 metres). The rapidly-growing Tasmanian blue gum tree *(Eucalyptus globulus)* imported from Australia is an im-

side of the island are the Levada dos Tornos, Levada do Norte, Levada do Curral et Castelejo and the Levada Calheta – Ponta do Pargo. They support a wide selection of flora, ranging from the chrysanthemum *(Argyranthemum pinnatifidum)*, the *Senecio petasites*, the *Ageratina adenophora*, and the *Solanum maritimum* to the service tree *(Sorbus maderensis)* and Canary ivy which clings to the trunk of the *Pittosporum undulatum.*

Water-splashed rock faces, with a thick covering of ferns – some of which are so tall that they look more like trees – and moss, alternate with dense thickets of shrubs, con-

portant source of building timber. It is not only the aromatic odour of the leaves – which in some countries was for many years believed to ward off malaria – but also their diversity which characterise the eucalyptus tree. While the young leaves are blue and ovute-shaped, the older leaves are dark green and crescent-shaped. The predominant vegetation at the foot of the eucalyptus trees consists of erica bushes and particularly common gorse *(Ulex europaeus)*, a thorny bush with yellow flowers even disdained by grazing cattle.

Laurel woods: As Madeira's traditional vegetation, its remaining laurel woods are an extremely attractive feature of the island's flora. They grow at a height of 2,300–3,900 ft (700–1,200 metres) and form the nucleus of the new national park. The basic conditions necessary for their preservation are an average annual rainfall of over 60 inches (1,500 mm), high humidity and steady, moderate temperatures. To prosper fully, a laurel wood requires at least a dozen different varieties of trees.

The dominant four species in the woods are the *Laurus azorica*, the "Til" tree *(Ocotea foetens)*, the Madeira mahogany or "Vinhático" *(Persea indica)*, a tropical tree of the mimosa family, and finally the ironwood tree *(Apollonias barbujana)*. All of these varieties are evergreens and have leathery leaves, which exude an aromatic odour, green/yellow-coloured flowers and black berries.

Before electricity arrived on Madeira, the islanders used to extract oil from the *Laurus azorica* to burn in their lamps. Some of Madeira's other plants are still put to good use. Dye is still obtained from the "laurisilva", the yellow flowers of the sow-thistle *(Sonchus fruticosus)* and the "Musschie" *(Musschia wollastoni)*, the red inflorescence of the Madeira geranium *(Geranium maderense)* and the blossoms of the yellow foxglove *(Isoplexis sceptrum)*.

A really impressive feature of the laurel woods is their wealth of ferns. There are over 70 varieties, and one of the most striking is the curious liverwort *(Adiantum reniforme)*, whose rounded kidney-shaped frond is not really typical of a fern at all.

In several places, for instance on the Encumeada Pass, the laurel woods give way to a bush landscape reminiscent of the *macchia* found in much of the Mediterranean region. Characteristic forms of this vegetation include tree heath *(Erica arborea)*, heather *(Erica scoparia)*, and the spurge *(Euphorbia mellifera)*. Interspersed with these colonies grows the Madeira bilberry *(Vaccinium padifolium)*. It grows to a height of 2 ft (60 cm) and yields copious quantities of berries which are easy to gather but are not highly flavoured.

All that remains of the former glory of the

island's laurel woods are the *Laurus azorica* and the "Faia" *(Myrica faya)*. Today, Madeira's laurel woods cover an area of 25,000 acres (10,000 hectares). To discover their rich ferns, mosses and lichens, nature lovers should explore one of the following four routes: the route along the Levada do Norte, the walk from Ribeiro Frio to Portela, the environs of Fajã da Nogueira and Boa Ventura, across the Caldeirão do Inferno, the "Green Inferno".

Mountain flora: The moor-bush region found above 3,900 ft (1,200 metres), with its dense bush vegetation, is reminiscent of the Highlands of Scotland. The vegetation of this zone, with its rock bed of basalt lava rock covered with a layer of tufa, is dominated by

heaths *(Erica arborea)* and heather *(Erica scoparia)*.

The fissured rocks, scree and small patches of grass at these heights also form ideal habitats for many rare species of plants that are indigenous to Madeira.

Among them are the Madeira violet *(Viola maderensis)* and *Odontites hillana*, both with their lovely lemon-coloured flowers, the white-flowered Madeira saxifrage *(Saxifraga maderensis)*, and *Aichryson villosum*, the *Ranunculus cortusifolius*, with its characteristic waxy yellow flowers, and navelwort *(Umbilicus horizontalis)* with its fleshy rounded leaves.

AGRICULTURE –
A MIXED BAG

The very first thing visitors notice as their plane lands on Madeira, or at the very latest on their first expedition into the countryside, is the complex patchwork of terraces covering the island's hillsides, particularly in its southern part. These giant "steps" testify to the industriousness of the local farmers, who have spent millions of working hours converting the island's steep and unpromising slopes into arable plots of land.

Naturally, the landscape did not always look so well cultivated. In fact, in 1419, when João Gonçalves Zarco and his crew – dispatched by Henry the Navigator – discovered the archipelago, the island was completely covered by woods.

Clearing operations: Nowadays all that is left of the original woodland is confined to about 25,000 acres (10,000 hectares). It represents roughly 15 percent of Madeira's total land area and is mainly concentrated in the higher regions of the northern part of the island. These laurel woods, which are also interspersed with other hard-leaved vegetation, are called *laurisilva* in Portuguese and represent the remains of a Mediterranean flora once spreading as far as the Azores in the middle of the Atlantic.

Today, these laurel woods are protected by Madeiran law, but the first settlers were less considerate in their treatment of the island's woodlands and quickly set to work burning down most of them to clear the land for cultivation. While such efforts were rewarded with large expanses of arable land, well fertilised by the ashes of the burnt trees, most of the fauna and flora inhabiting it also perished in the blaze. The loss of the protective carpet of vegetation subsequently resulted in serious soil erosion.

How long it took them to clear the land is not clear. According to the chroniclers of the times, at one point the early Portuguese settlers were unable to get their inferno under control. It is recorded that the blistering heat of the flames drove back the settlers, forcing them to flee to their ships for safety and leave the island to continue burning for seven whole years. Those people that were cut off by the blazing fires and unable to reach their vessels only managed to escape by taking refuge in the Ribeira dos Socorridos valley near Câmara dos Lobos, situated just to the west of Funchal.

However, if we try to sift the historical truth from this dramatic legend, the following explanation is probably the most feasible one: that it took the early settlers seven whole years to burn down the woods and clear the land for cultivation.

Terraces and water channels: Once the fires had subsided, the early settlers began to build the terraces, or *poios,* that we see today. Beginning at sea level they rise to a height of about 2,500 ft (800 metres), the maximum height at which crops can be grown on the island. Supporting walls were built to pre-

private ownership with loans and other means of support; on the other hand, despite this policy, about one-third of the island's arable land is still farmed on a *latifundia* basis, i.e. large estates belonging to single landowners and worked by tenant farmers.

This system has a long history on the island. When the Portuguese arrived on Madeira, the *fidalgos* – "sons of someone important" – were rewarded by their king with gifts of land, just as they might have been under the northern European feudal system. The land was cultivated by the *colonos*, tenants, who had to give the landowners 50 percent of the so-called *culturas ricas*, the valuable field crops: sugar cane,

vent the erosion of the rich reddish-brown soil and narrow water channels installed to carry irrigation water from the main *levadas* *(see pages 119–120).* To ensure that the precious water runs off from one terrace to the next plot below, each terrace was designed to slope gently downwards.

Not even the smallest tract of land was spared; everything that could be levelled on this small island was rendered arable. The partition of the land into minute plots might seem to indicate that it is owned by many smallholders, but this impression is misleading. The government wants the land to belong to those who farm it, and promotes

bananas and grapes. Since the tenants could hardly subsist on what was left over they soon began to grow their own fruits and vegetables. These they were permitted to keep all for themselves.

The landowner owns not only the land, but also a share of the island's water. This is allocated to him according to a system of quotas. The tenant, on the other hand, owns all the structures he builds himself: retaining walls, buildings, stables etc, and any trees he plants. When the landowner sells the land, he must pay the tenant a sum of money to reimburse the cost of the improvements made to his estate.

You will notice that many farmers still work the land equipped only with a simple hoe and carry in the harvested crops on their backs. Contrary to what many outsiders think, on Madeira this is not a sign of backward farming methods, but a necessity dictated by the island's topography: most terraced fields are far too small and inaccessible for modern machinery or draught animals to be used effectively.

Historically the resulting low level of productivity in the agricultural sector eventually rendered its produce uncompetitive on the European market. For instance, demand for Madeiran sugar cane, once the leading industry on the island, plummeted when a far

and bananas. Due to the low level of income in the agricultural sector, farmers are being forced to earn supplementary income or abandon farming altogether.

When there are no longer enough young people willing to follow their parents and seek their living tilling the island's terraces, this unique agricultural landscape is doomed to disapprear.

Year-round harvests: Vines originally came to Madeira from the island of Crete. Henry the Navigator had *Malvasia* grapes shipped to Madeira for planting purposes. They are said to have taken their name from the town of Monemvasia on the Peloponnese. The wine they produce is the same "Malmsey"

cheaper variety grown on the vast plantations in colonial Brazil flooded the international market.

It is a difficulty which has still not been overcome. Since becoming a member of the European Community in 1986, Portugal has been facing the very same problem with respect to its major export products, wine

Preceding pages: Tree heath and protea; terraced fields on the north coast; bananas are harvested green; tender young taro plants. **Left**, cattle grazing freely are not a common sight. **Above**, sheep cope better with the precipitous terrain.

savoured to excess by Sir John Falstaff and his boisterous drinking companions in Shakespeare's *Henry IV*.

A great number of these vines were destroyed by a leaf disease caused by mildew and then by the vine louse *phylloxera* at the end of the 19th century. As in other European vineyards ravished by these diseases, imported American vines were then crossed with European varieties to produce hybrids, which today occupy some 60 percent of Madeira's total wine-growing area.

But in compliance with the higher quality stipulations of the European Community, the cultivation of the average-quality hybrids is gradually being supplanted by high-quality varieties such as *Verdelho*, *Boal*, *Sercial*, etc.

The island's volcanic geology, with its bed of rock and fertile soil, and the climate, with its main rainfall in spring and long warm summers, offer optimum conditions for the cultivation of vines. On the other hand, such advantages are countered by other considerations – for example, too much sun makes the grapes over-sweet at the expense of their aroma.

To counter this, the vintners have built sun shields, which also serve to protect the vines against adverse winds. After planting, the vines need 6–8 years before they produce

Vegetables, French beans, haricot beans, potatoes, pumpkin, sweet potatoes, marrows, etc. are also planted between the vines. Superfluous leaves are trimmed from the vines in early summer and the actual wine harvest takes place in August and September, depending on the variety of grape and the location of the vineyard. After the vegetables have also been gathered in, green animal fodder is planted; its roots are worked into the vineyard soil the following year to act as natural fertiliser.

The cultivation of bananas also has a long tradition on Madeira. Originally indigenous to South-East Asia, the plants were introduced to Africa by Arab seafarers, where

grapes for harvesting, but from then on, they can produce ripe grapes for several decades if tended properly.

Vineyards need intensive care all the year round. Work begins in winter (February, March) when the vines are radically pruned back. The soil is then ploughed and prepared for the planting of new vines where needed. In contrast to the Continent, where the planting of new vines is carried out in the early part of the year, in Madeira this is not done until the autumn.

As soon as leaves and flowers appear on the vines, the vintner sprays them with sulphur and copper sulphate to ward off pests.

they were given the name by which we still know them: *banana* probably comes from the Bantu language.

The fruit was introduced to Europe by the Portuguese, reaching the Atlantic islands at the beginning of the 16th century and South America a little later.

The main variety grown on Madeira is the so-called Canary banana or miniature banana (*Musa cavendishii*), a tallish tree bearing relatively small fruit which are golden-yellow in colour and aromatic in flavour. There are also isolated plantations of other banana tree varieties, which are even taller and bear far more fruit.

Used to tropical climates, bananas do not flourish along the north coast of the island, and in the south they don't grow above a height of 65 ft (20 metres). Their ideal habitat is the wind-protected bay of Funchal, though they are being squeezed out by the expanding suburbs of Madeira's capital. The once extensive plantations on the fringes of Funchal are gradually being devoured by new housing and the ever-expanding hotel developments.

Because the cultivated form of the banana plant yields seedless fruits, called "berries" by botanists, they are propagated by seedlings, which sprout up next to the parent plant. After only one year, the new plants are

Due to their form, the individual fruit are compared with fingers, and a row of fruit with a hand. After the harvest, the involuted sheath of the tree stem is cut down and used as animal fodder.

Besides bananas, Madeira's farmers grow a series of other tropical and sub-tropical plants: custard apple *(anona)* avocados, figs, guavas, loquats (Japanese medlar), mangos, papayas, pineapples, passion fruit *(maracujas)* and citrus fruit *(see Tropical Fruits, page 124)*.

A hut for every cow: On such a small island, there is obviously not much room for livestock production. The only large expanse of grazing land is on the plateau of Paúl da Serra

capable of producing a bunch of about 200 bananas, or "paradise figs" as they are also called locally.

It is fascinating to inspect such a huge bunch of fruit (which hangs in the "wrong" direction due to its considerable weight). At the very bottom, i.e. at the tip, the reddish-blue supporting leaves have male flowers, which are followed by several underdeveloped hermaphrodite flowers and then the actual bananas, which grow from the female flowers without being pollinated.

<u>Left</u>, a patchwork quilt. <u>Above</u>, the banana grove is just as important as the vegetable patch.

in the western part of Madeira. Very few goats and cattle can be seen grazing in the open; most of the island's farm animals "live" in *palheiros*, thatched-roof huts. The shelters constitute another attractive feature of Madeira's terraced landscape, though those with animal welfare in mind might well disagree. The cows are shut up in their *palheiros* for days on end.

The green fodder required for these "incarcerated" animals is cut and gathered along the side of paths and other unfarmed terrain. When you see a farmer staggering under a bundle of hay, he is invariably off to feed and exercise his cow.

WHITE GOLD

Funchal's coat of arms bears five sugar cones, testimony to the significant role once played by the growth, processing and sale of sugar in Madeira. In Portuguese such a cone is called *pão de açúcas* which, when literally translated, means sugar loaf - the same name given to the famous rock in Brazil's Rio de Janeiro. Coincidentally enough, it was this country, having seen its own rubber boom come to an abrupt and economically-damaging end, which was responsible for bringing Madeira's developing sugar industry to a similarly speedy halt with the introduction of its cheaper product.

However, let us start at the beginning. Sugar cane was introduced to the island in the early part of the 15th century around about 1425, when Portugal's Prince Henry the Navigator had seeds imported from Sicily. The tropical crop had already been known to the inhabitants of India for centuries, under the Sanskrit name *sakkara* which became *sukkar* in Arabian, since it was Arabic merchants who introduced it to the west. The present plant's origins can be traced back to the New Guinean plant *saccharum robustum* which grows wild and is eaten and enjoyed as a vegetable by the Papuans.

The so-called "Moors", Arabian Berbers from North Africa, were shipped in to carry out the strenuous work demanded in the fields and processing procedures. One of their toughest jobs was to cut through the stalks just above the soil - where the concentration of sugar (at 20 percent) is at its highest. The sugar was cut in the spring (March/April), the exact timing being based on the yellow colouring of the leaves. Once it was cut the cane had to be processed straight away, since the sugar - especially at high temperatures - quickly "runs out of puff" as the industry's jargon puts it. In the early days, the slicing and pressing of the stalks was done by hand or with the aid of livestock and from about 1450 onwards watermills took over. Madeira's first mill was located in the valley of Ribeira Santa Luzia, the middle tributary of three small rivers which flow into the sea in Funchal.

This process has changed little over the years. The extracted juice is first cleaned and then boiled to make it thicken. After that the crystallised brown sugar is separated from the thick syrup and refined. The remaining molasses, which still contains a high sugar content, is used as fodder or for distilling alcohol.

In the old days the refined white sugar was formed into a pointed cone, covered in a blue wrapping and sold as a sugar loaf. Since the "white gold" was easily "mined", the market for it expanded rapidly. Thus, just as honey had been the main sweetener during the Middle Ages, so sugar now took the lead in the royal kitchens. Around the beginning of the 1500s Madeira exported 1,500 tons to Europe and even the republican towns of Venice and Genoa which, until then, had provided the continent with Asian sugar, were among the clientele. This new wealth led to the development of an equally flourishing building trade. Traders from all over the world opened subsidiaries in Funchal and one street was actually called the *Rua dos Mercadores* (the Merchants' Street).

The island's most important trading partners were Great Britain and Flanders. In the case of Flanders sometimes payment for the sugar was made with paintings, which were normally hung in the churches. Consequently Madeira managed to acquire a number of valuable works of art. A few can still be admired today in Funchal's Sacred Art Museum and various churches along the south coast.

However, just a century after the introduction of sugar cane to Madeira, the first large plantations appeared in the Spanish and Portuguese colonies of South America, where the Madeiran know-how was put to the best advantage. The tiny island could not compete with the productivity of its larger competitors and within a short time most people in Madeira were abandoning the market.

Today the production of sugar in Madeira no longer boasts anywhere near the same position it once held, although its role has not been completely extinguished; nobody in Madeira, for example, would for a moment dream of importing ingredients for the island's ubiquitous and potent sugarcane spirit, *aguardente*.

SOLVING THE WATER PROBLEM

While Madeira was still densely forested there was nothing to worry about as far as the water table was concerned. However, the deliberate burning of large areas of woodland by the first settlers threatened to upset the island's delicate ecological balance, as trees are able to store water far better than an area planted with sugar cane. It is thanks to the ingenuity of the Moorish slaves that the island's naturally dry southern region did not turn into a desert.

The problem was exacerbated by the topology of the island. A belt of volcanic rock, rising in areas up to almost 6,000 ft (1,800 metres) cuts a horizontal west-east line across Madeira. Clouds drifting in from the Atlantic are caught on this belt and empty their contents on to the northern face. Up to 78 inches (2,000 mm) of rain has been recorded, almost as much as in the Alps. Yet given the land, soil, temperature and average amount of sunlight of the northern regions, with the exception of a few valleys agricultural conditions are far more favourable in the south of the island.

The only problem is that the south does not get enough rain, sometimes not for six or seven months at a time during the long summer. What is more, a sloping away of the belt towards the north means that even heavy rain falling on the southern slopes of the "central highlands" ends up in the north.

In theory, the solution to the problem was quite simple: all that had to be done was to transfer some of the abundant water supply from the north to the less fortunate south. However, owing to the almost non-existent communications system, putting this theory into practice was no simple piece of engineering. It was eventually accomplished by installing canals across hundreds of miles. The name for these aqueducts, *levadas*, comes from the Portuguese word *levar*, which means to carry.

Since even the earliest settlers needed a great deal of water, both for farming and to power their mechanical sugar mills, the

levadas date almost as far back as the discovery of Madeira itself. Moorish slaves, who knew about irrigation from the developed engineering in their own country, were employed to construct these canals.

Sometimes the slaves were forced to climb to dizzying heights to blast out tunnels or dig channels into the sides of the cliffs. Their aim was to obtain a gentle gradient, since the best sources of water north of the belt are well above the level of even the highest fields in the south. Many slaves perished in the work, falling into precipes when the ropes from which they were suspended gave way.

It was not until the end of the sugar boom, with its initially disastrous effects on farming, that the expansion of *levadas* ceased. At the turn of the century it was estimated that there were 200 of these irrigation channels, providing water for about half of the total farming area.

Levada law: Because the water was so much in demand it was perceived as a potential cause of disputes and it was immediately made subject to government supervision. The Portuguese kings and their governors passed laws to guarantee that water was distributed as fairly as possible, employing civil servants to patrol the *levadas* and ensure that their laws were observed. Each landowner had to accept responsibility for the construction or maintenance of the aqueducts on his property.

This law was not changed until the second half of the 19th century. Then water was privatised by the government, which meant that, regardless of the consequences for the person on whose land the water was, its flow could be controlled or modified to suit the new owner's purposes. This inevitably led to some very underhand dealings. Bands of speculators bought water holes and then sold access to the water at whatever price they pleased. Farmers could be left high and dry if they refused to cooperate.

Thankfully, the *levadas* are now back under government control and since the end of World War II a public water commission has been concentrating on modernising and expanding the canal system.

The last major *levada* to be built (dos

Tornos near Monte, overlooking Funchal and Santa Cruz on the east coast) was built in the 1960s; it is over 62 miles (100 km) long, passes through several tunnels and powers the Fajã da Nogueira electric plant. Thanks to both the new and renovated aqueducts a large percentage of the agricultural land can now be irrigated. A *levada* was also responsible for the improvement of the capital's entire water supply.

Some of the smaller water holes still remain in the possession of private individuals. Like the earlier royal overseers these people are called *heréus* (singular: *heréu*). Most of them belong to a trade association and are responsible for maintaining the *levada*

as well as for the distribution of the water, a service for which they charge a fee called a *levadeiro*.

Standing in line: In theory anybody belonging to a water cooperative should be able to open the sluice gates at the designated time and water their fields for one or two hours. In practice, however, this is not always the way things turn out.

During the height of the summer any delay in water delivery can have disastrous consequences for certain crops, and inevitably lead to a lot of head scratching: is the channel blocked because somebody has dumped rubbish into the canals, or has a neighbour simply "forgotten" to close the gates, or has a tourist interfered with the sluice gates?

The scenario is reminiscent of the days when the millers used to sit around the pond squabbling over who should be able to use the water for their mill. It is not mere coincidence that the word rival is derived from the word Latin word *rivus*, i.e. the rivulet that neighbours coveted. The *levadas* of Madeira provide constant ammunition for old and new feuds.

Visitors to Madeira, however, are seldom aware of such quarrels. They have come to appreciate the *levadas* for other reasons, notably the paths alongside the canals. Called the *passeios dos levadas*, these paths were laid in order to facilitate the regular maintenance of the canals, and they provide excellent walking territory for tourists. With the exception of the climb up to the ridge, the *levada* paths are more or less flat, and at the top it is possible to enjoy a long ramble through the beautifully varied Madeiran countryside uninterrupted by development of any kind.

The biggest advantage for walkers is that in the mountains, although the *levadas* pass through large areas of unspoilt countryside, it is still comfortable – not up hill and down dale – walking. The *levadas* cross wild *barrancos* (gorges) by means of specially constructed bridges and, further down ramblers pass cultivated land and mills, where the canals branch out in many different directions. The paths, which are also used by the locals, have numerous other forks, many of which lead right up to the front door of private houses. Local children can often be seen splashing in the water, women wringing out their washing and husbands ploughing the fields.

Be warned, however: not all *levadas* are suitable for a lazy afternoon's stroll. Some, owing to their exposed position, should only be attempted by the sure-footed and avoided at all costs by anybody suffering from vertigo, especially since, in some cases, there is no hand-rail.

For details of suggested *levada* walks, see the chapter entitled "Island Walking Tours" starting on page 252.

Left, some of Madeira's most beautiful pathways run alongside the *levadas*. **Right**, cactus as modern art.

TROPICAL FRUITS

A native of the New World, the pineapple has found its way into many other tropical regions. In the 19th century the growing and export of this fruit was one of Madeira's leading industries, but cultivation has been curtailed considerably in the last few years. The Azores have taken over as the main supplier. Since both these groups of Atlantic islands lie outside the tropics, these bromeliad plants, which love heat and humidity, are grown in hothouses.

What we find so tasty is, from a botanical point of view, not actually a true fruit, since the plant is reproduced in the same manner as a vegetable, i.e. from cuttings, the "fruit" taking 10–12 months to ripen. It was christened *piña* by its Spanish discoverer because of its resemblance to a pine cone.

Whilst the pineapple – at least the tinned variety – is a common feature on domestic menus all over the world, the relatively unknown **anona** remains something far more exotic. This "custard apple", described by one early visitor to Madeira as "most delicate and toothsome", is likely to retain its mystery, since its tender flesh will probably never be able to survive transportation.

The anona tree, which can grow up to a height of about 39 ft (12 metres), originally comes from the Caribbean. Its magnolia-type blossoms produce berries which merge to form a fist-sized fruit. "Sweet sop" is just one of the many names used to describe this aromatic fruit with scaly, misty-grey skin. From the Latin name *annona* comes the Portuguese word *anona*, and in Madeira the main variety grown are called *cherimoya*.

Whoever says "A" for **avocado** should also say "B" for "butterfruit", since the ripe fruit really does slip off the tongue, which is more than can be said for the "pear's" original Aztec name: *ahuacatl*. Since only the Aztecs could pronounce it properly, it became known as *aguacate* and then by the American word avocado. Some even refer to it as an alligator pear. The evergreen tree, upon which the avocado grows, is a member of the laurel family and reaches a height of 65 ft (20 metres) in tropical forests. Just one blossom in every 5,000 produces a fruit.

Everybody has heard of **figs**, even if there is a huge difference between the dried specimens bought in Europe at Christmas and the fresh green-violet, pear-shaped fruits which melt in your mouth on Madeira. Even when not laden with fruit a fig tree is easily recognised by its white, phantom-like branches and hand-shaped leaves. The fruit ripens in August and September, when it is gathered for preserving.

Similar in name only, the **cactus-fig** can be seen everywhere during the summer. This prickly orange or pink-coloured (when it is ripe) "egg fruit", belonging to the *opuntia* family, demands a great deal of care if it is to

be properly enjoyed –– never pick and peel these fruit without gloves. A few freshly-peeled fruit make a tried and tested Arab remedy for stomach complaints.

The **guava** belongs to the myrtle family and originates from South America. The approximately 33-ft (10-metre) high gnarled tree produces oval-shaped "berries" the size of a peach and with a rough, lemon-like skin.

The fruit contains an orangy, juicy interior and tiny kernels rather than a stone. Like the pineapple, it was once a major Madeiran export. Its tasty flesh, similar to quinces, is pressed and made into marmalade, but it is also eaten raw or cooked. Apropos quinces, which also grow in Madeira, the term "marmalade" comes from the Portuguese word *marmelo* used to describe quince cheese – before it was taken over by the British to refer to their orange marmalade.

Loquat or Japanese medlar is the name given to a tree from East Asia, which reached the Mediterranean area and Madeira about 150 years ago. Belonging to the rose family, the loquat is one of the earliest false fruits known. Its shiny yellow fruits ripen early and can already be picked at the end of the winter. The fruit's large juicy centre is covered by a thin layer of sweet-smelling, rather sour flesh, often protected by a leathery skin.

If you buy a **mango** at Funchal's market don't try and bite it straight away - it is not a fruit you can eat in the street. The delicious, golden flesh, often connected by fibres to the relatively large stone, is not easy to deal with; by the time you have taken a bite or two you will probably need a shower. Two long parallel cuts above and below the flattened stone will produce the cleanest result.

Even 4,000 years ago, the Indians described the mango with appropriate awe and respect. It is thought that the tree probably originated in Burma and Assam. The Indians were responsible for replanting it throughout Southern Asia, from where it was taken to West Africa and Brazil by the Portuguese. In their natural habitat mangos ripen in spring, but in Madeira they are not picked until the autumn.

The **papaya** (paw paw) is, for some reason, referred to in some areas as a "tree melon", but in the true botanical sense the papaya is no more than a leafy plant, and as far as the comparison to melons goes, the only similarity is possibly the taste. This fruit, originally of Central American origin, is now to be found all along the tropical belt. It is also grown in some sub-tropical areas, Madeira being a good example.

The papaya is an hermaphroditic plant. The fruit is produced when the plants are pollinated by insects (all year round on Madeira, although there is a significant summer peak). The bunches of "berries", which weigh between 1–11 lbs (0.5–5.0 kg), tend to hang from a flimsy, leafy branch and thus look similar to melons.

Under their light golden to bottle-green skin of a papaya is an orange, almost red flesh. Once sliced in half, the peppercorn-type juice is removed from the hollow centre and the contents are scooped out with a spoon. The dull taste can be livened up by using the juice of limes, although lemons are equally good. Papayas are extremely good for you since they contain abundant quantities of both Vitamin C and Vitamin A.

The **passion fruit** boasts many different names in Madeira. The Spanish conquerors of South Africa (the natural home of this fruit) called it *grenadilla* (small pomegranate) because of its tiny pomegranate-type seeds, and occasionally on Madeira it is known by its botanical name, *passiflora*.

The more common name, passion, is said to derive from the distinctive form of the flowers. An imaginative Christian is supposed to have interpreted the shape as symbolising the suffering of Christ: the stigmas represent the nails of the cross; the five anthers symbolise the scars of Christ; the filaments around the flower, his crown of thorns; the ovaries, the cup used at the Last Supper; the ten petals, the Apostles (excluding Peter and Judas who were not present at the Crucifixion); the stalk, the whip; and the pointed leaves, the sword. But don't let that put you off.

Last but not least is the **tomarillo**. This egg-sized fruit grows on tall bushes, is rich in all vitamins and it tastes absolutely delicious.

For most people, the name Madeira is more likely to evoke thoughts of a mellow, sweet wine than a beautiful island in the Atlantic. Even wine-bibbers may have no idea where to look on the map for the small archipelago whose sunshine is responsible for the wine's famous flavour.

Shakespeare must have tasted the Madeiran wine at one time or another. In *Henry IV* Falstaff's comment on poor Bardolph's nose, which has a rather distinctive hue, reveals a familiarity with the wine: "Thou hast saved

me a thousand marks in links and torches, walking with thee in the night betwixt tavern and tavern: but the sack that thou hast drunk me would have bought me lights as good cheap at the dearest chandler's in Europe." And just a couple of scenes further on, Falstaff himself does not escape ridicule when he is accused of having sold his soul for the sake of Madeiran wine.

Yet Shakespeare probably knew little else about the island of Madeira. In fact, its inclusion in the play is one of Shakespeare's famous anachronisms. *Henry IV* is set during a period when the island had not even been discovered, let alone planted with the noble vine. It was only after the arrival of Prince Henry the Navigator, at the beginning of the 15th century, that young vines were planted on the island – offshoots from the equally famous Cretan grape.

In less than a century after its introduction Madeiran wine had become a legend in its own right. When, shortly before his execution in 1478, George Duke of Clarence was asked, in accordance with the court etiquette of the day, how he would like to meet his maker, he asked to be drowned in a barrel of Madeira wine. Whether this was just a last desperate bid for attention or a sincere expression of his love for the famous Madeiran tipple is unclear.

Luck and the power of fate: It was not without reason that the English soon began to "top up" their proverbial dry humour with the sweet product of the island. The enthusiasm the upper classes had shown for sugar was soon to be matched by an equal enthusiasm for wine.

In 1750 three factors led to the opening of totally new markets for this export winner: Madeira's production of sugar cane was drastically reduced owing to the stronger competition from the South American colonies, which meant that there was more land available for planting vines. Then love (or more probably politics) resulted in England's Charles II marrying the Portuguese aristocrat, Catherine of Braganza, a particularly lucrative match for English traders, since part of her dowry included trade privileges on Madeira.

In 1651, the Navigation Act was passed by the normally severely sober Oliver Cromwell. It gives a good indication of the place this wine already held in the English heart. The Navigation Act forbade the importation of all non-English wares to Britain from the colonies – with the sole exception of Madeiran wine.

From then on there was no looking back. Drinking a glass of Madeiran wine during dinner was considered the right thing to do, irrespective of whether you were an officer sitting in your mess in India or the Caribbean or a member of the upper classes sitting around the dining table of your stately home in England's home counties. The "Madeira-Shippers" made certain that no matter where you were in the world further supplies were always available.

In 1700 the quality of the wine was substantially improved by an accidental and surprising discovery. An ordinary sailor was apparently responsible for the find. The boat on which he was sailing was carrying crates from Funchal which, for some unknown reason, were refused in Hong Kong. Shortly before returning to Madeira, the captain ordered that the barrels of "spoilt" wine be thrown overboard.

The sailor – and who could blame him – thinking this a tragic waste, opened a cask and tried some of the wine destined to be tipped away. His face lit up as the first taste touched his lips and trickled over his palate. Over the course of the voyage the grape had been tipped in another, completely new, but positive direction.

At the time, the general consensus of opinion was that the secret behind this special wine had to be somewhere along the journey over the equator. Was it the rocking of the ship that had done the trick or the great difference between the temperatures recorded during the day and those at night? Or had seawater, either when transporting the wine on to the ship or else just splashing around in the stern, managed to penetrate the barrels of Madeira?

Perhaps it was a combination of various factors which contributed towards the new taste. Even today there is no logical, scientific reason for the change from an ordinary sweet table wine to Madeiran wine as we know it. One thing is certain, however, and that is that no other wine would put up with such rough treatment.

Naturally, people endeavoured to get round the necessity of transporting the wine over the equator by trying out all sorts of alternatives, including some which were very strange. There is one story which tells of a

tradesman who hung a barrel over the entrance to his office so that every customer that came to visit him had to move it before entering. But even this simple and original technique proved – fortunately for the customers one might add – not to work. Thus the barrels were shipped back and forth over the equator until 1794 when a technique was discovered of artificially heating the wine in large ovens.

Just at the time when things were not looking very rosy for the island, luck sur-

faced once again and led to a further improvement in Madeiran wine. It was in 1800 when Napoleon's brother Joseph occupied the entire Iberian Peninsula, hoping that by blocking the sea route to Madeira the French could strike a nasty blow against England's prospering trade.

The wine stocks in Funchal grew visibly by the day, as did the general fears that all this precious liquid would go to waste. In desperation the tradesmen started to experiment with the stockpile, endeavouring to prolong the wine's shelf life by blending it with spirits.

It was a method which subsequent sampling proved to be extremely successful. Further variations of this "fortification" process improved the quality of Madeiran wine even further.

This new luck lasted another 50 years and then a new disaster struck with a vengeance. The mildew epidemic that occurred in 1852 destroyed a massive 90 percent of all the grapes on Madeira. This time the wine merchants were devastated. Almost all of the established British shippers subsequently left the island for Spain and of the 70 British establishments on the island in 1850 only 15 were left five years later.

Staying power and pure British pig-headedness helped the remaining tradesmen

ever since. The old wine reserves which could be used for blending with the poorer quality wines were soon exhausted, and the replacement of such wine could not be expected for many years. This meant that some compromises had to be made in wine production, a trend that led to a general fall in standards.

In 1979 the new state wine institute was founded (*Instituto do Vinho da Madeira*) and this heralded a new start. The role of this Institute is to observe and control the entire process of Madeira's wine production. This means that there is somebody supervising right from the planting of the vine itself, through the fermentation and maturing proc-

survive this period. They used the opportunity to stock up on old wine, a worthwhile investment, because this wine was necessary to blend with the grapes picked from the young vines. In 1873, however, fate dealt another blow. A vine pest, brought from America (*Phylloxera vastatrix*), completely destroyed the existing plants. It was only by importing resistant American vines, a measure instigated by the Blandy and Leacock families, that the Madeiran vines could be revived at all. This pest had the same disastrous consequences in Spain and France.

Madeira's wine-growing industry has suffered the consequences of these two events

ess and not stopping until the cork is pushed into the newly filled bottle.

It is the Institute's responsibility to ensure that Madeira's wine is authentic, controlling every step. Only then is the wine granted its official stamp (*selo de garantia*) and individual number. In addition, it is responsible for the education of wine specialists.

The alchemy of wine making: Madeira's wine harvest begins punctually on 15 August, and lasts well into November. The different kinds of grape ripen at different times. Last to ripen is the Sercial.

Today, lorries collect the harvested grapes, which are left in baskets along the side of the road. The grapes are then sent to the wine centres, where they are pressed using mechanical presses. In the old days the whole process had a far more romantic touch to it. Then, the grapes were put in large containers and trod by the bare feet of the grape-pickers. This was more than a bit of country fun at harvest-time, however, since this method had a particular advantage that can elude mechanical methods; it guaranteed that the seeds and panicles were not damaged and thus that no tannin (tanning agent) entered the juice of the grape.

There is much more to making Madeiran wine than just pressing the grapes, and filling and bunging the barrel. In fact, once the process which is a mystery to vintners and scientists even today, and which would cause other wines to turn sour.

In the course of the last century different methods have been developed to mimic the process. Even the shortest and quickest method lasts another two months. This method entails heating the wine in enormous tanks where the wine (sometimes with the additional aid of a circulatory pump) is kept in constant motion.

In another procedure the wine is left in the barrels which are piled into so-called *estufas* (hot houses) and slowly brought to a temperature of 113°F (45°C). Slowly means over a period of 6–12 months. The additional

fermentation process has been completed, i.e. the transformation of the fruit sugar into alcohol, the real work begins. It is only then that the complicated and extremely delicate procedure can be started – reconstructing the peculiar conditions experienced by the wine on that legendary trip to Hong Kong all those years ago.

It is a masterpiece of alchemy. The most important factor is the heating process, which caramelises the previously ordinary wine, a

Left, visitors are always welcome in Funchal's wine cellars. Above, the noble vintage awaits the connoisseur.

effort, care and quality entailed in this process is clearly visible in the result, since the wooden casks lend the wine a completely different character to that of the wine heated in the steel or concrete tanks.

Of all the methods, the simplest, oldest and, in a sense, most modern from an ecological point of view is the *vinho canteiro*. Using this method, the wine is left to mature in the sun, under the glass roof of an *estufa do sol*, sometimes for a period of over 20 years. Pure sunlight is decisive in helping the maturing process and every drop of this first-class wine tells how perfectly it has soaked up the sun's rays.

The normal maturing process – after a sharp cooling period – takes place in barrels made of American or Polish oak, although chestnut, mahogany or teak are also used. The important thing is that the sealing of the barrel is controlled by the Wine Institute. It is the Institute's officials who close the barrel, leaving the characteristic banana leaf around the bung. Around this is wound a band of linen, held in place with a wax seal bearing the Institute's coat of arms. This acts as a guarantee that nothing is added or taken away without it coming to the attention of the authorities.

The finest wines will be left in their barrels for 20 years and the minimum time allowed

Anybody who buys Madeiran wine, either at home or in Madeira, and decides to leave it in the cellar for a few years to mature is advised to leave it standing up, so that the cork lets in some air. Only then, with this small amount of oxygen can the wine continue to mature.

The long road to maturity: After all these years of waiting we should eventually get round to some drinking. When and on what occasion should one drink Madeiran wine? In the early days Madeiran wine parties were given, but now the general rule recommends the *Sercial* or the *Verdelho* as an aperitif, a Portuguese *Vinho verde* to accompany the main course, followed by a *Boal* for the

for any Madeiran wine to reach maturity is 18 months. A good-quality wine will be bottled at the very earliest after three years and even then the various decanting processes are far from over.

The true connoisseur of Madeiran wine does something with his 30, 50 and 150-year-old wines that would make the hair of any other self-respecting wine connoisseur stand on end. Every five to ten years he empties the wine out of the bottle, washes the bottle, dries it thoroughly and then puts the wine back in. This is meant to give the wine that extra breath of fresh air necessary for its further "growth".

dessert and the *Malvasia* as the crowning finale of a meal.

These classic Madeiran wines are named according to the type of grape. The Sercial is dry to extra dry and has an extremely powerful bouquet. The Verdelho is a rich golden wine pleasing on the eye and with a dry finish. The Boal is a medium-coloured wine with a rich flavour and well-rounded character. It is Malvasia though, full-bodied, sweet and heavy, almost similar to a liqueur, that is responsible for Madeira's fame in the wine industry.

As most tourists quickly discover, the vintners frequently open up their cellars for wine-tasting and whoever wishes to learn more about the island's wine can, for a small fee, try a few small glasses of different wines and come to their own conclusions. Using this method aspiring connoisseurs can "work" happily at their preferences, and purchase a few bottles or cases of any that they particularly enjoy. They are recommended to take their own white bread with them, since the practice of clearing the palate between the different wines is completely foreign to the islanders.

Naturally, it is not possible to have a quick sip from the real vintage bottles of Madeiran wine. After all, who is likely to open a 30, 80 or 120-year-old bottle for sampling? Some

ing to ship wine abroad. They are extremely reliable and there is never any worry about receiving an incorrect delivery or your cases not turning up at all. It is worth considering since, even with the customs' duties, it still works out a great deal cheaper than buying the wine at home.

The table wine, called *vinho da casa*, produced in the country villages is not exported, but it is served to visitors in the local restaurants. Such table wines are generally of a very high standard, even if some of them are actually blended.

Often these have come from family-owned concerns and are made from grapes which have been grown in tiny but lovingly-nur-

of the top-class wines of such vintages sell for £100 a bottle.

Sadly, Madeiran wine which has made the journey over the equator is no longer for sale. Whether bottles of this legendary wine are still available is very doubtful, since the owners of such a treasure are hardly likely to want to part with it, although – if the experts are to be believed – it would still be an enjoyable wine.

If desired, many wine merchants are will-

Left, on Madeira the cooper's job has not died out. Above, the proof can be seen in these fine examples of his work.

tured vineyards. Therefore, the wine is absolutely pure, without any additional sweeteners and hence, on the whole, extremely dry. Occasionally, a wine with an undefinable after-taste will be served in one of the small restaurants but this is due to the type of grape and the soil in the area. You will find that the wine you sample in the next village will be different again.

The name of the most popular table wine in Madeira is *Vinho verde* (green wine), initially brought over from the Portuguese mainland. This light, sparkling wine with a green tinge is served chilled and is exceptionally refreshing.

Madeira and its small neighbouring islands of Porto Santo and the Desertas literally rise straight out of the blue. Yet their sudden appearance on the surface of the Atlantic is matched by an equally sudden falling away of the sea bed. At the edge of the 1½-mile shelf around Madeira, the water takes a vertical dive of 10,000–13,000 ft (3,000–4,000 metres). The reason is that the island is the crowning summit of a 19,000-ft (6,000-metre) mountain range.

Small and large fish: With such a narrow shelf of shallow water surrounding it, Madeira does not possess the conditions conducive to the support of abundant marine life, and despite relatively low water pollution (the damaging oil slicks of 1990 excepted) only a small food chain has managed to establish itself. There is more than enough light and oxygen in the clear water, but there is a distinct lack of the organic particles and other suspended substances needed to produce new life and continue nature's inexhaustible cycle.

Such a dearth of primary life made up of phytoplankton (plant plankton) leads inevitably to an even poorer secondary chain of zooplankton (animal plankton). The azure-blue ocean might look inviting to humans, but beneath the beautiful veneer it is little more than a desert.

The few large fish which can be caught off Madeira and used commercially are usually caught en route between their spawning and feeding grounds. These include *freira*, tuna, marlin, swordfish, mackerel, sardines and sharks. The flying fish are also worth mentioning. Capable of swinging themselves on their pectoral fins, these fish are able to glide like birds when they wish to escape a persistent predator.

Also living in the narrow shelf area is the parrot fish, regularly appearing on the menu as *Bodião*. Living and swimming close to the shore, the male and female of this species are easily distinguishable owing to their different colouring. Whilst the female is red and

brightly coloured, the male is far duller, almost grey. Their parrot-like mouths explain their names.

Other native inhabitants and popular catches include grey mullet, which the locals regard as the "poultry of the sea", the predatory barrcauda, served in homes but seldom in restaurants; the extremely tasty *cherne* (a member of the perch family); regular perch; beam and barbel.

Seafood includes cuttlefish, octopus and shellfish, and a particular speciality is the *lapa*, a species of snail which the fishermen prise off the bottom of the cliffs with knives. Trout-farming schemes which have been set up in the mountains ensure that this freshwater fish is also available

The relative dearth of marine life is exacerbated by the practices of some of the area's fishermen. The coast around the islands has suffered immeasurable harm owing to their ignorance or plain idiocy. It is their persistent misuse of dynamite for fishing purposes that has been responsible for most of the damage. Naturally, there are laws forbidding such wanton practices, yet as long as dynamite is freely available for such things as road building, it is not difficult to obtain it for less worthy causes.

Some fishermen are naive enough to believe that they can expect better catches as a result, others use it because they wish to catch the tiny plant-eating fish which can neither be baited nor caught in a net. They do not seem able to grasp the fact that though by using dynamite they find exactly the fish they want floating "keel up" on the surface, leaving them little arduous work to do, they also destroy all life forms in that area – all the way from the primary plankton to the large fish. Inevitably, in the end they will ruin the food chains and threaten the existence of the very fish they seek.

Divers have no difficulty seeing the results of this over-exploitation. Whereas 10 or 15 years ago there was a teeming ocean of colourful life forms, including sea urchins, bristle worms, coral, sea cucumbers and various species of fish, today what the diver is more likely to encounter is all too visible evidence of "civilisation": rubbish of every

Preceding pages: the grim-looking espadas are caught in deep water. **Left,** Câmara de Lobos – the headquarters of the fishermen.

description, scrap metal and huge quantities of non-biodegradable plastic. Another problem is the number of abandoned nets, mainly around the Ilhas Desertas, which still trap unsuspecting fish. These are pointless deaths, since the fish are are never collected and simply perish through want of food and freedom.

On a happier note, written laws are at last being backed up by organised action. A coastal patrol service has been introduced in the form of three young men on the otherwise uninhabited Ilhas Desertas. The *cagaras*, the Atlantic shearwaters which breed on the Deserta Grande, are also thankful for the presence of these young guardians. Despite

Pirates of the deep: When the *freira* is being sold at the market, the local fishermen, quoting an old Madeiran saying, warn that a time of hardship is not far off. The dark brown fish with its grim, sad appearance and enormous eyes is present in Madeiran waters from February onwards. By June it will have completely disappeared from the markets' fish stands.

Little is known about this "sea bream-mackerel". Nobody knows where it comes from or where it goes and even the experts do not know in which category to place it: sea bream or mackerel? It does not seem to fit either of them exactly. Also known by the name *brama brama*, the fish can reach up to

rulings to the contrary, fishermen and poachers continued to climb the cliffs either at night or when it was foggy to steal the young *cagaras* birds (considered by some Madeirans to make an excellent alternative to roast chicken).

Here again, not until the situation was completely out of hand did the fishermen realise that they had done themselves more harm than good. Without the modern radar systems which can show the precise position of fish, and then suddenly without the *cagaras* either, the fishermen found it even more difficult to tell exactly where the shoals of fish were swimming.

a good 29 inches (75 cm) in length.

Living as it does at a depth of 328–1648 ft (100–500 metres), this high-backed, flat fish, with its crescent-shaped tail fin and medium-sized mouth, full of sharp teeth, is not the easiest of catches. Indeed the Madeiran fishermen are the only "hunters" who take the trouble to search for it, despite the fact the *freira* can be found in other regions of the North Atlantic and the Mediterranean. There is a limited market for it in Spain, but on the whole its white flesh is not in great demand outside Madeira.

Since the *freira* is so elusive fishermen in more fertile waters do not find the end justifies the means. Not so their Madeiran counterparts who haul them out of the sea one after the other. The tool they use is the "long line". The Madeiran fishermen are specialists in this type of fishing, since they have always had to contest with the treacherous, fissured sea bed around their coast, and know from experience that they cannot use drag nets. They have worked hard developing this skill and are now able to obtain optimum results when fishing off their shores.

That explains why, for example, whatever the season the *espada* or scabbard fish has a regular place on the fish stalls each morning. As the large eyes and the black colour of this eel-shaped fish lead one to surmise, the

seas" in the same way as the *freira*, using a line measuring over 1 mile (1½ km). This will have upwards of 150 individual flies with baited hooks spaced at 6-ft (2-metre) intervals. Specialists in catching *espada*, the team of fishermen from Câmara de Lobos, Madeira's most important fishing centre (just west of Funchal), bring in a total catch of more than 1,500 tons every year.

Nonetheless, this thin fish with its sharp rapier-type teeth is an absolute mystery to scientists, especially its breeding habits, about which nothing is known even today. Marine biologists like the former Director of Funchal's Municipal Museum, Günther E. Maul, have not, despite long research, come

espada lives in even deeper waters than the *freira*. The *espada*, whose Latin name is *Aphanopus carbo* is the most important fish in the archipelago and lives at depths of between 656 and 2,566 ft (200 and 800 metres). This is considerably deeper than most professional fishermen choose to fish and for that reason the *espada* in the waters off Madeira are not disturbed as often as they might otherwise be.

The Madeiran fishermen pursue the up to 3.2-ft (1-metre) long "pirates of the deep

Left, the cod is dried on huge wooden frames.
Above, tuna is rarely available in the market.

up with much enlightenment. Nobody knows at what depth the *espada* spends its first few months, or even knows if the fish is hatched as an egg or born already formed like a shark – which is also possible.

According to Günther Maul it was only 150 years ago that: "João Gomes or José Figueira or whatever his name was, sailing far out at sea, earned a just reward for his spirit of adventure when he caught the first fish of this kind. He was using a line that was at least 2,625 ft (800 metres) long. To his eyes, what he saw dangling on the hook was a strange, unknown, monster, weighing about 5 lbs, over 3 ft (1 metre) long and as black as coal. It had a huge mouth full of razor-sharp white teeth under a pair of enormous eyes." This example was kept for research purposes and can still be seen today in the British Museum in London.

Only four years after its discovery by the scientists it came to the attention of the gourmets, who developed an appetite for its delicious white flesh.

Long-line fishing for the *espada* led to the discovery and description of 12 unknown species of fish at depths of around 3,300 ft (1,000 metres) in the waters off Madeira – and this long before the deep-sea expedition of the *Challenger* (1873–76). Today, about 100 different edible salt-water fish are served

on the tables of Madeira. Obviously these never all appear on the fish stalls at the same time. But the *espada* is always on the market, whatever time of year.

Tunny on the line: Tuna and marlin fishing in Madeira is still a job for the tough guys. It is no love of sport fishing, but rather stark necessity which forces the men out to sea. Their fishing equipment is not sophisticated, and consists of a simple rod and line plus the ability to endure a tiring fight. Such fishing has enormous ecological advantages over the net fishing used extensively in the Mediterranean (as already said, not practical here) . It is an indirect method of controlling the

balance, a considerate method of fishing which does not threaten to force the species into extinction.

Everybody has probably eaten tuna at one time or another, if only the tinned variety in a sandwich. One of the best known species of this "tinned fish" is the true bonito, called *Katsuwonus pelamis* in Latin. Like all tuna the bonito is one of the ocean's most adept predators. The torpedo-shape of its body gives a very clear indication of its lifestyle. It is an exceptionally fast swimmer, needing a great deal of oxygen, as the dark colour of its flesh indicates. The fish is constantly on the move and is at home in tropical as well as sub-tropical waters. It swims in schools, searching for food or on its way to its spawning grounds.

Madeira's fishermen appear to have – in addition to a lot of spare time and a constant thirst for the island's red wine – a sixth sense which tells them where to find a school of tuna. During the summer months the bonito, or *gaido*, as it is called here, can be found in the waters of Madeira, and in the autumn the red tuna, *Thunnus thynnus*, makes its annual appearance.

Should there be a small lull in the fishing calendar the fishermen use the opportunity to maintain their equipment. Faulty boats are serviced and new vessels are built in the neighbouring shipyards in Machico, Caniçal or Câmara de Lobos. Such shipyards are fascinating places and make for an interesting visit: entire or partial wrecks in picture-book colours, rusted canisters, chickens and other animals rummaging around in the debris, and wooden planks of every possible length and width, distorted, bent, and stacked on top of each other, give an impression of hopeless mess.

One might think there is nothing but rubbish here – or at least nothing suitable for building a boat. Yet, surprisingly, it is just such twisted bits of wood that are so sought after by the boatbuilders. They offer the hull, the beams and stern the best resistance to the waves. The different-shaped planks, guaranteed not to warp, are fitted together like a puzzle. Even in the old days the shipowners had trees specially trained so that they grew curved for ship-building.

Left, tuna are gutted on the boats. **Right**, this is what a tangled line looks like.

The Madeiran fishermen are usually very easy-going characters who do nothing in a hurry. But occasionally you'll see them rushing to their boats in the dead of night. When you do, this can only mean one thing: they want to reach Desertas before sunrise to do some tuna fishing. It takes them two or three hours to get there, so on the way they prepare the necessary rods and the large tank they use for transporting the live bait.

If tuna condescends to bite at all, which, even given normal conditions, is not very often, then they will only do so if live bait is used. During the spawning season, though, tuna will not eat anything at all, the egg-laying being done in batches and sometimes taking many months. This spawning process appears to follow a strict order. The younger fish lay first, followed by the older ones. What still remains a mystery to the fishermen, however, is the exact location of these spawning grounds.

Normally a school will consist of tuna of more or less the same size. Less strictly observed is any sort of blood relationship, so "stranger" fish can join the group without any problems. At the school's spawning time no members will go anywhere near a hook. Even the most tempting bait will fail to lure stragglers.

Unfortunately, however, modern fishing has outwitted nature's happy plan to ensure the breed's survival. Japanese and South Korean fishermen, for example, get round it by using a sort of "lasso" technique. The entire school is surrounded with nets which are gradually drawn together; the trapped fish are then heaved on board with iron hooks and slaughtered.

To catch the bait: The first job of the fishermen on the way to the tuna fishing grounds is to clean out the tank to take the live bait. Young mackerel – the left-overs from the day before – dead or swimming listlessly on their backs, are fished out and put through the mincer. This fish mince is used to catch the live bait – fresh mackerel – to tempt the tuna fish.

The boat then heads out to the place where the mackerel are to be found. The bare volcanic rocks of the Desertas tower vertically above the water, as steep at the bottom as at the top. Surrounding this unwelcoming pile of rocks is a narrow shelf with a tiny area of calm water. This small shelf is the breeding ground for many of the fish later found swimming out at sea.

Catching the mackerel is the easy part. The fishermen shine a spotlight on the water and scatter newly-made fish paste on its surface. Within seconds hundreds of small fish – a school of mackerel – dance in the light's beam. Yesterday's bait attracts today's. The fish pump is turned on and starts sucking. Gallons after gallons of fish and water enters the tank.

At daybreak the real work of tunny fishing begins. Still without a definite destination the boat sails across the water. All eyes will be expectantly watching the water. Now is the time to spot the prey and no sounder facilitates the task. The boy brought along to handle the bait throws a constant stream of small fish into the water – a sort of pre-baiting. Hours can be spent doing this without anything happening. Sometimes a whole day is wasted.

Yet, as soon as something takes a bite things start happening on deck. The bait is thrown overboard in bucketfuls and a whole school of tuna will appear to attack it. The surface, so smooth seconds beforehand, will churn madly as the fish bite. The hose, attached to the rear of the boat, is turned on and water bubbles out.

The tuna, wild with hunger, snap at anything and everything in the water. Their torpedo shapes shoot in like arrows – creating a shimmering hubbub of every shade from metallic blue to silver – the typical colouring of pelagic fish, i.e. fish living in the surface waters or middle depths of the sea. They are ideally camouflaged: on their backs they are blue like the ocean, and to blend in with their sea-bed surroundings if viewed from the bottom, they have a silver-grey stomach.

In a school of fish a strict code of conduct prevails. A school knows no aggression, no class difference, but also no independent actions – there is only group action and this is synchronised. Fishing for such tuna is not comparable in any way to the romanticised image of young boys fishing with a hook and line on the quayside. On a tuna-fishing expedition sheer pandemonium reigns.

Doing battle: A successful catch depends to a large extent on how fast the fishermen can react, not least when feeding the bait. The live bait, forced mercilessly on to the large metal fishing hooks must still be wriggling in the water. The line is cast and within seconds pulled in again. There is no pause, just a continual in and out action. The tuna bite

It is no wonder the men attach the line to a wooden capstan when they hook a large tuna. This way they let the fish swim itself to death. If they did not, even the strongest man could be tugged unexpectedly overboard by his catch. The fish fly rapidly on to the deck where they toss about energetically trying to escape. Their energy seems boundless. The wriggling, colliding bodies make a horrendous noise, like a furious drumroll.

Their scales glisten with all the colours of the rainbow – a fascinating sight just before

immediately. If there is no fish on the hook it means the bait has been eaten and has to be quickly replaced.

To pull the rod in successfully, mastering the correct swing is all important. It is impossible to try simply to heave the tuna aboard. The fish fights far too well for that. Sometimes a long, flexible rod on the deck will start to wave madly, bending right over and getting tangled with the rod next to it. There is no way to control it. The fisherman has to let out more line and try again.

Once the trail of a school of tuna is discovered the hunt begins in earnest.

their death. Yet as quickly as life leaves their body so, too, the beautiful colouring deserts the scales. Nonetheless the tuna still keep coming to the hooks. The entire school goes down together.

As the boat sails home the fish are gutted, their insides thrown overboard to be eaten by the seagulls and other fish. In other areas, once gutted, the tuna would be refrigerated immediately, but such ideas are, as yet, too advanced for the Madeiran fishermen. As soon as the fishermen are back home, the cleaned fish are laid out on the quay to attract a buyer. Meanwhile the deck is swabbed down ready for another day.

Madeira does not actually have a cuisine that it can call its own. What there is could probably be best described as Portuguese, with a touch of Arabian spice.

Madeiran women tend to cook light, simple dishes, using island produce as far as possible. Taking pride of place is the range of superb fresh fish, headed by the incomparable tuna and the black eel-like *espada*. A close second are the exotic, native fruits which come in all shapes, colours and quantities. Due to the small size of the island and low agricultural production, a large proportion of the meat and vegetables have to be imported. These are consequently rare and fairly expensive.

The most popular methods of cooking in Madeira are: *frito ou grelhado*, namely roasted or grilled. However, it is possible to order dishes which are *cozido*, "cooked", or *assado*, braised. That does not mean that the food is boring, though, since it is the seasoning that counts. The aromatic smells of fennel, garlic, lemon and laurel which float around the Madeiran gardens and countryside in summer also waft from its cooking pots. Caraway seed is also used in abundance and no cook would dream of leaving out a dash of local wine.

Local produce: Madeira owes its rich choice of locally-grown fruits to the fertile volcanic earth and the mild ocean climate. Available in abundance are *cherimoya*, papaya, *maracuja*, guavas, mango, citrus fruits of all kinds, avocados, bananas, cherries and apricots. Nonetheless, customers in many restaurants are more than likely to be served fruit salad out of a tin. This is mainly due to the fact that a large proportion of the fruit is exported and fresh fruits are consequently fairly expensive. Those who would like to stock up with fresh fruit should pay a visit to the *mercado* in Funchal, the largest market on the island. There are always plenty of bargains to be found there.

Unfortunately though the waters around Madeira are crystal-clear, they are consist-

ently over-fished and some kinds of fish, such as the grouper, have already become expensive rarities in restaurants. Fortunately the *atum*, as tuna is called in Madeira, is still widely available. Found on almost every menu, it can be eaten *frito ou grelhado*, on its own, or just with lemon and a seasoning of salt and pepper.

Another typical fish to be found on Madeira is the mysterious and delicious tasting *espada*, the coal black, scaleless scabbard (not to be confused with the Spanish bull-

fighter-type *espada* complete with sword). This eel-like fish is fished extensively only in the waters around Madeira and Japan. Fishermen say that it can only be caught at night using deep-sea fishing techniques (*see feature on fishing*).

The *bacalhau* is nothing more than dried salted cod. Drying used to be the only method of preserving this cod. The cooking of dried cod is a fairly complicated process, since it has to be soaked for around 12 hours, otherwise it tastes awful. The water it is soaking in must be changed frequently to ensure that the salt is washed away. Only then can the fish be cooked.

<u>Preceding pages</u>: picnic in the open – a favourite pastime of the Madeirans. <u>Left</u>, the *mercado* sells everything. <u>Above</u>, fishermen.

Not so often found in the frying pan or under the grill are *sarda* (mackerel), *pargo* (plaice), *truta* (trout) and the grouper fish. The same goes for shellfish. Mussels are occasionally available in restaurants but unlike tuna, prawns and langoustine they are not easy to find.

Fish kebabs: Compared to the fish dishes available on Madeira, meat, for reasons of expense, has a lower profile. Most of Madeira's beef, pork, chicken and ham – *bife, porco, frango* and *fiambre* – is imported from the European mainland.

That said, one of the most delicious Madeiran specialities is *espetada*, skewered beef grilled over an open fire with laurel

croquettes the *milho cozido* or *bolo de cado*, cooked in stone ovens and served while still warm. Unfortunately, there is only a limited choice of salad and vegetables. Tomato salad usually served with just a couple of green leaves, onions, or, in the best cases, a few olives, and every sort of tinned vegetable, are the norm.

A wine for every course: Madeiran wine ripens in huge oak barrels which are called "mother barrels". This name refers to the fact that the wine that is left over in the barrels is topped up with new wine – the idea being that the old wine will pass on its taste to the youngster. The four most important wines are the pale dry Sercial, the medium-dry

leaves and onions. *Espetada* can be bought on every street corner and in every food shop. On its own it makes a good hors d'oeuvre; when served with a salad and *bolo de cado* (warm sweet potato bread), a main course; with chips, a snack.

Also popular is *carne de vinho e alhos*, the name given to a delicious dish, prepared by braising meat, that has first been marinated in a wine sauce, with garlic and laurel or fennel. You should definitely try this during your visit.

In addition to rice, potatoes, bread and noodles, other typical Madeiran side-dishes served with meat and fish include the maize

amber-coloured Verdelho, the medium sweet red Boal and the sweet, full-bodied Malvasia (known as Malmsey). The first two are normally drunk before a meal and the last two afterwards.

On the whole Portuguese wines are served, and these are actually very good. The delicate Matéus Rosé is enjoyed at its best when it is well-chilled. It accompanies any course perfectly. Another ideal table wine is the light and sparkling *vinho verde*, the "green wine" – actually made from unripe grapes. The *vinho de la casa*, a light, dry table wine is available in open carafes at a very reasonable price.

Anybody wishing to sample the local beer should ask for *cerveja*. Imported beer, mainly brands from Germany or Denmark, is normally only available in the island's larger hotels.

Madeiran dishes to try out at home:

Bacalhau Dourado – serves 4
500 g dried cod
⅛ litre olive oil
500 g potatoes
6 eggs
Oil to fry
1 large onion
freshly ground pepper, 1 sprig of parsley

of salt. Cook it for approximately 20 minutes until it is soft. Drain off the water, leaving the fish in the pan. Peel the onion, chop it up finely and fry it in the oil until it is golden. Cut the fish up into pieces and add it to the onions and fry for a minute or so. Beat the eggs and whisk them together with the pepper. Add them to the fish and stir until it thickens. When this is all done add the potatoes. Taste it, adding extra seasoning if necessary, and serve sprinkled with chopped parsley.

Porco de Vinho e Alhos – serves 4
¼ litre white wine
1 kg pork (shoulder)
2 tbsp wine vinegar

Soak the dried cod the day before in a container full of water, changing the water frequently, for at least 12 hours.

The following day, preheat the oven to 200°F (100°C). Peel the potatoes and cut them into small chip-size pieces about 4 cm long by ½ cm wide and then fry them in a frying pan for 3 minutes. Drain them on kitchen paper and then put in the oven to keep warm. Take the fish out of the water and wash it thoroughly to remove the last traces

Left, simple Madeiran dish: tuna, potatoes and fresh bread. **Above**, *bol de caco*, a sort of honey cake.

4 cloves of garlic
3 tbsp salt
1 tsp caraway seed
3 slices white bread cut in diagonal pieces
1 lemon
salt and pepper to taste

Put the wine, vinegar, crushed garlic, caraway seed, slices of lemon and salt and pepper into a bowl and mix thoroughly. Cut the pork into strips of about 4 cm long and 1 cm wide and add them to the bowl. Marinade them for 6 hours, turning occasionally. Remove the meat and drain it on kitchen paper. Melt half the fat in a large frying pan and fry the meat until it is golden brown. Drain away the remaining fat and add about 1/8 litre of the sauce. Bring to the boil and then simmer for 30 minutes.

In another pan melt the other half of the fat and fry the pieces of bread until the croutons are golden. Season the meat with salt and pepper, remove the lemon and serve with warm bread.

Pudim – serves 6
¼ litre milk
3 egg yolks
⅛ litre cream
2 cl Madeira
75 g sugar

Preheat the oven to 350°F (175°C) and prepare a *bain-marie* with six fire-proof pudding bowls. Bring the cream and milk to the boil in a pan. Melt the sugar carefully to make a caramel and then slowly add the cream and sugar, stirring all the time until smooth. Beat the egg yolks with a hand whisk. Add the hot caramel milk and the Madeira. It is important that everything is whipped until stiff.

Divide the pudding mixture equally between the six fire-proof pudding bowls in the *bain-marie* (the water should cover the bottom half of each bowl), place them on the

middle shelf of the oven and cook for 40 minutes.

The best way to test whether it is cooked is to stick a knife into one of the puddings. If it comes out easily the pudding is ready. It is best to leave them overnight in the fridge before removing them from the pudding bowls. As the pudding cools the caramel sinks to the bottom of the bowl. If it the puddings are left for a while, they will have an attractive and delicious caramel top when turned out.

To help you order:

sopa de peixe, caldeirada – fish soup
sopa de tomate – tomato soup
con cebola – with onions
acorda – bread soup with egg and garlic
omeletas de peixe – fish omelettes
queijo e fiambre – ham and cheese
con cogomelos – with mushrooms
bacalhau dourado – dried cod with eggs and potatoes
ameijoas na cataplana – mussels with ham and sausages
prego no prato – beefsteak
ovos e bacon – egg and bacon
frango assado – roast chicken
costeletas porco – pork chop
espetada regional – beef kebab
carnede vinho e alhos – meat in a wine sauce
minho cozido – Maize meal
bolo de caco – honey cake
bolo rei – honey cake with candied fruits
pudim – pudding
Sercial – dry Madeira
Verdelho – medium-dry Madeira
Boal – semi-sweet Madeira
Malvasia – sweet, full-bodied Madeira (Malmsey)
Dão – Portuguese red and white wine
Matéus Rosé – Portuguese rosé
Vinho verde – young wine
vinho de la casa – house wine
poncha – hot rum grog with honey
aniz escarchado – aniseed cocktail with a twig of fennel
aguardente – locally distilled spirit
ginja – cherry brandy
sumo de maracuja – passion fruit juice
chá de limão – lemon tea

Left, shell fish and **right**, dried fish are important ingredients of the Madeiran cuisine.

TALE OF THE WHALE

Marine biologist Petra Deimer mourns the loss of Madeira's whales and tells what is being done to restore their numbers

"Whales – the whales are here!" The young lad can hardly suppress his excitement as he rushes into the supermarket to break the good news to the busy shoppers. My curiosity aroused, I dash out on to the promenade to scan the horizon. Lo and behold, there they are, about 2 miles off the southern coastline, where their "spout" is clearly visible above the surface of the calm sea.

Spout is the name given to the air which the whale expels under high pressure through its nostrils. It condenses on striking the colder outer air forming a dense column of spray, which quickly disappears again. There must be four, five or a good half dozen of the sea mammals. To go by the size most probably they are sperm whales.

Their movements cause the sea to heave. An occasional tail rises out of the water and smacks down on to the waves making a great splash; a glistening head like a dark submarine tower breaks the surface of the sea and silently disappears again. Then suddenly, a whole whale, nearly 50 ft (16 metres) long, soars out of the water, hanging for a moment like a Zeppelin in the air, before plunging back into the ocean, leaving behind a cascade of sparkling water.

I hurry to the nearest telephone kiosk to tell Eleuterio Reis, the ex-commander of the whaling station, about the spectacular show. I imagine that the news will really stir up his hunting instinct. But Eleuterio will have to leave his harpoon at home; a cease-fire has been in force between man and sea mammal in Madeiran waters since 1981.

We were able to watch the whales for well over an hour. They seemed to be engrossed in some form of playful activity, which went on for the best part of their visit. When they had had enough, they swam leisurely away.

We all set off to Reis' house to celebrate this memorable event – naturally, with a glass of Madeira *Sercial*, which is served by the islanders whenever there is the slightest reason to celebrate.

We observed this gala performance given

by the whales in early 1986, and we know now that we were extremely lucky to be on the spot when they arrived, because sperm whales are absolutely unpredictable, suddenly appearing and disappearing with no seasonal regularity whatsoever.

It has been observed that at least the young cow whales and their calves spend the whole year in the waters of the archipelago, including the islands of Porto Santo and the Desertas. The "old ladies" travel further, possibly to the Azores or the Canaries and back. But that is mere speculation; even the islands' veteran whalers admit that they know very little about the migratory movements and travels of the sperm whales.

Swimming leisurely at a speed of up to 3 miles (5 km) an hour, small herds of whales move around the deep, crystal-clear waters of the Atlantic – aimlessly it would seem, at least to us. About once a day or at night, several of the whales get together for a rendezvous. Up to two dozen sperm whales have been observed at such meetings, where a lot of physical contact is involved. They rub themselves against one another, as if trying to compensate for being unable to embrace and caress each other with their short pectoral fins. With their heads put close together they look as though they are exchanging endearments or some item of spicy gossip. They relax in their "water-beds", and evidently enjoy idling away the time, propping one another up in the water and giving their offspring rides on their backs. The whales' social behaviour expresses a high degree of group solidarity and affection.

The bulls are apparently only tolerated at mating time. Such a matriarchy, which also prevails among elephants, plays an important biological role: the far bigger bulls are in this way prevented from becoming food rivals for the cows and their calves. But to safeguard themselves more effectively against attacks by sharks and killer whales, several females will band together, perhaps led by an old experienced cow.

While the young female offspring of the mother whales would appear to stay in these schools, the young males are driven away as soon as they have grown to the size of their mothers and aunts and reached sexual maturity. Adolescent males form their own schools and behave rather like teenage louts. At the age of 25, the males are sexually and socially mature and can become fathers.

This complicated social structure – with a very slow rate of reproduction – has had catastrophic consequences, especially in the North Pacific, where the slaughtering of far too many sexually mature male whales has caused a continuing decline in whale populations. Even if no further sperm whales are killed, populations will not be able to recover until the coming decade due to the lack of potential fathers.

Pollution also kills: Nevertheless, whales are still being killed, if not in Madeiran waters and not with the harpoon. An immense problem has been caused by one modern fishing technique: the use of drift-nets in the tropical seas, which destroys millions of commercially useless marine creatures. In addition, environmental pollutants also take their toll of marine life. The "seal epidemic" which killed some 18,000 seals in the North Sea in 1988 was most probably caused not by a virus but by toxic substances such as heavy metals and mercury. There is ample proof that these substances seriously damage the immune system of seals, and presumably of other creatures too. It is quite conceivable that the deaths of dolphins and whales are also caused by toxic substances.

I shall never forget my first trip to Madeira. What started off as a strictly scientific project eventually developed into a small nature and wildlife conservation project. It all began in 1973, when I was at work on my thesis in marine biology. Its subject was whales. In those days, Madeira was a whaling island.

"Whales? Research work?" The dark, thick-set man peered at me over his horn-rimmed glasses and grinned broadly: "A few male students have been here to do the same, but at the first sight of a dead whale on the quay they disappeared."

Eleuterio Reis, then the commander of Madeira's whaling station, continued rooting around his disorderly desk, while I tried my best to persuade him that I was really whale," I tried to explain. "I'm writing a thesis on these bones, which, because whales don't have legs like other mammals, are only rudimentary in whales." And that sort of work, I thought to myself, is best done safely on land, well after the dead creatures have been sliced up and processed. "Of course," he countered, "but if you really want to study whales, you have got to go out to sea to observe them."

Reis was quite right, of course. And through him, I was able to observe whales in their natural habitat, in the vast expanse of the open sea. How else could I have got to know anything at all about this fascinating leviathan? After all, he is a bit too big for a zoo or

serious about my project. "All right, young lady," he suddenly announced, "if you promise not to get cold feet, you can come along and get to know Moby Dick personally out on the ocean!"

Come along? What on earth did he mean by that? I didn't want anything to do with whaling. "I'm really only interested in the whales' bones, the pelvic bones of the sperm

Preceding pages: sperm whales can reach lengths of up to 50 metres. Whales were harpooned off Madeira until only a few years ago. Left, the whalers were accompanied by a speedboat. Above, this whale has breathed its last.

an aquarium. At that time I would never in my wildest dreams have thought that one day I would be swimming about in those very same waters for a peaceful underwater rendezvous with the dolphins and whales of Madeira. We now set sail every year to study their habits on the *Song of the Whales,* a marine research boat operated by the International Fund for Animal Welfare (IFAW). But we still have a long way to go before our hopes of saving the whale are realised.

The Madeiran whaling station was launched in 1941 under the command of Eleuterio Reis, who had moved to Madeira from the Azores. He brought with him the whalers' battle call: "*baleia, baleia...*" "Whale, whale, there he blows!"

The commander was a young man in those days, but he was a born whaler and with a seaman's sixth sense he set out in search of whale oil. He and his 25 comrades were not to be disappointed either, because the sperm whale, which is still a source of industrial oil today, is a cosmopolitan creature, at home in all of the world's oceans.

When I returned to the whaling station, Reis was more than astonished to find me back at his office, having given up on me long ago. "All right!" he said, and gave me a turbulent trip on his speedboat to test my seaworthiness. I managed to pass this test, and having gained the commander's confidence I took to wandering down to the whaling station every morning. But there were no signs of any whales. "It's entirely different from going out to catch fish," Reis said, "Whales don't turn up every day, and certainly not by appointment!"

The whaling boats are always ready for the fray. The long, hand-made wooden sloops are small and fragile compared with the huge whales. Well-greased harpoons, spears and other heavy iron implements are stacked in the boats ready for action. Long ropes lie neatly coiled in their hulls. These have to hold the whales, and they are always made of Manila hemp; the whalers hold the ropes in their bare hands, which would be severely lacerated by plastic rope.

In some ways time has stood still for Madeira's whalers. I feel as though I've been taken back into scenes depicted in old prints in which the famous figures from Herman Melville's *Moby Dick* suddenly come to life. I can almost see before me the monster whale of biblical legend which swallowed Jonas. There is, in fact, only one of the 90 different species of whale featured in all the many myths and yarns about men and boats being swallowed by denizens of the deeps, and that is the sperm whale. Its has the following vital statistics: It can grow to 50 ft (17 metres) in length; its head is huge and bulbous and terminates in a heavy snout; its wide jaws are armed with enormous teeth, which it is quite prepared to use if provoked.

But to return to my whaling story! Every morning at dawn, three or four men clamber up Madeira's coastal mountain peaks, armed with binoculars, to scour the sea for schools of whales. The observations posts are occupied every day until 4 o'clock in the afternoon during the year-round whaling season.

When the sea rages and the waves are white-capped, the whales enjoy a period of brief respite, because the spout which betrays them is no longer visible from land. More often the sea is as smooth as glass, and the whale's steaming breath rises like a white cloud above the sea - a fatal signal visible from afar. When the look-out man sees a whale blowing, he notifies the whaling station by radio. Commander Reis is the first to react, and he shoots a signal rocket into the air. The whalers in the nearby village of Caniçal drop everything and rush down the stony path to the whaling station. Their wives and mothers quickly pack baskets of provisions and follow them down. Amidst the excitement and confusion, four-men crews set about getting their boats ready for sea. Levers are used to launch all three of the station's boats into the water.

In the meantime Reis has started the engine of his speedboat *Vedetta*. This piece of modern equipment was an important asset to the whaling "fleet", and escorted the boats to help the crews should they get into trouble. The *Persistentia,* an old converted steam trawler, has also weighed anchor and chugs off slowly, its engines grinding, towards the spot where the school of whales was sighted.

All at once Reis falls silent and begins to scan the tranquil surface of the sea with a look of intense concentration on his face. Our whaling guru has obviously got the scent and is in no mood to answer any further annoying questions from his inquisitive passenger.

Suddenly, right in front of us, we witness a breath-taking wonder of nature. This is no mountainous mass of bone and blubber wallowing on the surface of the water, as depicted in historical illustrations. No, the whale glides smoothly and leisurely through the water – a wonderful, elegant creature. Noiselessly, and without even the slightest turbulence testifying to its titanic strength, the whale's gleaming body glides forward, nose downwards. The single blowhole closes almost automatically before it disappears below the surface of the water. A vital adaptation to life in the sea, it keeps the sea mammal's lung absolutely watertight.

Then, all of a sudden, the whale turns and

swims head on for our boat. I must admit that with Moby Dick at such close quarters I feel a bit weak at the knees. Prior to this turn of events, I had been quite convinced that we had set out for a rendezvous with a gentle, harmless creature, but now I'm beginning to think that perhaps this ocean "playmate" is a bit to big for me.

For the whalers, however, this 30 ft (10 metre) specimen is still a baby and not yet ready for the sharp end of the harpoon. What they do instead is to take the blunt end of the murderous instrument and vigorously prod the back of this juvenile member of the whale family. Strangely, he seems to relish this unfriendly treatment and keeps coming

whalers to unpack their picnic baskets and fortify themselves with wholesome bread and red wine for the imminent trial of strength.

They know very well that sooner or later the whale will resurface for air, and since none of its fellows has yet been tormented by the whalers' sharp harpoons, "word" will not have got around the school that danger is lurking above. They continue to glide down to the ocean depths in search of squid – a speciality on the sperm whale's menu.

Battle commences: So far, everything has been relatively harmless. But once the battle between whale and whaler begins, the operation becomes a horrible experience – a gruesome and repugnant bloodbath. At close

back for more. But the harpooners, hoping for bigger booty, soon tire of the game and start beating a loud tattoo on the bows of the boat. They know whales are extremely sensitive to noise, and this ruse causes our friend to take a hasty plunge into the deeps. I breathe an inward sigh of relief.

The whalers now set course for another, larger whale. But before they can get anywhere near, this colossus turns head and tail to make for the deeps, where it will probably stay for a while. That is a signal for the

The magnificent creatures are processed for their oil and other products.

range, a whaler plunges the harpoon deep into the whale's back, just below the dorsal fin. The huge body shudders violently. The whale bends and writhes in pain, and tries to dive down to the safety of the deeps. But even if it succeeds, the poor creature is forced to resurface for air. Its breathing becomes shorter and shorter and it is obvious that the animal is suffering from great stress.

The whale's efforts to dive become more and more desperate, and it can't get enough oxygen. Its mighty head rears out of the water, its back arches and it battles to escape from the enemy to which it is fettered by the harpoon and rope. Once the battle has begun, the other members of the school become restless; their breathing and movements become more and more erratic. The warning signals emitted by their captive comrade are audible miles away. They are all on the alert, quickly diving and then suddenly reappearing in the distance. Some swim back, wanting to help a fellow member of their herd now fighting for its life, and vainly hoping they will find safety in numbers.

It is mainly the cows which form groups for defence purposes, a practice which may succeed in warding off attacks by killer whales but which only makes it easier for the whalers to continue their slaughter.

Even when they realise that a comrade is

heart. The sea is now clouded dark red with blood. Some whales are still blowing, but their spout is also red – stained by blood. The harpooned whale rolls from one side to the other like a huge empty bottle. Now in its death throes, the whale's great head once again rears out of the sea, its wide jaws gaping, and, emitting a final strident wail of reproach, it collapses on its side. The poor creature is dead.

The men, relaxed, grin. I sit there numbed, but relieved that the slaughter has finally ended. The harpooner straightens his bent spear with a few blows of a hammer and gets the tools of his trade ready for the next unequal duel. Another member of the crew

doomed, the whale is not left to die alone at the hands of the whalers. Its fellow creatures form a circle, heads pointing inwards and their tails outwards ready to be used as a powerful weapon. In this position, with only the lobe of their tail fanning the water, they neither attempt to attack nor to escape, but stay motionless at their post until the bitter end. Faced with this group behaviour, the whalers don't bother to use their harpoons on the rest of the school. They can easily slaughter them with their spears.

A volley of spear thrusts bores deep into the heads and the backs of the defenceless creatures; only rarely do they directly hit the

plunges a marking flag deep into the eye cavity of the dead whale – to me, a final act of brutality – but apparently the only place where the marker will stay put. It will enable the parent ship, the *Persistentia*, to find the whale, hitch a rope to its tail and tow it slowly back to port.

The next day, just after dawn, the carcasses are hauled on to the platform by the whaling station's old and creaky winch. One by one, the whales are flensed and the chunks of flesh thrown into the cauldrons, where these once splendid marine creatures are reduced to industrial oil. The oil they yield is of very high quality, resistant to heat and pressure, and obviously extremely useful for industrial purposes. The meat, which not even the dogs will touch, is processed into a flour-like substance and used as fertiliser and animal fodder additive.

That's how things used to be at the Madeira whale station. Fortunately for the whales, however, a law was eventually passed in June 1981 forbidding the export of sperm whale products like oil, flour and teeth, in the hope of saving the marine animals from extinction.

An ocean refuge: In 1985 the Society for the Protection of Sea Mammals published the following declaration: "Everybody is talking about protection of the environment...

The fact that it is the Madeirans themselves who have taken up arms to protect the whales has its reasons. The Society for the Protection of Sea Mammals has submitted a unique concept to the island government, providing for the setting up of a "national park" for ocean mammals. The 77,000 sq. mile (200,000 sq. km) reserve will be an ocean refuge for many endangered species like the sperm whale, finback, and humpback, as well as various dolphin varieties hunted by the whalers as a source of meat, and the monk seal, which is already on the verge of extinction.

Obviously, thousands of other marine species will also benefit from such biotopes.

One small island in the North Atlantic is taking this seriously: Madeira. After whalers had managed in just 40 years to slaughter no less than 5,885 whales – most of them sperm whales – in the waters of the archipelago, the whale-killers have finally given in to the conservationists. Instead of pursuing Moby Dick with harpoon and spear, ex-station commander Eleuterio Reis and his men are now devoting their best efforts to saving their former prey from extinction."

Left, whalebone carved into a tourist souvenir. **Above**, the *Song of the Whale* – the research vessel of International Fund for Animal Welfare.

And so will the islanders themselves, who, living as they do from a good half million tourists a year, will reap the rewards of being associated with such environmentally friendly projects.

Tourists and scientists, schoolchildren, students and other interested visitors will discover a wealth of information on the historical and practical aspects of whaling, on marine biology, and especially on whales and other ocean dwellers. A real highlight of the project is a model of a 45-ft (14-metre) sperm whale made of fibre glass.

It is over 10 years since Reis killed his last sperm whale. In the meantime, a whaling museum has been opened in Caniçal, the former whaling village, which is now the headquarters of BIOS (Associacão para a Protecção da Natureza), an organisation for the protection of the environment set up on Madeira in May 1990.

The pride of the museum is a model of a huge sperm whale mounted on the wall above an original whaling boat, collections of scrimshaws (shells, carved and coloured by the whalers in their spare time), and other relics from Madeira's whaling past. That is one further reason for us to look a little closer at current progress being made by the whale conservation project.

The transition from commercial use to

continue to man their posts on the islands of the Desertas. They won't be scanning the sea for schools of sperm whales, however, but keeping a sharp look-out to ensure that fishing boats keep well away from the protected "desert islands" so that the rare monk seal can enjoy the sheltered childhood it needs.

Home on the Desertas: The sailing boat *Song of the Whale* is moored off the islands of the Desertas, not for pleasure, however, but for the serious business of scientific research. After completing over 300 hours of marine biological investigations, the research vessel of the International Fund for Animal Welfare returned to Madeiran waters in 1990.

Naturally, we want to renew contact with

conservation of whale populations obviously needs substantial funding, and for that reason the International Fund for Animal Welfare (IFAW) has decided to support the project. IFAW chief Brian Davies came, saw, and donated 10 million escudos to get the museum project off the ground and to help solve some of the social problems.

Former whalers, for instance, are not being left without a livelihood. On the contrary, they are continuing to make harpoons, albeit not to kill whales with, but to sell to tourists as souvenirs. They will carry on building whaling boats, in the form of handy little models. And as in the old days, others will

the sperm whales, now that they have been under protection for the past ten years. We shall compare monochrome photos of tail fins, which serve as a sort of passport photo, to see if we can recognise any of our old whale friends from the Azores.

What route the sperm whales actually take from those islands is still a mystery to marine biologists. And research is being done to shed light on the social life and family relations of these peaceable sea mammals. The scaled-off skin of the whales can be conserved. In the laboratory, DNA analyses can be carried out to determine its protein composition, which is as individual and unique as a finger-print. This indicates which whale is related to another.

For me, there is no sea as beautiful as the waters of Madeira. Surrounded by the deep-blue Atlantic, the volcanic island rears up from unfathomable deeps. Naturally an attraction for the huge sperm whales. The great depth of the Madeiran waters also explain why pollution of the ocean environment is not immediately visible (except in the case of the recent oil spill which was fortunately less serious than comparable catastrophes). The waters of Madeira are a natural ocean habitat for sea mammals like whales, dolphins and seals, as well as for turtles and sea birds, whose natural habitat is respected by human

prey. And, of course, they also communicate and whistle to one another. What a pity that as yet we have not yet learned to understand these intelligent and fascinating marine creatures.

Common dolphins, for instance, grow to a length of about 8 ft (2.5 metres), and are relatively small members of the whale group. They live in small family groups, the males, females and their offspring frequently forming larger schools for the purpose of hunting. These dolphins are really fast sprinters, spurting to 25 mph (40 kph) in a mere two seconds. They can also jump far higher than other dolphin species and love to ride on the bow waves of passing ships. Just like surfers,

beings. Unfortunately, however, few visitors to Madeira will have the luck to sight a whale or a dolphin.

Our *Song of the Whale*, with its sophisticated acoustic equipment, can easily detect the enigmatic sea mammals and even find them at night. The hydrophone – an underwater microphone – can pick up the clicking sound made by sperm whales, pilot whales or dolphins over relatively long distances. The sea mammals switch on their echo sounder to gain orientation or to detect their

Left, a manta with attendants. **Above**, threatened with extinction: the monk seal.

they exploit the pressure of the waves to save energy while swimming.

Of all the many species of dolphin, the most well-known is the bottle-nosed dolphin of "Flipper" film fame and a popular performer in oceanaria all over the world. It is mainly grey in colour and grows to a length of 14 ft (4.2 metres). This ubiquitous aquatic mammal is found in all warm seas, and like other dolphin species is intelligent, playful and inquisitive, which is why they seek contact with humans and enjoy escorting fishing boats.

Humpback and finback whales have become extremely rare, and the North Atlantic right whale can be considered extinct; the last specimen was killed by Madeiran whalers some 20 years ago.

Relatively little is known about the fairly prolific pilot whale, thus named because of its very close social ties, which frequently lead to an outbreak of mass hysteria and subsequent stranding of the herd. Between 1,600 and 1,700 pilot whales are still slaughtered every year off the Danish Faroe Islands, despite worldwide protest.

Madeiran waters are also occasionally visited by the killer whale or grampus. Despite its ugly name and reputation, it is not a killer at all, but a sort of sanitary policeman patrolling the seas. There is not a scrap of evidence that human beings have been attacked by killer whales.

Like sperm whales and pilot whales, most of the dolphins in Madeira's waters rely on squid as a source of food, though dolphins certainly don't turn their snouts up when a tasty fish swims by.

Precious seal: The sea mammal most in need of protective measures, in the opinion of marine biologists, is the monk seal, which is adapted to its warm-water environment. Only eight specimens were counted in the last seal population census carried out in the coastal regions of the archipelago, which means that monk seals must be rated as one of the most endangered species of fauna in Europe. The situation of this shy seal species is really precarious.

The Caribbean monk seal, prized for its blubber and its hide, probably became extinct in the 1950s. Its cousins living off Hawaii are on the verge of suffering the same fate, and it is currently estimated that only 200 to 500 monk seals still exist in the Atlantic and Mediterranean.

Before Portuguese seafarers discovered Madeira, large colonies of this warm-water seal species lived in the island's coastal waters, where they inhabited the coarse-sand bays backed by the steep protective cliff walls. Although seals are adapted to life in the sea, they also need a natural habitat on dry land, where they can bear and suckle their young. For that they need to be undisturbed, for baby seals remain dependent on their mothers for a far shorter period of time than is the case with other mammals and only by producing numerous offspring are the seal colonies able to survive. That also calls for plenty of space for the younger seals.

Monk seals inhabit caves along rocky coastlines, preferably those with one or two underwater entrances. Resting on sand or algae, the warm-blooded sea mammals shelter from the hot summer sun. Extremely shy, these aquatic mammals may have also chosen to lead this sheltered life in their caves in a desperate effort to escape persecution by human beings.

There is a small fishing village near Funchal called Câmara de Lobos, the "Bay of the Sea Wolves", as the monk seals (*Lobo do Mar*) are popularly named. Unfortunately, no monk seal has been sighted at Câmara de Lobos for many a year. The survivors of what used to be a flourishing colony eventually fled to the Desertas, which being more rocky and inhospitable for humans than the bigger islands of the archipelago, are an ideal natural habitat for the seals.

There is no fresh water on the islands of the Desertas – and therefore no civilisation. Nothing that grows there has been planted by human hand, and animal life has its own vital rhythm. Rare spiders like the big wolf spider, which can grow to 1.5 inches (4 cm), or the many varieties of lizards find an ideal home in the rocks and fissured crags of the coastline. And the wild goats which roam the deserted island are really wild and were not originally shipped there by seafarers and settlers to serve as a source of milk cheese and meat like their distant "cousins" on other islands in the archipelago.

Following a meeting of marine biologists held in September 1989 to discuss measures for protecting the monk seal, 50 percent of the group of islands was placed under the strict protection of the government, with a "No Entry" ban which applies to everyone. To make sure that this important piece of wildlife legislation is effectively enforced and observed the region is continually patrolled by three young wardens, for even a discreet and well-meant visit by genuine nature-lovers to a monk seal's den can cause the mother seal to desert her brood. Fortunately, *Monachus monachus,* as the monk seal is called in Latin, has been given a last chance to survive by this judicious piece of government legislation.

From Saul to Paul: Eleuterio Reis is today a protector of whales.

A STITCH IN TIME

Madeira is the home of wineries,
And extremely expensive embroidered
fineries.
I seem to sense a relation tender
Between vintner and embroidery vendor.
Free sample sippings of the grape
Inflate the tourist to a shape
In which, by the time he's embroiled in the
embroidery imbroglio
He will pay for a dozen doilies the price of an
authentic First Folio.

Ogden Nash

Ogden Nash may have been a bit fanciful in his conclusions about the relationship between Madeira's vintners and needlewomen but he correctly identified their importance on the island: wine is the most famous of Madeira's export commodities, but manufacturing industries based on traditional handicrafts, in particular embroidery, come a close second. Since its large-scale introduction to the island in the middle of the last century embroidery has become pre-eminent among the high-quality products made in Madeira.

It is doubtful whether crowned heads reposing on the tenderly embroidered flowers of their Madeiran cushions really appreciate all the hard work that goes into their production. But the embroiderers know. And one doesn't have to look far to see the importance the Madeirans attach to this art. The *bordadeira* – embroiderer – is one of the island's most popular motifs. Embroidery features on murals, on postcards and even on stamps. Aged between 8 and 80, the embroiderers mainly work in their villages, plying their trade as they sit chatting contentedly together in the shade of the vineyards. Traditional embroidery songs accompany the steady, perpetual rhythm of their hands.

Cottage industry: For many Madeiran women outworkers and their families, the products of this mainly home-based industry provide a vital contribution towards the family income. But, despite the high prices the

Preceding pages: Madeiran embroidery: admired all over the world. **Left** and **above**, a painstaking craft.

needlework fetches on the international market, the share that trickles down to the women who actually do the work isn't great: "My father is a fisherman and my mother is an embroiderer," says Lília, who is sent by her parents to beg on the streets.

Mainly it is women from the traditional fishing villages or the villages deserted by emigration who spend their time embroidering. They do it while waiting for their men to return. It is still a craft passed on from mother to daughter, although nowadays, un-

like in decades past, few daughters are around for much of the day. School is now compulsory and it is illegal for girls under the age of 14 to be registered as embroiderers.

Since the revolution in 1974, all people working in the embroidery industry have had to be covered by National Insurance. Leandro, an embroidery designer and employee of the *Instituto de Bordados, Tapeçãria e Artesanato da Madeira* (IBTAM – Madeiran Institute of Embroidery, Tapestry and Handicrafts) which supervises the industry of the island's handicrafts of embroidery, tapestry and wickerwork, believes that the often-quoted figure of 30,000 is a little exaggerated. "We have perhaps 10,000 true embroiderers," he says. All the processes other than the actual embroidery are carried out in the numerous "embroidery factories", most of which are located in Funchal.

Visitors will find it difficult to ignore the industry. Wherever you go, vendors spread out tablecloths, collars, napkins, table runners, scarves and handkerchiefs with an incessant stream of sales talk. The eyecatching patterns of rich foliate motifs make it difficult to resist the temptation to buy. The price of these works of art often dampens the enthusiasm, however, but resistance along the lines of: "What happens if somebody knocks over a coffee cup?" will be met with

deira have embroidered since time immemorial. Many of the vestments which can be viewed in the museums were made on the island. It would also appear to be the case that – like everywhere else in Europe – socially aspiring daughters of housekeepers strived to copy the beautiful dresses worn by the aristocratic ladies. Over the years quite a few Madeiran girls will certainly have helped embroider materials towards the dowry of high-born daughters.

Even today some of the finest families have retained their own family crest.

Perhaps it is due in part to the British dominance of the island over the years and the colonial spirit they instilled that Miss

a stream of reassurances. Nothing to worry about: Madeira's fine embroidery is both washable and long-lasting – a claim that is not always true, unless products bear the special seal of the *Instituto*.

Before and after Phelps: Leandro, who also trains embroidery designers, is keen to emphasise that embroidery was not introduced by the English as commonly claimed. He points to Gaspar Frutuoso who, in his historical work of the 16th century – interestingly enough in a chapter concerning the psychology of the Madeira women – wrote about the skilled work that the women produced on cloth. And the nuns in the convents of Ma-

Elizabeth ("Bella") Phelps, daughter of the wine merchant and school teacher Joseph Phelps, is so often presented as the mother and originator of Madeiran embroidery. Elizabeth Phelps, an unmarried English lady with a delicate constitution, had connections with the Santa Clara convent which still exists today. In this way she came into contact with an orphanage in Santana in which she spent a certain amount of time herself, since the climate on the north coast was better for her health. While she was there she taught the orphans how to embroider cotton.

On her regular trips back to England she took some of their work with her in the hope

that she would be able to make some money for the convent and for the children. She succeeded more than she dared hope.

In England the Phelps family was well-known for its missionary work, and it is very probable that it was Miss Phelps herself who was successful in bringing Madeiran embroidery to the attention of the ladies of the royal court. However, she could not, even in her wildest dreams, have suspected the tremendous effect her act of charity would have on Madeira economically. It is therefore not without a certain amount of justification that Elizabeth Phelps's name is linked with the industrialisation of embroidery on the island. Proof of this is the small business in the

Madeiran embroidery won great favour at Victorian ladies' tea parties in England. In 1851 Bella was invited to display her wares at the world exhibition in London. The English entrepreneurs Frank and Robert Wilkinson became her agents and established themselves on Madeira in 1862, thus laying the foundation for industrialisation and export on a large scale.

At this time the official published figure of people working in the embroidery industry was 1,029, and one can assume that the embroidery industry was then in a position to help, at least partially, towards counteracting the disastrous economic and social consequences of the mildew attack on the vines

Rua das Pretas called Figueira and Phelps.

But the claim that "Bella" Phelps introduced the Madeirans to embroidery would seem to be rather presumptive. While it appears that there was no commercial production of embroidery before 1850, in that year Madeira held its first trade fair at which embroidery was exhibited and awarded prizes. This implies that embroidery must, as Leandro of the *Instituto* stresses, have been around at the time.

Left and **above**, young girls are no longer as enthusiastic about embroidery as their mothers were.

between 1854 and 1856.

But fashions change and from 1880 onwards the sophisticated English ladies grew weary of the fine Madeiran embroidery. The export quota stagnated, even decreased. New markets were necessary if the industry was to survive. Then, from 1891 onwards, German traders took over the market and export was concentrated on Germany, France and the United States.

With typical German thoroughness, Otto von Streit rationalised and reorganised the production process. Instead of being arduously pre-stitched, the patterns were transferred directly on to the material with colour.

This was done using a new machine called a *máquina de picotar*. After the design has been transferred on to heavy-duty tracing paper, this perforating machine picks the tiny holes along the traced lines. The tracing paper is then laid over the cloth to be embroidered and the surface of the paper wiped with a cotton wad, the *boneca de algodão*, soaked in a mixture of aniline dye, paraffin and wax. In this way the pattern is transferred on to the material underneath. The cloth and thread to be used are then sent to the outworkers. A special measuring instrument is used to count the stitches, to ensure the pattern is according to specifications and to calculate the embroiderer's payment.

quality of their work and even the area in which they live; generally it fluctuates between 12,000 and 30,000 escudos – about £50–120.

In the factory the various articles are washed, ironed and subjected to any modifications necessary before being sold or exported. The final step is the coveted seal of approval, which proves that the work is authentic Madeiran – but then what is really meant by authentic?

After 1850 white cloth was stitched with white threads. The idea for this came from the British embroidery industry. This was followed by the "Richelieu", "Renaissance", and "Venetian" styles and even the Germans

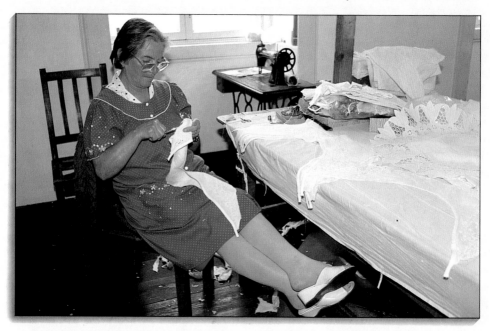

Loops, buttonholes and Richelieu: The agents, working on a commission basis, who provide the embroiderers with new material and collect the finished work, no longer travel up to Rosse, but otherwise everything is still much the same as it was. Some of the country women even manage to cut out the middleman and go to the factories themselves. Then their high-quality handiwork, prepared in the spare moments between feeding the pigs and cleaning the house, is registered and paid for on the spot. Inferior quality is paid proportionately less.

The monthly income of the embroiderers varies, and depends on their diligence, the

made their contribution to the new trends. Sewing with blue and then with brown thread was eventually accepted. Nowadays it isn't just cottons that are the background to the bouquets of flowers; high-quality materials – linen, organdie, batiste and silks – are sewn using a variety of skilful techniques, such as satin and cord stitch. New ideas are still welcomed by the market and many designs have been imported from abroad. Surprising though it might seem, the largest portion of Madeira's embroidery production today is exported to Italy.

While on Madeira, the visitor should try and take the time to observe the craft at close quarters by visiting one of the factories. It is a fascinating experience, where the visitor really gets a whiff of the past, of the patina that surrounds so many things Madeiran and Portuguese.

Painting with the needle: It isn't only embroidery in which the needlewomen of Madeira are skilled; they also excel at tapestry. This is, of course, an age-old craft, but its commercialisation on Madeira is relatively recent. Once again, the historians are unable to agree on the exact course of events. In this instance, it is the Germans rather than the British who seem determined to take all the credit, although there are documents available which prove that a written request for

landscapes, old master copies and floral pieces – on to canvas, and these were then sewn. It took only 16 years for tapestry to become an important and lucrative local craft industry.

The Kiekeben company remains the repository for the wool used to produce an original Madeiran tapestry. The enormous range of 2,500 colours that the company uses is first divided into main colour groups and then subdivided into colour tones, such as sweet and dry, bright and soft, fresh and old.

The production process is very similar to that already described, the main difference being that in this case, the needle is used to "paint" or copy. The tapestries are mostly

the protection of *tapeçaria* had already been made as early as 1780.

Nevertheless, it was not until the late 1930s that large-scale production of tapestries got under way on Madeira, under the Kiekeben family. The Kiekebens are of German origin. Father Max Kiekeben had been involved in Madeira's embroidery industry since 1909 and in 1938 his son Herbert introduced this new branch of the needlework industry. An artist in his own right, he painted pictures –

Left, embroidery is a thriving cottage industry. Above, it is also a popular hobby. Above right, in the Institute of Embroidery in Funchal.

copies of well-known masters. It is possible to obtain everything from Rembrandt's *Man with the Golden Helmet* to Leonardo da Vinci's *Mona Lisa*. For those who wish to embroider their own masterpiece, canvases are available with just the painting traced in.

The pattern for a new tapestry is drawn up and then transferred to the "artists' studio" where Kiekeben's full-time embroiderers copy it using their own interpretation of the overall dimension and style. These are then copied again and distributed to the embroiderers working at their homes in the countryside. About a fifth of the money earned from the sale goes to these workers. Like the embroiderers, they too now have to pay National Insurance contributions.

Visiting the Kiekeben factory, one gets a distinct feeling of having taken a journey back in time, as time-honoured methods are still the order of the day. Ronald Reagan and Princess Di are both proud owners of an original Kiekeben tapestry.

Recent history: The history of the Kiekeben company mirrors the development of the Madeiran embroidery industry. In 1906 six of the eight existing embroidery firms were under German control. It was a time of prosperity: more and more wealthy people were embarking on cruises to Madeira and the beautiful embroidered goods were packed

obvious that Madeiran embroidery was no longer the skilled craft it had been. In the general desire to make as much money as possible the true originality of the product was lost.

With the advent of the slump in the 1930s the Americans relinquished the market to the Portuguese. The Kiekebens, however, managed to keep their heads above water, at least until their business burnt down in 1937 and they were forced to start again from scratch. Strangely enough, this coincided with a radical change in the industry as a whole. An umbrella organisation, the *Grêmio*, was founded.

This organisation was responsible for in-

into small boats and transported to the cruise liners where they were sold to the passengers. World War I had disastrous consequences for the Germans on the island and from 1916 the business was largely taken over by Americans of Syrian-Jewish origin. It was they who were responsible for developing the industry and giving it the status it had hitherto been lacking.

By 1923 about 70,000 people were involved either directly or indirectly in the embroidery industry. The standard of living of many Madeiran families improved, whereas the quality of the embroidery itself sadly deteriorated. It became increasingly

troducing strict standards of quality control, starting embroidery schools, calculating prices for the different articles, granting subsidies towards housing and making sure that the industry was represented at international trade fairs. A percentage of the income earned by the industry as a whole was reserved for this organisation.

During the 1974 revolution, this organisation was dissolved and replaced by a commission. This meant a change for Kiekebens too. Since then the firm – which even in the days of Max Kiekeben was called *Casa Americana* – has concentrated on the American market.

Quality and art: The Madeiran Institute of Embroidery, Tapestry and Handicrafts was established in 1978. Housed in the imposing building in the Rua Visconde Anadia near the market and right next to the fine embroidery firm belonging to Patrício and Gouveia is a museum; it is open to the public on weekdays. The oldest exhibits date back to 1870. The exhibition housed on the first floor gives a good overall picture of the traditional skilled industries in Madeira, thereby fulfilling the role of folklore and ethnography museum. If you are intending to buy needlework, it is worth paying a visit to the museum before doing a tour of the 50 or so embroidery firms in Funchal. You will

industry hold out? Until now the embroidery industry has helped to keep the threat of female unemployment at bay. But it is a painstaking craft, hard to learn. A poem from the "Embroidered Songs", *Toada Bordada*, written by Leandro F. Jardim says it all:

> *Alma à roda*
> *roda e urde*
> *Borda.*
> *A vista turva*
> *faz a curva*
> *mete o ponto*
> *ponto a ponto...*
> She puts her soul into her work
> holding the circle, turning the circle,

then have some sort of critical basis on which to work when you are deciding what to buy. A price and quality comparison is advisable.

Often the small and medium-sized firms are housed in beautiful *fin de siècle* buildings and these are easily recognisable by the company logos outside. Most of the buildings look in need of renovation, a fact which would indicate that it is obviously not possible to make large investments in such a slow-moving industry. This leads to the inevitable question: how much longer can such a noble

Left and above, some items of local handicraft are more affordable than others.

she sews.
Her tired eyes blur.
She closes the circle
arriving at her goal
stitch by stitch

Will the modern, young girl of the next century still sit with her mother and grandmother in the shade of the vines and join in the refrains of an embroidery song? There is strong competition from the Far East, especially China but, thank goodness, originals and fakes are easy to distinguish – and if they are not, you can always look for the seal to guarantee true quality!

"Yes my father makes baskets, but he's sleeping at the moment", says the young boy playing with his ball in the entrance to the small, split-level house built into the hillside in Camacha.

The smell is reminiscent of a farmyard. No wonder: Agustinho Jesus Freitas is the proud owner of three cows. "Tax reasons," he growls, still half asleep. As far as his social security payments are concerned, he is a farmer, although the money that actually feeds the family comes from his wickerwork, or *vimes* as it is called locally. Among the wicker workers of Camacha, Agustinho is regarded as the artist. His speciality is animal reproductions. These demand a great deal of skill, and occupying pride of place in his *tenda*, which translates more or less as "workshop", is his masterpiece, a team of oxen pulling a cart in true-to-life scale – well almost. It took him six months to complete, working at it day and night . "I also have a monkey, a lion and a pig," adds Agustinho with modest pride.

Family trade: He began to weave at the age of seven, following in his father's footsteps. Today he works together with his wife and a few relations, depending on how much there is to do. Wickerwork is very much at the mercy of economic factors. Regular income, holidays or hours are not things Agustinho and his family know anything about.

It is not a life that appeals to everyone. His 17-year-old daughter only helps out during the holidays, if then. She is planning to finish her schooling, gain good results and go on to join a "modern" profession. She beams with self-confidence. Her mother, on the other hand, keeps her eyes fixed on the ground.

It is amazing how fast Agustinho and his wife divide the willow canes into four piles, the *liaça*, using a plate-sized machine called a *rachador* – a name which is impossible to translate (the sound of the word is exactly the same as the noise the machine makes). A basket awaits completion and soon there is a demonstration of how fast and skilfully the experts can weave.

Before the willows arrive on Agustinho's doorstep they have to be peeled and cooked in enormous vats, which bear a striking re-

semblance to a witch's cauldron! After the harvest, which takes place from January to March, thick clouds of steam hang over the village, filling the air with a distinctive aroma. This is the so-called "warm" method during which the canes adopt their typical brown colouring.

The long, drawn-out "cold" method is rapidly dying out and is only used when furniture made out of "white" cane is specifically requested by the customer. Using this method, the cane is soaked in cold water for

four to six weeks – approximately as long as it takes for them to sprout a second time. After peeling the cane is soft and white enough to be made into exceptionally hard-wearing baskets. The processed cane is bound according to strength and size into sheaves and can be sold at various prices per kilo.

The basins that were once used for soaking the willow can be seen, now largely overgrown, rising in small terraces above the road as you drive into Camacha from Funchal. Camacha, a small village on the east side of the island, is where Madeira's wicker industry began and where it is still concentrated today. There are people who claim that 90 percent of the population is directly involved in the industry.

In fact, there are 1,400 wicker-workers, middlemen and export salesmen in Camacha, with another 310 in Caniço on the south coast. The focal point of the village appears not to be the church but the Café Relógio: this is the centre of attraction for the dozens of tourists who flock here every day to take a look at the wicker goods for themselves. It would be difficult not to be enchanted by this packed wicker supermarket. There is an ex-

art. Among these is the "Zoo", and most of the animals "kept" here are the result of Agustinho's efforts. However, among so many practical products, the wicker animals do tend to look rather out of place.

Top of the sales chart has to be the clothes basket, which airlines usually allow to go through as a suitcase. Particularly appealing is the furniture, the kind which one would otherwise normally find in super-expensive furniture stores back home. Such pieces really do make living more beautiful. Freight

tremely good chance that when you leave the round building – after having visited the excellent restaurant on the first floor which serves local specialities and boasts a superb view – you will be carrying at least one of its wonderful baskets on your arm. In addition to the baskets, which are available in every possible and impossible shape and size, there are over 1,200 other articles for sale. Some of the wickerwork products are real works of

Preceding pages: wickerwork makes an ideal gift; after all it does not have to be something as large as a chair. Left and above, it takes a great deal of work to prepare the willow for weaving.

can be arranged, although a 40 to 50 percent surcharge on the actual sale price should be expected as well as a two- to three-month delay before the goods arrive. Small articles will be accepted by the airlines without any problems, but not large items. When in doubt it is worth inquiring with the respective scheduled flight or charter airlines.

Funchal itself also has a few wicker centres (in the Rua da Carreira, the Rua do Carmo and the Rua do Castanheiro), which you can browse through at your leisure, although there is not the same amount of choice as in Camacha.

The willow plants stem from a cross between *Salix alba* and *Salix fragiles*. They thrive above all in the small, well-watered valleys of the north, around Boaventura and Ponta Delgada. The landscape in this area with its fields full of towering canes seems, especially at dusk, to have an eerie quality about it.

After the harvest, which takes place between January and February, only the bald *cabeças* – heads – of the canes are left standing. Every plant delivers between 4.5–11 lbs (2–5 kg) of cane. They reach their peak of production when they are four years old, remaining productive for up to another 12 years, depending on the quality of the soil and the amount of water they receive. Dry

domestic purposes, to carry fruit and vegetables, although it will still sometimes be used to transport stones on building sites if a crane isn't available.

When baskets were first produced as pieces of handicraft on Madeira, they were made not of willow but of broom, and the smaller, more delicate pieces continued to be made from this material right up until the 1950s. Unfortunately, this craft has now completely died out. The small baskets on display in Café Relógio are all made in China.

There are many different versions concerning the origins of the wickerwork industry on Madeira. One story goes that a man from Camacha used the time he spent in

and windy seasons can severely reduce the willow harvest.

Long tradition: The Madeiran wicker industry has a long history. Even during the building of the first *levadas* at the time the island was settled, workers were lowered down the steep cliffs sitting in baskets. The oldest and most typical basket is the *barreleiro* made of raw, untreated willow, which even today is still exported to wherever Madeirans are living and continuing this craft. This includes places as far away as South Africa.

It is mainly at the market that the *barreleiro*, with its distinctive plate-shaped rim, can be seen. Nowadays it is only generally used for

Limoeiro Prison in Lisbon to acquire the trade from a fellow prisoner. Upon his return he shared this knowledge with his fellow villagers. Others claim the craft took root in Funchal's prison and give the year as being 1845. Yet others are wont to maintain that the beginning of the industry dates back as far as 1827 when a delegation came over from Gonçalo, a village near Guarda in Northern Portugal, the hub of the Portuguese wicker industry, and left only after having imparted their skills to the people of Madeira.

Still more people point to William Hinton, the 19th-century sugar industrialist, as the originator of wickerwork on Madeira. The secret of weaving is said to have been unveiled by a certain António Caldeira as he took apart a mat that had been imported from England for Hinton. Certain it is that Hinton, whose descendants continue to operate businesses on Madeira to this day, was the main driving force behind the industrialisation of the craft. It was in Camacha that the Hintons and other British families had their summer residences and the wickerwork industry really got off the ground when British families found themselves wanting replicas of the cane furniture that was so popular in England and Germany at that time. Soon, pieces were also produced for the hotels in Funchal and they became so popular that wickerwork

cheaper goods, whose quality leaves a great deal to be desired, are often preferred by the profit-seeking exporters. This is obviously detrimental for the experienced craftsmen.

The wicker-workers do not have a full-time contract, so are also at the total mercy of their clients. There is nothing like a recognised quality control on all products as there is in the island's embroidery industry, although the wicker industry also falls under the umbrella organisation, the Madeiran Institute of Embroidery, Tapestry and Handicrafts (IBTAM), which supervises the island's handicrafts.

In addition, Camacha's young generation no longer wish to enter the wicker industry.

developed into a booming export industry. Baskets were even brought in from Italy to be used as models.

Economic factors: The industry has always been susceptible to slumps, as one can see looking at the ups and downs in the export figures over the years. Fashions change, weather can never be relied upon, and since wicker goods take up so much space, transport costs were always high. In addition,

Far left, practice makes perfect. <u>Left</u>, the artist among the wickerworkers – Augustino Jesus Freitas. <u>Above</u>, he doesn't make simple baskets like these anymore.

They tend to opt for clean, nine-to-five jobs, and it is often only members of the older generation who still know how to make particular wicker products. The competition from both China and, since Eastern Europe started opening up, Poland is also regarded with trepidation. Entering the EC has not brought any advantages so far. The basket-makers in the southern part of Portugal, including the archipelago, still live with the fear that they will be neglected in the general European euphoria. Agustinho's daughter, the daughter of the artist wicker-worker, is one who has no intention of stepping into her father's shoes.

AZULEJOS – THE BLUE ART

People for whom the word "tile" means nothing more than the type of wall-covering used in bathrooms and kitchens have clearly never been to Madeira or even Portugal, where these small squares hold a respected place in decorative art. In many cases, tiles comprise an integral part of the architecture they are adorning. The tiles of Madeira are known as *azulejos*.

The word *azulejo* does not actually have the remotest thing to do with *azul* – the Portuguese word for blue – even if most of the tiles it refers to are indeed that colour. The etymological roots of the word are Arabian, and in Arabic "azulejo" means nothing more than "small, polished stone". This immediately tells us something about the country of origin of this decorative art; it originally came from Arabia, over the Iberian Peninsula.

One can certainly be forgiven for confusing *azulejo* with *azul*. Most of the tile mosaics are executed in a combination of cool blue and white colours. It is predominantly these refreshing colours which adorn surfaces in houses, staircases, benches, floors, church interiors and church towers. The fact that, in the case of churches particularly, they are sometimes used externally shows that they are an effective method of protecting buildings from the wind and the rain.

This may, in part, explain the character of some of Madeira's modern villas: many of the families who have returned to Madeira after living overseas have chosen to use cheap, mass-produced tiles to cover the outer walls of their houses. The less charitable explanation, however, is pure ostentation. These gaudy homes were once described rather laconically as "maisonettes" by the Portuguese journalist Joaquim Letria. He did not come to any conclusions as to why so many returned ex-pats and other recent arrivals on Madeira have chosen to turn their houses inside out.

Recently, the government has been leading a fierce television campaign for the preservation of the typical Madeiran architecture. Many of Funchal's churches and monasteries mirror the styles of the great epochs in the history of art.

The earliest style of tilework has Spanish-Arabian origins, the so-called *Mudejar* style. *Mudejars* were Muslims who had converted to Christianity. They were familiar with the decorative tilework of the Arabs.

The most beautiful example of this kind of work has to be the floor surrounding the high altar in the Convent of Santa Clara. The writer Henry Nelson Coleridge said when he visited the convent in 1825, "If your whim or your necessities should lead you to Madeira, go, for my sake, to the nunnery of Santa Clara." To this day art experts come from all over the world to see the convent's floor, crawling around on their hands and knees to take in all the detail.

These tiles are recognised by their strict, geometrical pattern, so typical of Arab-inspired art. No figures are depicted, as portrayals of animate subjects were held to be taboo by the strict Islamic precepts of the time. The old techniques of production are clearly evident; before the tiles were put in the kiln, threads soaked in oil and magnesium oxide were laid across their surface to prevent the colours from running into each other. Small furrows dug into the clay while it was still wet served the same purpose. *Azulejos* prepared in this way were therefore never as smooth or uniform as the tiles produced in the following century, when methods were improved.

In Funchal, the oldest example of glazed tiles *in situ,* dating back to the 16th century, can only be seen from a distance: the green, brown, blue and white tiles of Funchal's cathedral. They were originally put there to protect the spire from the damaging effects of wind and rain.

Another site which was famous for its Spanish-Arabian tiles was the Santa Cruz nunnery. This, alas, no longer exists (the remains lie buried under the runway of the Santa Catarina Airport), but the best-preserved examples of its tiles were extricated from its ruins and taken to the safety of the Quinta das Cruzes Museum. Visitors can still admire them here today.

Simple, yet possessing great beauty, is the so-called *enxaquetado* ("divided into squares") style. The best place to witness it is in St Peter's Church and on the spire of the Convent of Santa Clara. This style was the inexpensive answer to the question of decoration during the economic crisis suffered by the island during the last 25 years of the 16th century.

By this time the art of the Mudejars remaining after the liberation of the Iberian Peninsula had already been superseded by the *majólica* method. The name of this procedure stems from the Balearic Island of Mallorca, but it was the Italians who were responsible for introducing the new method to Europe, in particular to Spain and the Netherlands.

The same technique was later called faïence. Using this method, the metal oxide was applied directly on to the tile's white enamel. It was a technique already used by Turkish and Persian craftsmen. Over the years, the patterns became gradually prettier; You can find examples in the Convent of Santa Clara.

This new and simplified method encouraged people to think of covering much larger expanses. Designs were multiplied on the same surface and patterns grew into what could justifiably be called "tile carpets". Again, it was commonly used in churches, and entire naves were decorated in this fashion, for example, the one in the Collegiate Church (Church of Saint John the Evangelist), which also contains the biggest collection of tiles dating from the 17th and 18th centuries.

Also worth seeing is the "Chapel of the 11,000 Virgins" in the Jesuit church. By the end of the 17th century people had begun to tire of such endless geometry. The first depiction of figures appeared. Next came plant motifs, and on Madeira corncobs and camellia were especially popular motifs. Blue on white colour combinations, influenced by the Chinese ideas which had come via Holland and Portugal, suddenly became fashionable. This same colour combination is found in Delft china.

The Quinta Vigia Chapel contains impressive examples of such tilework and is worth a visit if you can get in. However, Madeira's governor carries out his state business in the house so, understandably, entrance is discretionary. The terrace has a mosaic portraying the fables of La Fontaine. The skilfulness of the tiles' design makes them worthy of special attention. They are a fine example of Madeira's rococo period.

The baroque period found fitting expression in the blue and white tiles. Some of the best examples appear on church walls – such as that in the small chapel of Nossa Senhora da Nazaré just north of Nazaré's residential area. A similar example is more freely accessible on the rear entrance of Funchal Cathedral. The finest examples tend to be in the chapels of private *quintas* or in country churches. In this connection, the Saint Roque Chapel in Machico is well worth seeing, although it is unfortunately very rarely open.

The 19th century saw the start of the mass production of tiles. The expert eye and creativity of the tile-makers were replaced by stencils. Tiling in Portugal was influenced by developments in Brazil, where it was discovered that tiled walls provided ideal

are therefore difficult to find. It was not until the turn of this century that the tiling industry was given a new lease of life through historicism.

Under the influence of historicism, staircases were adorned in imitations of majólica and exterior walls were embellished with unassuming but nevertheless clearly visible elements of neo-baroque – in fact everything "Neo". It is very rare to see an original Art Nouveau frieze such as the one on the house behind Funchal's cathedral.

The blue and white tilework that immediately catches the eye of anybody wandering around Funchal all comes from the 20th century. It includes the fountain in front of

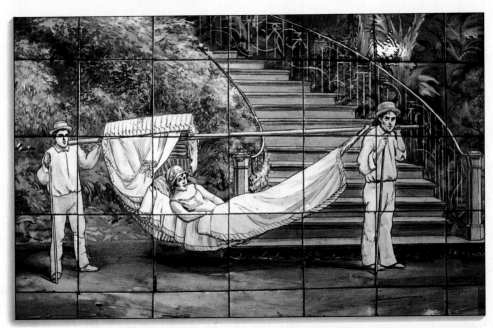

protection against damp and heat. People started to render entire walls with plain tiles, integrating them into the architecture.

Many ceramic factories launched themselves into this new market with enthusiasm. But in Madeira this industrialisation was despised and scorned. In Funchal, there is not one house to be seen from this time, only the aforementioned lurid imitations that the returned ex-pats favour.

Traces of 19th-century tiling on Madeira

Preceding pages: flower vendors in traditional costume. Above, it was easier for travellers in the old days: they were carried in sedan chairs.

the Carlton and the beautiful corner decoration on the former Ritz Café, where the local literati used to congregate. At Reid's Hotel perfect harmony reigns between the tiles and architecture on the terrace. Modern art can be seen in the graveyard of the Chapel of S. Martinho, where the tiles depict Saint George defeating the dragon.

Funchal's municipal museum, located in the town hall, offers a fairly comprehensive guide to the history of Madeira's tiles. Eagerly awaited is the anticipated addition of Dr Frederico Freitas' valuable collection to the museum, until now only accessible to teacher and scholars.

In the past, Madeira had one of the most unusual transport systems in the world. Before the advent of more modern means of locomotion – cars and buses are now as common as they are anywhere else, though there is no railway (the distances are too short and the island is too rugged and mountainous) – the contraptions used for transport were like nothing to be found anywhere else in the world. Their designs were amalgamations of elements from a wide range of international cultures.

There were good reasons for this. Madeira's mountains are so steep and inaccessible that the people living in the outlying villages were obliged to think of a solution if they wanted to be able to share in the island's wealth. This wealth was based on exports of home-produced goods, and without good communications systems, the inhabitants of these villages could not transport their bananas, their sugar cane and, above all, their wine to the outside world.

The only place with factories in which the products could be processed was Funchal. It was also the island's only port capable of handling large ships. Consequently, cross-country routes had to be built. However, since the Madeirans wanted to sacrifice as little of their precious agricultural land as possible, roads were built in places where it was believed they would cause the least interference.

Naturally this policy posed different problems. The roads were often so steep and narrow that today it is hard to believe they were ever seriously conceived as such. Often the paths were constructed like staircases and surfaced with smoothed basalt stones, the reason being that the transport of goods was mainly done on foot and steps were the most comfortable means of ascending and descending heights.

The Madeirans developed a particularly original and specialised transport system. Each product had its own guild of porters, all

Preceding pages: the toboggan drivers from Monte wait for customers. Left and right, visitors can still take a toboggan ride today – just like in the old days.

of course kitted out with the correct equipment. There was the milkman, who carried his cans of milk on a yoke around his neck, the onion man who transported the onions tied together on a stick, the fisherman who balanced his catch in a basket on his head and the vintner who humped his wine into town in goatskins. Only really heavy products were ever packed on to a donkey or a mule; occasionally, however, they were packed on to a board which would be dragged over the ground by two oxen.

The Madeiran people were quite happy with these methods of transportation. They have always had more than enough time, and walking never bothered them. It was the foreigners living on the island who were responsible for looking into methods of improving the transport system which would make getting around the island less laborious. As these people were generally well-travelled, it was possible to pool the many different methods of transport which they had come across. They then adapted the best modes to meet the special needs of Madeira. Inevitably this led to a rather weird mixture of vehicles.

Pick up thy bed: Hammocks and sedan chairs were among the most popular modes of transport on the island in the 19th century. These conveyances were called *palanquins*, or *lazarettos* (since they were often used for transporting sick people who could no longer walk – numerous in Madeira because of the benefits of the climate).

The Madeiran sedan chairs are not at all like their Indian or East Asian equivalent, except for the fact that they fulfil the same purpose. Isabella la França, the talented and humorous writer featured on page 85, described them perfectly. This English lady moved to the island with her Madeiran husband in 1853 and recorded all her experiences and observations – which she also illustrated – in a diary which now ranks as one of the most enlightening works ever written about the island.

ders and support themselves using a stick that they hold in their other hand."

Compare Isabella's description with her painting of the palanquin on page 193. Being humped around on such a sedan-chair must have been about as comfortable as travelling in one of the island's hammocks which Isabel describes on another page: "The descent is perfectly frightful… At every curve one is left hanging over a chasm or dangling over a gorge, without having the consolation of being able to see any trace of the road." Yet she is full of admiration for the *portadores* who carry their loads so sure-footedly up and down the mountains, never tripping or stumbling along the way.

Of the palanquin Isabella wrote: "The Madeiran palanquin… consists of a board which is just long enough for a person to stretch out their legs. The end at which one sits is slightly higher and cushioned. The rest is covered in a piece of carpet. There is a small iron railing all the way around which is about 7 or 8 inches high and the entire contraption is attached at both ends to an iron pole which is secured with two vertical rods. Two men balance the poles on their shoul-

The hammock, a piece of strong cloth tied at both ends and – like the palanquin – secured to a pole, made its appearance around the beginning of the 17th century. It followed much the same principle, in that the "passenger" still had to be carried. The hammock was a method of transport much favoured by the inhabitants of Monte. For a long time it was considered chic to be carried to church or even up to the summit of Pico Ruivo, the island's highest mountain. Naturally, the social status of the owner was very much reflected in the appearance of the "vehicle". The luxury model consisted of embroidered cloth, complete with a small awning-type arrangement to cover the passenger's head. It served two useful purposes, offering both protection from unwelcome curiosity among the *hoi polloi* and shade from strong summer sunlight.

The oxen-drawn sleigh: However luxurious and comfortable the hammocks might have been, a certain Mrs Buckley was never given an opportunity to benefit from them. She was unfortunately so overweight that even the *portadores*, who had had to put up with a lot in their time, were extremely reluctant to carry her all the way into town. Walking was out of the question because Mrs Buckley suffered so terribly from arthritis. Her dutiful husband, Major Buckley, determined that

a simple chassis – but Mrs Buckley was quite happy with it, and people soon began to follow her example.

In the course of time this *carro de bois* came to be fitted with springs, and gradually other improved features appeared as well: a sturdy wicker carriage, colourful cushions, curtains and an awning of oilcloth.

By 1850 somebody had hit upon the idea of making a sleigh available for the tourists. The sleigh was operated by the *boieiro*, the driver, and a young boy whose job it was to walk in front of the oxen and keep them on course. The sleigh was an ideal form of transport on the small, slippery cobbles which paved the capital's streets. By 1900 it had

his wife shouldn't be a prisoner in her own *quinta*, set about finding a solution to the problem, and it wasn't long before he came up with an ingenious sleigh drawn by two oxen, a *carro de bois*.

Pulled in such a vehicle across the round basalt stones, Mrs Buckley was now able to slide into town whenever the fancy took her. True, the first sleigh was a rather rudimentary affair – a box with four seats nailed on to

Left, until just 10 years ago, ox-drawn sleighs could still be seen regularly on Madeira's streets. **Above**, the lazaretto or palanquin – a sturdy sedan-chair.

become as familiar a sight as the corporation buses are today.

It was not until 1980 that this wonderful vehicle was finally taken off the streets – much to the chagrin of today's tourists. There is still talk of bringing it back, but until the capital's disastrous traffic conditions can be improved the chance of a ride on such a sleigh remains remote. Nostalgic visitors can see examples of it in the museum or in the O Boieiro restaurant, where the sleighs have been painstakingly and cleverly remodelled into tables.

Toboggans: Madeira's toboggans (*Carro de cesto*) also have a long history and of all the original methods of transport, this is the only one that can still be experienced on the island. The toboggans take exactly the same route as they always did, from Monte down the approximately 3-mile (4.8-km) stretch into the centre of Funchal. You should really try this out, even if on first glance it looks like the worst kind of tourist trap. These toboggans represent one of Portugal's first methods of public transport. Of course Isabella la França tried out this method too: "The toboggan", she writes, "looks even stranger than the oxen sleigh and the speed has to be experienced to be believed!"

Naturally, compared to what we are used to today this speed is hardly record-breaking.

Even at the steepest points, the toboggan rarely exceeds a speed of 6–7 miles (10–12 km) an hour. The ride is still fun though. You can book one of the many organised bus tours which include the toboggan trip in its programme, available in every travel office and in many hotels, or catch either the number 20 or number 21 bus to Monte. From there it is only a couple of metres to the starting point of the route.

The toboggan drivers always dress in white. Each toboggan is operated by two men, who run alongside the contraption as it slides down into the valley, steering, braking when necessary, pushing or on occasions even

pulling. The confidence with which they handle the toboggans soon allays any fears provoked by the many empty (and full) bottles of Madeiran wine lying around at the starting point. It's also reassuring to remember that though the toboggan was introduced at about the same time as the sleigh, in 1850, so far there has not been one accident.

Disasters strike: This is more than can be said for other methods of transport. In the 50 years between 1893 and 1943 tourists travelled to Monte by rack railway. It must have been a wonderful ride. The small railway needed about 20 minutes to make the 3,000-ft (920-metre) climb. The foreigners, who mainly came to live in Monte for its salubrious air, loved this ride past the *quintas* belonging to the wealthy Madeirans.

At the time there were plans to extend the railway to Pico do Arieiro, but disaster struck in 1930. A boiler suddenly exploded killing a large number of people. As a result, the shocked inhabitants turned their back on their formerly favoured rack railway and in 1943 it was closed down completely. The rails were dismantled and shipped back to England.

An equally tragic fate awaited the popular seaplane, the pride of the Madeiran people for many years. Following its first successful landing in 1921, there was a regular plane service between England and Madeira. The Aquila Airways' machines used to take off from the Isle of Wight, stop off in Lisbon and then land in the bay of Funchal – no small achievement considering the often stormy conditions of the Atlantic. In those bleak days the seaplane seemed like a godsend to the Madeirans, not least because it meant the arrival of a fresh batch of wealthy tourists. Until then many would-be visitors had declined to visit Madeira because they did not want to undergo the traumas of a long journey by ship.

Islanders and English alike were naturally upset when in 1958, after two plane crashes, these flights were discontinued. To this day, many older Madeirans remember this old seaplane with affection.

Left and **right**, porters – on the mountainous island this job is still as important today as it ever was. **Following pages:** the Fortaleza do Pico in Funchal; the Madeirans take pride in their beautiful fountains; a flower lady with orchids.

Much of this second part of the book is devoted to routes that can be taken on the island either by car, by bus or on foot. Indeed, visitors wishing to appreciate the full beauty of Madeira must be prepared to do some walking, and what more convenient way is there than strolling along the footpaths that run along the island's man-made irrigation channels, the *levadas*? There, where the only sound is the trickling of the streams, the gushing of waterfalls and the crackling of the foliage underfoot, where you can breathe the scent of the wild flowers, you will discover the best of Madeira.

The old port city of Funchal, with its narrow streets, now has to contend with the congestion and exhausts of automobiles, but there are still plenty of reminders of the days of the age of discovery, the sugar boom and the heyday of the wine trade. The restaurants of the old town invite you to sample grilled *espada*, and the tasting bars and cellars to try the island's famous wine.

The parks and gardens of the old *quintas*, the residential mansions of the island's former aristocracy, are a veritable paradise of blooming rarities, containing exotic species indigenous to the island and others imported from all over the world. They provide a convenient retreat from the hustle and bustle of the city.

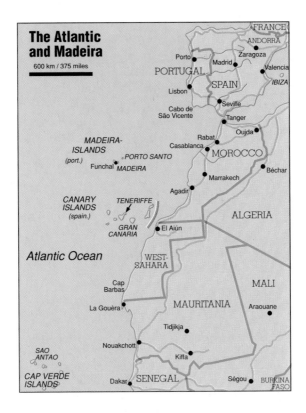

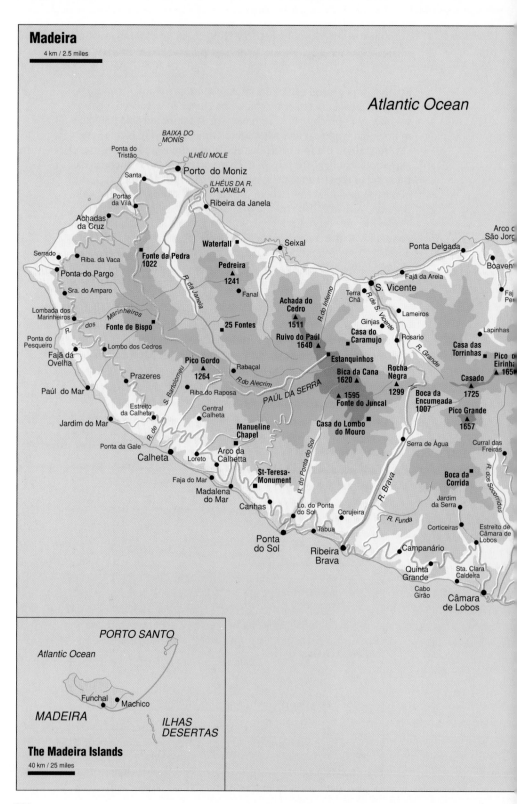

Madeira

4 km / 2.5 miles

Atlantic Ocean

BAIXA DO MONÍS

Ponta do Tristão

ILHÉU MOLE

Porto do Moniz

Santa

ILHÉUS DA R. DA JANELA

Portas da Vila

Ribeira da Janela

Achadas da Cruz

Waterfall

Seixal

Ponta Delgada

Arco d São Jorg

Serrado

Riba. da Vaca

Fonte da Pedra 1022

Pedreira ▲ 1241

Fanal

Fajã da Areia

Boaven

Ponta do Pargo

Sra. do Amparo

S. Vicente

Terra Chã

Faj Pei

Lombada dos Marinheiros

Marinheiros

Fonte de Bispo

25 Fontes

Achada do Cedro ▲ 1511

Ruivo do Paúl ▲ 1640

R. do Inferno

Ginjas

Lameiros

Rosario

Lapinhas

Casa do Caramujo

Ponta do Pesqueiro

R. dos

Lombo dos Cedros

Casa das Torrinhas

Pico Eirinha ▲ 165

Fajã da Ovelha

Pico Gordo ▲ 1264

Rabaçal

Estanquinhos

Bica da Cana 1620 ▲

Rocha Negra ▲ 1299

Casado 1725

Prazeres

R. do Alecrim

PAÚL DA SERRA

▲ 1595 Fonte do Juncal

Boca da Encumeada 1007

Pico Grande ▲ 1657

Paúl do Mar

Riba do Raposa

Central Calheta

Casa do Lombo do Mouro

Estreito da Calheta

Jardim do Mar

Manueline Chapel

Serra de Água

Curral das Freirás

R. dos Socorridos

Ponta da Gale

Arco da Calhetta

Calheta

Loreto

Faja do Mar

St-Teresa-Monument

Boca da Corrida

Madalena do Mar

Canhas

Lo. do Ponta do Sol

Corujeira

Jardim da Serra

Tábua

Corticeiras

Estreito de Câmara de Lobos

Ponta do Sol

Ribeira Brava

Campanário

Quinta Grande

Sta. Clara Caldeira

Cabo Girão

Câmara de Lobos

R. da Janela

R. de S. Bartolomeu

R. de

R. do Ponta do Sol

R. Brava

R. Funda

R. de S. Vicente

R. Grande

PORTO SANTO

Atlantic Ocean

MADEIRA

Funchal

Machico

ILHAS DESERTAS

The Madeira Islands

40 km / 25 miles

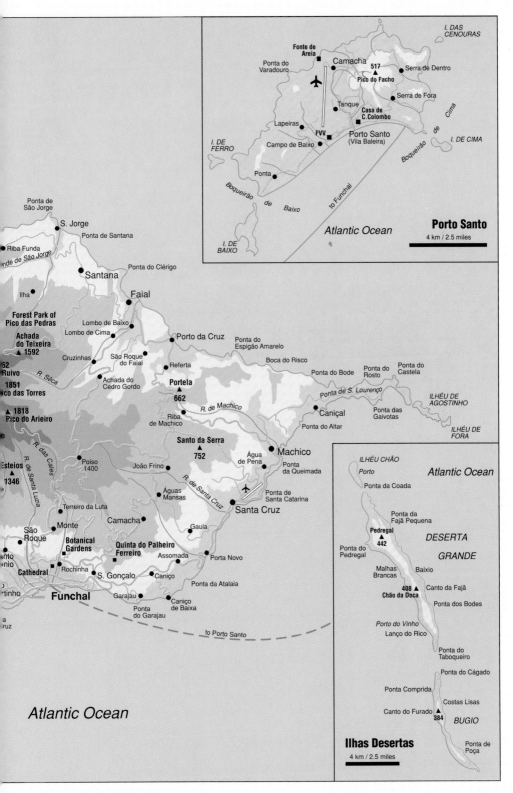

Porto Santo

4 km / 2.5 miles

I. DAS CENOURAS

Fonte de Areia

Ponta do Varadouro

Camacha

▲ 517

Serra de Dentro

Pico do Facho

Serra de Fora

Tanque

Casa de C.Colombo

Lapeiras

FVV

Porto Santo (Vila Baleira)

I. DE CIMA

I. DE FERRO

Campo de Baixo

de Cima

Boqueirão

Ponta

to Funchal

Boqueirão

de

Baixo

I. DE BAIXO

Atlantic Ocean

Ponta de São Jorge

S. Jorge

Ponta de Santana

Riba Funda

nde de São Jorge

Ponta do Clérigo

Santana

Ilha

Faial

Forest Park of Pico das Pedras

Lombo de Baixo

Achada do Teixeira
▲ 1592

Lombo de Cima

Porto da Cruz

Ponta do Espigão Amarelo

Cruzinhas

São Roque do Faial

Referta

Boca do Risco

52 Ruivo

R. Sêca

Achada do Cedro Gordo

Portela

▲
662

Ponta do Bode

Ponta do Rosto

Ponta do Castela

1851 ico das Torres

Ponta de S. Lourenço

ILHÉU DE AGOSTINHO

▲ 1818 Pico do Arieiro

Riba. de Machico

R. de Machico

Caniçal

Ponta das Gaivotas

ILHÉU DE FORA

0

R. das Cales

Santo da Serra
▲
752

Ponta do Altar

Esteios
▲
1346

R. de Santa Luzia

Poiso 1400

João Frino

Águas Mansas

Água de Pena

Machico

Ponta da Queimada

Ponta de Santa Catarina

R. de Santa Cruz

Santa Cruz

ILHÉU CHÃO

Porto

Atlantic Ocean

Ponta da Coada

Terreiro da Luta

Camacha

Gaula

Ponta da Fajã Pequena

São Roque

Monte

Botanical Gardens

Quinta do Palheiro Ferreiro

Assomada

Porta Novo

Pedregal
▲
442

DESERTA

Ponta do Pedregal

GRANDE

nto nio

Cathedral

Rochinha

S. Gonçalo

Caniço

Ponta da Atalaia

Malhas Brancas

Baixio

tinho

Funchal

Garajau

Caniço de Baixa

408 ▲
Chão da Doca

Canto da Fajã

Ponta dos Bodes

a ruz

Ponta do Garajau

to Porto Santo

Porto do Vinho

Lanço do Rico

Ponta do Taboqueiro

Ponta do Cágado

Ponta Comprida

Costas Lisas

Atlantic Ocean

Canto do Furado
▲
384

BUGIO

Ilhas Desertas

4 km / 2.5 miles

Ponta de Poça

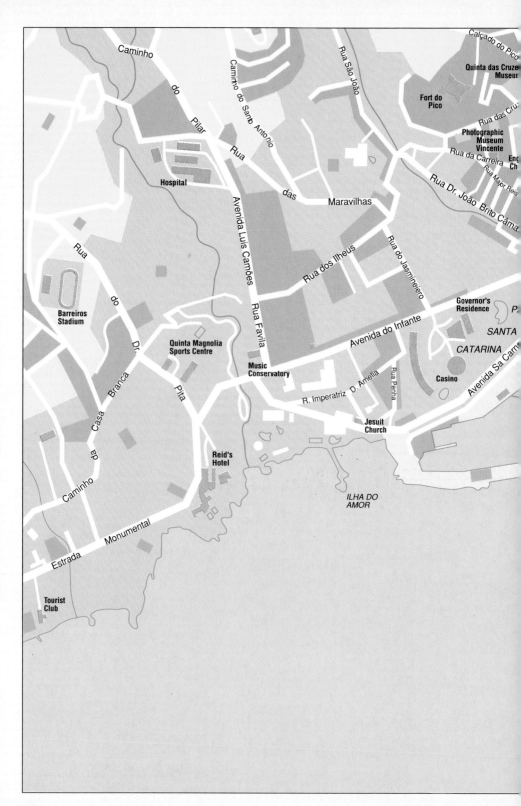

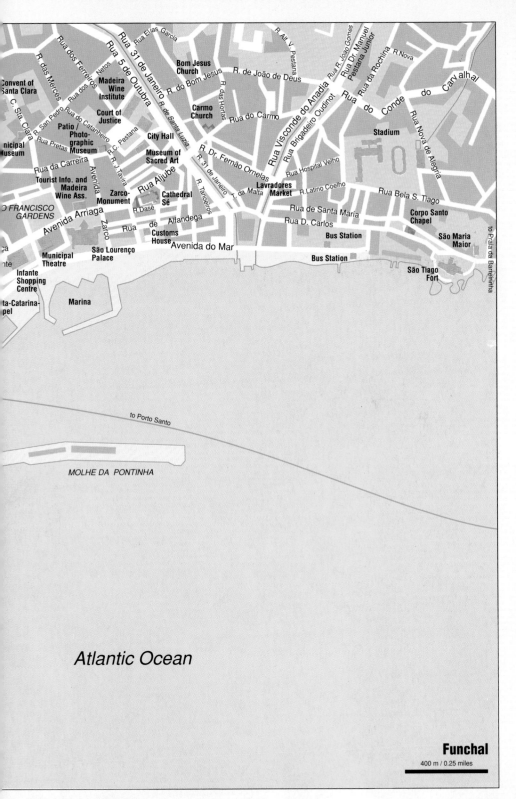

Convent of Santa Clara

C. Sta. Clara

Municipal Museum

O FRANCISCO GARDENS

Rua das Merces

R. San Pedro

Rua dos Ferreiros

Rua dos Netos

Madeira Wine Institute

Court of Justice

Patio / Photographic Museum

Rua Pretas

Rua da Carreira

Tourist Info. and Madeira Wine Ass.

Avenida Arriaga

Municipal Theatre

Infante Shopping Centre

ta-Catarina-pel

Marina

Rua 5 de Outubra

Rua 31 de Janeiro

Rua Elias Garcia

Bom Jesus Church

R. do Bom Jesus

R. de Santa Luzia

R. de João de Deus

R. Alf. V. Pestana

Carmo Church

Rua do Carmo

R. das Hortas

Rua Visconde do Anadia

Rua R. João Gomes

Rua Dr. Manuel Pestana Junior

R. Nova

Rua da Rochina

Rua do Conde

do Carvalhal

Rua Nova de Alegria

City Hall

Museum of Sacred Art

R. Dr. Fernão Ornelas

Rua Brigadeiro Oudinot

Rua Hospital Velho

Stadium

Rua Aljube

Zarco-Monument

Cathedral Sé

R. Dasé

R. 3 de Janeiro

R. Tanoeiros

T. da Malta

Lavradores Market

R. Latino Coelho

Rua Bela S. Tiago

Corpo Santo Chapel

Zarco

Rua de Alfandega

Customs House

Avenida do Mar

Rua de Santa Maria

Rua D. Carlos

Bus Station

São Maria Maior

São Lourenço Palace

Bus Station

São Tiago Fort

to Praia da Barreirinha

Atlantic Ocean

to Porto Santo

MOLHE DA PONTINHA

Funchal

400 m / 0.25 miles

A WALK THROUGH FUNCHAL

Funchal enjoys a particularly dramatic setting. Slopes rise up from the coast in a semi-circle like banks of seats in a huge amphitheatre, reaching heights of up to 3,600 ft (1,200 metres) above sea level at the northern edge of the basin.

The city is supposedly named after the wild fennel (Portuguese *funcho*) which, in 1419, Zarco and his men found on the banks of the three rivers which flow into the sea within the boundaries of the modern city. It was the sheltered location of the bay which persuaded the first immigrants to found their settlement here.

In the few empty spaces between the built-up areas the remnants of what these people encountered, a rich sub-tropical vegetation, still thrives. The character of the rivers, **Ribeiras de São João, de Santa Luzia** and **de João Gomes,** however, has been changed beyond recognition. Under the pretext of flood prevention they are now bedded in concrete in order to regulate their flow. On top of this they are now used by local residents as a rubbish dump, and have become an insult to both the eyes and the nose. Fortunately these former rivers, now degraded to mere gutters, are hidden in many places by the gorgeous hedges of bougainvillea that have been trained over the wires stretching between their banks.

Beginnings: In 1450 Captain Zarco was given Funchal and its surroundings as a fief duchy. The cultivation of sugar cane and vines, both introduced by Henry the Navigator, led to an undreamt-of level of economic prosperity in the settlements. In 1508 "Piccola Lisbonna", as it was jokingly called by Italian sailors who docked here, was given the status of a city by King Manuel I, and just six years later it became a diocesan town centred on the most important site in Funchal, the cathedral, where we begin our tour.

The Portuguese word for cathedral, **Sé**, comes from the Latin *sedes*, which means seat, i.e. the Bishop's seat, and thus has the same meaning as our word cathedral, which derives from the Greek word *kathedra*. The cathedral was erected between 1493 and 1514, and Pedro Eanes is regarded as the architect. Visitors enter the basilica, with its three naves, through a Gothic portal on the west side. The royal coat of arms can be seen above the entrance, and above this a simple rose window interrupts the gable wall. Inside your eyes will need some time to get accustomed to the light, before you can appreciate the Moorish-style ceiling of "cedarwood" inlaid with ivory (in fact, it is really a type of juniper wood indigenous to Madeira). The chancel is dominated by seating from the 16th century and a high altar picture from Flanders which was paid for out of the profits of the then booming sugar trade.

The Old Customs House, **Alfândega**, is situated to the south of the cathedral. It can be reached via the Direttissima, but the route around the Sé, past the flower sellers in traditional costumes, provides a delightful view of the apse of the Bishop's church with its spiral towers and other decorative details typical of the style at the time of Manuel I, the Manueline style. The Customs House is now the seat of the regional parliament and so only parts of it are open to the public and only at certain times. The north portal, with uniformed guards standing in front of it, is among the most famous examples of Manueline architecture on the island.

The south side of the old Customs Office looks on to the **Avenido do Mar**, Funchal's sea promenade. This is the terminus for buses to all parts of the city and to nearly all the other towns and villages on the island, as well as for boats to Porto Santo. The **Marina** is also situated here. Our route follows this street eastwards, crossing two of the rivulets mentioned above, which flow into the sea here. At the end of the promenade Avenida do Mar turns to the left, leading immediately into a pedestrian precinct on the right.

At the beginning of the precinct is the **Capela do Corpo Santo** dating from the Manueline period. It was built by

A toboggan driver pauses for a cigarette.

fishermen and is still maintained by them. Behind this the picturesque old city stretches out. It is full of bustling life, especially at night: bars, restaurants and discos are housed in many of the colourful old houses. Here it is possible to hear *fado*, a type of Portuguese ballad accompanied by the guitar and full of *saudade* (sadness). Contrary to what you might be led to believe, *fado* is a musical style typical of Lisbon but having little to do with Madeira.

At the end of the **Traversa do Porto**, which cuts through the old city, our route confronts the **Fortaleza de São Tiago**, the fort of St James, which was built at the beginning of the 17th century. Unfortunately, as this now serves as the headquarters of the military police it can only be admired from the outside.

With the fortress on your left, walk down to the **Praia da Barreirinha**, a beach covered with polished black basalt pebbles where local residents go to enjoy sun and sea in summer. Fishermen keep boats and stalls here, and there's a bar where their freshly-caught seafood can be sampled. **Santa Maria Maior**, which lies north of the beach, can be reached by the street to the left of the fortress. It is also called the Igreja do Socorro (the Church of Salvation), a reference to an epidemic in the 16th century that is said to have been ended by the apostle St James the Less, whose shrine can be seen in the church. The citizens' remission is commemorated every May by a procession of thanksgiving which starts from the church. The square in front of the church, the **Largo Socorro**, provides a fine view over Funchal.

To return, take **Rua de Carlos I**, which leads to the market area. Here there are many small bars where you can enjoy a cup of *cortado* (coffee with sweet Madeira) and *sandes*, a corruption of the English word, sandwich. The covered market itself is called the **Mercado dos Lavradores** (the Workers' Market) and was built in 1941. It is situated between two narrow streets north of the Rua de Carlos I. The hustle and bustle of Funchal

A view of Funchal's harbour.

life unfolds here daily, with particular gusto at the weekend when farmers from the surrounding areas join the local traders to display their produce. This is a good opportunity for visitors to introduce themselves to the wide variety of products available on the island. Flower women stand near the entrance, and the courtyard is packed with stalls selling vegetables, exotic fruits and, of course, fish. Two types of fish stand out amongst the seafood: huge red tunny, which is sold in slices, and the shiny black, streamlined *espadas*, the famous swordfish with bulging eyes and teeth as sharp as a razor blade.

Rua Dr Fernão Ornelas leads from the market back to the town centre. At the end of this street on the right is the **Carmo Church**, dating from the 17th century. Following the Rua da Conceicão northwards you come to a church called **Bom Jesus**, which dates from the same period. After crossing over the concrete bed of the Ribeira de Santa Luzia, with the Palace of Justice on your left and the town hall on your

right, you will arrive at the **Praça do Município**, the municipal square. The black and white paving of the square is reflected in the façades of the surrounding buildings. Dark volcanic lava stone was used both for paving the square and for the façades.

The **Câmara Municipal** (the city hall) in the northeast of the square was built in the second half of the 18th century. Diagonally opposite is the **Igreja do Colégio**, the Jesuit Collegiate church which was built some 150 years before. The front of the church is adorned by four statues portraying saints of the Society of Jesus, including the founder of the order, Ignatius of Loyola. The tympanum includes a huge municipal coat of arms. Three portals lead into the church with its single nave. The interior is lavishly decorated with tiles (*azulejos*), wood carvings and paintings from the baroque period.

The Jesuits were forced to leave Madeira in 1760. Their *Sacred Experiment* (the title of a play by Fritz Hochwälder about the Jesuit state in

Funchal possesses many attractive squares, such as this one between the Collegiate Church and the city hall.

Paraguay) aroused the disapproval of the men in power and this led to their deportation from South America, Spain and Portugal.

The southeast of the town square is occupied by the former bishop's palace, which is now home to the **Museum of Sacred Art** (entrance: 21 Rua do Bispo; closed on Sunday afternoon and Monday). It is most famous for its Flemish paintings from the 15th and 16th centuries, which found their way to the island as a result of the flourishing sugar trade with Flanders.

The greatest treasure in the collection is *The Adoration of the Magi*, which is presumed to be from the Antwerp school dating from the beginning of the 16th century. It was originally part of a triptych, but the other two panels have been lost. The most impressive exhibit from the collection of gold and silver pieces is the processional cross made in 1528 out of gilded silver, and donated to the cathedral by King Manuel I. Another piece which deserves special mention is a Flemish statue of the Madonna with child which Manuel I presented to the parish church at Machico.

After visiting the Museu Diocesano de Arte Sacra, described above, leave the town square going westwards by way of Rua C. Pestana. This street becomes Rua de Carreira where, on the immediate left, the **Fotografia Museu Vicentes**, Vicentes Photographic Museum, can be found at number 43 (open: Tuesday–Friday, afternoons only). The museum is reached by crossing the **Pátio**, which is planted with banana trees, and stands next to a café, an English bookshop and a health food shop.

The museum is named after the first-born sons of the Gomes da Silva family who were all christened Vicente. In about 1848, after the invention of the daguerrotype technique, the first of the Vicentes began to take an interest in photography. In 1865 he opened Portugal's first photographic studio and this existed until the death of the last Vicente in 1960. At the beginning of the 1980s the studio was converted into a museum showing historical photos of Madeira.

Funchal's typical cobbled ways. Stout footwear is advisable.

As at least 380,000 negatives exist, the vast majority of them are not on exhibition and are still waiting to be sorted and catalogued.

Leave the museum using the exit into **Avenida Zarco** and head south. Stretching along the street on the righthand side is the **Seat of the Regional Government**, the oldest part of which was built in the 17th century. On the right is the **Main Post Office** which is joined to the historical building of the **Bank of Portugal**.

In the centre of the junction of Avenidas Zarco and Arriaga, standing with his back to you, is the statue of **João Gonçalves Zarco**, the discoverer of the Madeiran archipelago. He can be seen gazing out to the sea – perhaps, one might be forgiven for thinking, to escape the exhaust fumes which plague this busy intersection. The monument was created by a local sculptor, Francisco Franco, in 1927.

Tourists can get any help or information they need from the friendly employees of the **Tourist Information Office** at 18, Avenida Zarco. It is open from Monday to Saturday from 9 a.m. to 7 p.m. and until 1 p.m. on Sundays.

At number 28 you can join one of the tours of the **Madeira Wine Company Lodge**. As usual, these tours are rounded off by an enjoyable session of wine-tasting so that those who are favourably impressed can buy a few bottles (or cases) to take home with them. As well as the tasting room you can visit the storage rooms, where the wine is kept in casks, on the upper floor, and an interesting wine museum (there is another wine museum, the Instituto do Vinho da Madeira, at 78, Rua 5 de Qutubro by the river Santa Luzia).

The other side of the street is dominated by the **Fort of São Lourenço**, built in the early 16th century. The east tower with its battlements and the coat of arms of Manuel I is a fine example of the architectural style named after this king. The following centuries saw substantial changes to the building. Nowadays the prime minister and the military commander of Madeira reside here, which is why the guards will steadfastly refuse entry to all unauthorised persons.

Beyond the fort the **Chamber of Commerce** is decorated with *azulejos* showing typical scenes on the island; embroideresses, basket-makers, ox-drawn sleighs etc. Beside this is the **Teatro Municipal**, an example of *fin de siècle* architecture. To the left of the municipal theatre Rua do Conselheiro José Silvestre Ribeiro, a narrow street which seems to be shorter than its name, leads to the Casa do Turista, a souvenir shop. The **Centro Commercial do Infante**, almost at the end of Avenida Arriaga at number 75, is a department store with an even greater range of goods for tourists to take home. Opposite the Chamber of Commerce and the theatre is the **Jardim de São Francisco**, a park containing tropical and sub-tropical trees and bushes, some of which even have edifying nameplates.

Avenida Arriaga leads into the **Praço do Infante**, a roundabout with fountains in the middle. The globe in the fountains symbolises the former worldwide importance of Portugal as a seafaring na-

The mountains drop steeply to the sea.

tion. Behind it, stretching south-westwards, is the **Jardim de Santa Catarina**, gardens laid out in the 1950s and '60s. Here the visitor can find many examples of exotic flora.

The gardens also contain a number of interesting monuments. At the entrance there is a statue of Prince Henry the Navigator standing under a neo-Gothic pointed arch and looking out over "his rotunda". "His rotunda", because the Infante mentioned in its name is none other than Henry the Navigator, the founder of the first settlement on Madeira. Inside the park there is a statue of Columbus, whose Portuguese name is Cristóvão Colombo. At the highest point of the park stands a statue of a sower trying to fertilise the ground around him. At any rate, he is obviously more successful than the sower who stands in front of the government buildings; this sower has been scattering his seed on the stony ground of the Avenida Zarco to no avail for years.

From the point of view of art history the most important monument in the park is the **Capela de Santa Catarina**, the saint who also gives her name to the park. The present chapel was largely built in the 17th century, although one already stood here in 1425, built by Constança Rodrigues, the wife of the discoverer Zarco. This was probably the first place of worship on the island. The belltower and the holy-water font under the canopy of the church are from the Manueline period.

Opposite the municipal park, on the other side of Avenida do Infante in another park, is the **Hospício da Princesa**. It was founded in 1859 by Dona Amelia, the second wife of the Brazilian emperor Pedro I, as a tuberculosis sanatorium in memory of her daughter, Maria Amelia, who died of consumption. The hospital chapel, which is often closed, contains a picture of the Virgin Mary donated to the chapel by Archduke Maximilian of Austria, who later became the emperor of Mexico. He was engaged to Maria Amelia, but she died before the marriage could take place. Later he married Princess Charlotte of Belgium instead.

A popular meeting place for visitors: the Patio in the city centre.

From the hospital park there is a view of the **Fortaleza do Pico**, which dominates the upper city. This fortress was built by King Philip IV of Spain, some time between 1580 and 1640, when Portugal belonged to the Spanish empire. As the navy now use the fortress as a transmitting station, there is no access for tourists.

The Jardim de Santa Catarina adjoins the casino complex to the west, which is mainly situated in the grounds of the splendid Quinta Vigia or **Quinta das Angústias** as it is also known. The pink-walled villa belonging to this estate now serves as the residence of the Governor of Madeira and guest house for state visits. However, you are permitted to look into the garden and sometimes into the chapel with its fine *azulejos*. Among the many illustrious guests from earlier days are the British queen mother, Adelaide, the two Amelias mentioned above and Elisabeth of Austria, the beautiful and beloved wife of Emperor Franz Josef I whom he called Sissi.

Next to the *quinta* is the ostentatious casino complex, consisting of a casino with a restaurant and nightclub, the Casino Park Hotel and a conference centre. This was designed in the 1970s by the prominent Brazilian architect, Oscar Niemeyer, who was also responsible for Brasília. Below the casino gardens is the **Molhe da Portinha**, the harbour wall in whose confines the cruise ships berth.

Most of Funchal's tourist hotels can be found just to the west of the casino complex along the **Estrada Monumental**. The majority of these have been built in recent years to meet Madeira's enormous increase in popularity as a holiday resort.

One outstanding exception to the standard tourist hotels is **Reid's Hotel**, run in the best British, or, more precisely, Scottish, tradition. Tradition, however, has its price – luxury suites can cost up to £350 per night. For those who cannot afford the luxury of staying here, afternoon tea offers a glimpse into the life of those who can, in particular well-heeled elderly English women. It is also worth

Funchal's polluted rivers are disguised by bougainvillea.

a visit on account of the view from the terrace over the well-tended garden to Funchal Bay.

A few hundred yards to the north of Reid's Hotel is another former estate, the **Quinta Magnólia**. It can be reached via Rua do Dr Pita and is situated behind the Quinta do Sol hotel. Formerly the British Country Club, it is now a public park with a children's play area, a swimming pool, squash and tennis courts, and a keep-fit track.

In the former clubhouse there is a restaurant belonging to the Hotel School where aspiring young waitresses serve the first-class food cooked by their fellow students. The restaurant enjoys such a good reputation that it is necessary to reserve a table. If it is not possible to secure a table for lunch, the traditional afternoon tea is worth catching. Unfortunately the restaurant is closed in the evening.

About 500 yards further along Rua do Dr Pita is the Barreiros **Sports Stadium**. The road past the stadium leads to the **Pico dos Barcelos**, a viewpoint which offers a breathtaking panorama in all directions.

Back in the city, the area around the **Church of São Pedro**, just north of the Jardim de São Francisco, is worth exploring. The **Municipal Museum and Aquarium**, housed in the Palace of São Pedro, was built at the end of the 18th century. The aquarium is on the ground floor of this natural history museum and contains a collection of fish from the waters of Madeira's islands. Upstairs you will find examples of flora and fauna and a range of geological specimens, as well as exhibitions of local history and contemporary painting. Bookworms may like to browse through the 30,000 or so volumes contained in the municipal library which is also housed here.

The church itself, which is opposite the museum in the Calçada Santa Clara, is worth a short visit to see the fine coloured glazed tiles which it contains. The steep hill leads up to the **Convent of Santa Clara** which was founded by the granddaughters of Zarco at the end of the 15th century. It stands on the site of a chapel, dedicated to the Immaculate Conception, which was built by the discoverers of the island. The convent has seen a number of alterations over the years and the only part of the original building which has survived intact is the Gothic pointed arch.

The walls of the adjoining convent church are covered with old tiles, and the richly decorated ceiling shows an Hispano-Arabic influence. The church also contains the tombs of Zarco, two of his daughters and his son-in-law, Vasconcelos, as well as some former governors of the island.

More tombs can be found in the cemetery of the English Church, dating from early colonial days, which lies just to the southwest of the convent. Because of its special importance, the Quinta das Cruzes, next to the Convent of Santa Clara, is dealt with in detail in a separate chapter along with two other particularly fine *quintas*.

Our last excursion takes you to the village of Monte, which lies 6 km (4 miles) north of the centre of Funchal at

Left, fish caught the night before are sold at the fish market. **Below**, narrow streets and a lot of traffic.

an altitude of 1,900–2,400 ft (600–800 metres) above sea level.

Monte is an absolute must, even for those tourists making a cruise, who often spend only half a day on Madeira. It can be reached by launch, hired at the harbour, by taxi or by public bus (numbers 20 and 21). The steep road up to Monte can prove rather strenuous for anyone who chooses to go on foot (the way is not shown on the street plan, but can be found on map tours 3 and 5). Unfortunately, the rack-and-pinion railway, which was used to take high society up to the health resort for half a century from 1893 to 1939, no longer exists (see page 194). All that remains from this time are the arches of the railway bridge over the Monte gardens and a few dilapidated "grand hotels". To enjoy the view at its best it is advisable to visit Monte in the morning as it often becomes cloudy in the afternoon.

Cars can be parked in the square, **Largo da Fonte**, with its fountain and statue dedicated to the Virgin Mary. From the square, steps lead up to the pilgrimage church, **Nossa Senhora do Monte**. This was built in the second half of the 18th century, replacing a chapel which was 300 years older and said to have been built by Madeira's first-born citizen, who was appropriately called Adam. On the high altar there is a wooden statue of the Virgin Mary which was found two kilometres above Monte at Terreiro da Luta. As a result of this find, the Virgin became the patron saint of the island. The statue is believed to work miracles and every year on 15 August it is carried through Monte in a solemn procession in which the most devoted pilgrims climb the steps up to the church on their knees.

Visitors with less faith in the power of miracles may be more interested in the **Side Chapel** on the left of the entrance. Behind a wrought-iron grille decorated with a coat of arms is the coffin of the last Austrian emperor, Charles I. He was forced to abdicate his throne after World War I and, following a long odyssey, came to live on Madeira, the place of exile chosen for him by the **City centre bustle.**

victorious powers. He lived close to the church in the **Quinta Gordon** together with his wife, Zita of Bourbon-Parma, and his children, Otto, Adelheid, Karl Ludwig, Rudolf and Charlotte. But within six months of his arrival Charles had died of pneumonia. Attempts by the family to have his body transferred to the Capuchin crypt in Vienna, where the emperor's widow was eventually laid to rest in 1989, have so far not met with success.

In nearby **Terreiro da Luta** (battlefield) the Virgin Mary is honoured in the form of a marble statue, **Nossa Senhora da Paz**, dating from 1927, which is over 15 ft (5 metres) high and weighs 20 tons. The statue was erected by the people of Madeira during World War I, following an attack by a German submarine. They prayed to Mary for peace and vowed to erect a statue to her if they were saved. The Madonna's remarkable rosary is made of the anchor chain of a French battleship sunk in 1916 and round stones carried up to the statue by the faithful.

The other well-known piece of statuary here is a statue of Zarco, the discoverer of the island, created by Francisco Franco in 1919, but most people come here to see the vista rather than such monuments. The view to be had from Terreiro da Luta is perhaps even more beautiful than from Monte.

The best way to return down to Funchal is by *carro de cesto*, the famous toboggans, steered by two traditionally white-suited men wearing straw hats.

The enormous friction between the toboggan's runners and the slippery cobblestone streets does not allow it to reach dangerously high speeds and the two *carreiros* have to push more often than brake. Even when the toboggan gains momentum there is no need to fear having an accident – the drivers are much too interested in getting a generous tip to take such risks. The end of the journey, either in **Livramento** or two miles further on at the southern end of Rua do Colombo in Santa Luzia near the old city, depends on how much the passengers are prepared to pay.

The tranquillity of an old villa on the edge of town.

REID'S HOTEL

Anyone who harbours a nostalgic desire for the days of grand hotels, those splendid old villas with the elegance and atmosphere of the last century, will find exactly what they are looking for on Madeira. You can't get much grander than Reid's, one of the world's leading hotels. Of course, actually staying at Reid's can cost a small fortune; the exclusiveness of the hotel is reflected in the rarefied prices.

Reid's was built by and named after the Scotsman, William Reid, who owned a veritable chain of high-class hotels on Madeira in the mid-19th century; in his guidebook to Madeira published in 1889, Anthony J. Drexel Biddle recommends six hotels, five of which are owned by the Reid family. Reid left the British Isles in 1836 at the age of 14 with £5 in his pocket and a fervent desire to make his fortune. In order to get to Madeira, he travelled by ship to Lisbon working his passage as a cabin boy. In Funchal he soon established himself as a wine dealer and, shortly afterwards, bought his own hotel. However, it was not until 50 years later that he achieved his greatest ambition: to build a hotel catering exclusively to the tastes of the *fin de siècle* nobility.

To build his dream he employed the architect of the famous Shepheard's Hotel in Cairo, choosing as a site the most striking viewpoint in Funchal. The hotel is located on top of a cliff and offers a magnificent panorama of the ocean as well as the bustling harbour and old city of Funchal. Alas, William Reid did not live to see the longed-for opening of his hotel. He died in 1887, and his two sons, Willy and Albert, were left to complete the project on his behalf.

The hotel no longer belongs to the Reids – it is now in the hands of the equally famous Blandy family – but it has remained what it always was: the epitome of discreet luxury. It stands in 10 acres (4 hectares) of grounds, scented, sub-tropical gardens where flowers are always in bloom. Narrow cobble-stoned paths, typical of Madeira, lead through gardens planted with roses and geraniums as well as cedars, cypresses, palms and other exotic trees of the island. Visitors can relax on benches in the middle of green lawns and watch lizards darting past or gaze out over the Atlantic lying far below.

However, the majority of the guests prefer to spend their day relaxing beside on of the swimming pools, particularly the one inside the hotel. The interior of the hotel is so inviting that it is hardly surprising that its guests feel no great urge to venture outside. The drawing rooms are light and airy, some with suites of pastel-coloured wickerwork chairs, others with flowery chintz-covered sofas which are perfect for post-prandial dozing.

Other facilities include comfortable lounges and lobbies, ideal for passing the time of day, as well as a billiard and snooker room, a bridge room and a conference room. In the writing room the guests are provided with writing

Left, the epitome of traditionalism: Reid's Hotel. Right, Churchill and his wife Clementine on Madeira.

paper, quills and ink. The hotel enjoys a wonderful sense of quietude. The reading room is disturbed by nothing more irksome than the occasional rustle of a newspaper; the salons are enlivened by nothing louder than the soft tinkle of china teacups and the quiet murmur of people versed in the art of small talk.

The old library is furnished completely in teak and contains row upon row of leather-bound tomes dating from colonial times. Guests not interested in those can find a good range of modern English novels as well as a number of foreign language books.

However, Reid's greatest attraction is afternoon tea on the terrace overlooking the sea. This is where aristocratic-looking guests, suitably attired in light but stylish dress, meet to enjoy the English version of an afternoon ritual: buttered toast, cake and tea.

Since its opening the hotel has always kept up the same British tradition which can be found in restaurants like Simpson's in London or in the best London clubs. However, it relies on the friendly Portuguese population for its staff and it is under German management. To quote the manager, Peter Späth: "Reid's is a typical *de luxe* resort hotel, with the most modern technical equipment, traditional comfort and a tendency to understatement."

From the beginning it has been a meeting place for celebrities from all over the world. As the guest book verifies, the hotel has played host to emperors, kings and queens; one of the first was the glamorous Empress Elisabeth of Austria. Dictators, both ruling and deposed, for example ex-President Batista of Cuba, have stayed here, not to mention writers such as the German poet, Rainer Maria Rilke, and George Bernard Shaw. Many of this select circle of guests came back year after year to spend the winter season at Reid's, some of them returning as many as 26 times.

During his stay Shaw even took dancing lessons, in spite of his advanced age of 71 years, and signed a photograph for his teacher, Max Rinder, with the dedi- **Other visitors to Reid's.**

cation: "To the only man who ever taught me anything."

Winston Churchill, another Reid's regular, must have been in equally high spirits when, one evening, he ordered the oldest bottle of Madeira in the hotel, dating from 1792. When the bottle was brought up from the wine cellar, Churchill placed a napkin over his arm and assumed the duty of serving his guests himself. Incidentally, the finest suites in the hotel are named after Shaw and Churchill.

Some famous personalities have had more dramatic reasons for staying at Reid's. The last emperor of Austria, for example, spent the first part of his exile here after being deposed from the Austrian throne. Another exile was Fulgencio Batista, the Cuban dictator, who was forced to flee from Cuba by Fidel Castro. He arrived with a large entourage and took over a whole floor of the hotel.

The history of Reid's itself has not been without its turbulent moments. During the strikes against the so-called "Hunger Law" in 1931 it functioned as an extension of the British Embassy and offered asylum to some of the rebels who were later forced to escape abroad. But normally a *de luxe* hotel like Reid's is, as already said, a haven of peace. This is one of the reasons for it being so popular among elderly people, some of whom, if they are wealthy enough, spend the entire winter season here. They arrive in September and depart after Funchal's famous celebrations at New Year. The British still make up 42 percent of the guests, but 12 percent are German and 8 percent Swiss. In the summer months families come from Spain or Italy, but it is rare that all the rooms in the hotel are occupied.

The rigid code of etiquette, particularly concerning dress, has relaxed only slightly in recent years. The British guests are still keen on dressing up in the evening, making dinner a formal occasion. For men wearing a tie is enough to comply with the hotel's standards, but dark suits or dinner jackets are generally considered more suitable. The women wear an evening dress, either long or short. As the manager, Peter Späth, says: "It takes a few days for those guests who are here for the first time to get used to the obligation to wear a tie, but they soon begin to appreciate it – after all, dining in formal dress is a part of our culture." In the main dining room a *table d'hôte* dinner is served to the sound of piano music in the background. The menu is written in French; the food, however, is predominantly English. The alternative is the grillroom, where guests can eat a candlelit dinner *à la carte*, choosing French or Portuguese dishes.

After dinner, guests can spend the evening in the ballroom where they are invited to dance to the music of a Portuguese orchestra. The side of the ballroom overlooking the sea is made entirely of glass, offering a view of the dark Atlantic Ocean far below and the twinkling lights of Funchal.

The formality of the evenings at Reid's contrasts with the relaxed atmosphere it offers during the daytime. Guests have a choice of three salt-water swimming pools, two of which are surrounded by green lawns and palm trees, one with a constant temperature of 27°C. The third pool is at sea level and is built directly into the rock. It can be reached by steps leading down the cliff or by a lift. Other facilities include tennis courts and, a recent addition, a herb and vegetable garden with access for guests.

When alterations were made to the hotel in the summer of 1990, those guests who have no wish to get dressed up for dinner every evening were taken into consideration. The most daring innovation was a restaurant where guests can appear for dinner in jeans if they wish, a custom normally reserved for the buffet lunch in the garden restaurant.

One other speciality which the hotel offers is a weekly walking tour of the *levadas*. This is carried out in the best British tradition, with a picnic lunch carried in hand-made willow baskets covered by fresh twigs. When the weary ramblers reach the most exquisite of the tour's beauty spots, the baskets are set down, bottles of cool Portuguese wine and delicious food are spread out on tablecloths and everyone tucks in.

THE PARKS AND GARDENS OF FUNCHAL

Visitors who take the time to stroll through the parks and gardens of Funchal will encounter an incredible variety of tropical and sub-tropical plants and trees. The following selection is based on those with particularly striking flowers or fruits or leaves.

A sea of flowers: From the stock of trees with red blossoms one deserves special mention; the flame-of-the-forest or tulip tree (*Spathodea campanulata*). Its scarlet bell-shaped flowers, like tulips, protrude in panicles over the outside of the crown. Equally striking are the fiery red flowers of the coral tree (*Erythrina* spp), which appear on the branches of the tree even before the foliage. In spring the flame tree (*Brachychiton acerifolium*) produces small, flaming, bell-shaped flowers which hang in bunches between the hand-shaped, lobate leaves. Another flame tree is the royal *poinciana* or "flamboyant tree" (*Delonix regia*) which is characterised by its clusters of red flowers with long stamens bending upwards.

The red gum tree (*Eucalyptus ficifolia*) is notable for the splendid colour of its flowers with their bright red, brush-like stamens. The *Brassaia actinophylla* can be recognised by its protruding, finger-shaped inflorescence and its hanging clusters of leaves in an umbrella-like formation.

The bottlebrushes (*Callistemon* spp) are richly blooming shrubs with red flowers arranged in cylindrical spikes reminiscent of a bottlebrush. The flowers of the *Plumeria rubra* are pleasantly scented. In Asia, where the plant originally comes from, it is considered to be a symbol of immortality and is therefore frequently planted in the gardens of temples.

In spring the sweet scent of the bead tree (*Melia azedarach*), reminiscent of a lilac, is particularly striking, as is the abundance of flowers on the jacarandas

Preceding pages: in the shade of the palm trees. Below, glowing bougainvillea.

(*Jacaranda mimosifolia*) which line many of Funchal's streets, bathing them in a delicate violet colour. The evergreen *Tecoma stans* can be recognised by its golden-yellow, funnel-shaped flowers which are in bloom for many months of the year.

Very similar to this is the *Markhamia platycalyx,* which has yellow blossom with a splash of red in the mouth of the flower. The cassia (*Cassia didymobotrya*) is a large shrub with winged pods notable for its candle-shaped flowers which rise above the foliage in clusters like candelabras. Occasionally you might come across acacias (*Acacia* spp), which originally come from Australia. In blossom they are completely covered by fluffy, yellow spherical or cylindrical flowers. One of the advantages of this tree is that its roots have a particularly beneficial effect on the soil, adding nitrogen.

The majority of trees and shrubs can be most easily recognised by their distinctive flowers, but there are a number which draw attention to themselves because of the unique or curious fruits they bear. Particularly impressive is the sausage tree (*Kigelia africana*), a small but imposing tree with curious fruits looking like sausages hanging from long stalks. Another curiosity is the kapok or silk-cotton tree (*Ceiba pentandra*), whose trunk is covered with thorns and is reminiscent of the hide of a prehistoric animal. It bears balloon-shaped seeds which have a coat of white silky fibre often used for stuffing pillows and teddy bears or for sound insulation.

The fruit of the *Couroupita guianensis*, which originally comes from the South American rain forests, has the shape of a cannonball weighing up to 10 lbs (5 kg) and grows directly on the trunk of the tree. Probably the two most distinctively formed trees are the *Euphorbia ingens*, a form of spurge, and the curious dragon tree (*Dracaena draco*), which has a straight cylindrical trunk from which the branches radiate in layers. In earlier times the red resin from this tree was collected and used to treat wounds.

Nature exceeds itself in Funchal's magnificent parks: mimosa.

Above all it is the numerous fan and feather palms which lend the parks and gardens their typically exotic character. The elegance of their slender trunks and the gracefulness of their overhanging leaves epitomise tropical vegetation for many visitors. Particularly impressive is the Washington palm (*Washingtonia filifera*), originally from California, which reaches heights of up to 80 ft (25 metres) and has large fan-shaped leaves and small black fruits. Its slender trunk thickens out at the base like an elephant's foot. Equally striking is the decorative *Archontophoenix cunninghamia* with its scarlet berries.

The flowers of the *Brahea armata* hang in panicles as long as 15 ft (5 metres) from its foliage and the trunk of the tree is notable for its thick, swollen base. The *Syagrus romanzoffiana* is not so densely foliated and has fewer leaves.

A type of date palm (*Phoenix canariensis*) which originally comes from the Canary Islands is frequently planted in Madeira. It can be easily recognised by its stocky trunk and its numerous overhanging leaves. Many roads are lined with hedges of bushy hibiscus shrubs (*Hibiscus rosa-sinensis*; H. *syriacus*) and 6-ft-high poinsettias (*Euphorbia pulcherrima*). The ubiquitous Swiss cheese plant (*Monstera deliciosa*) with its long, hanging roots and club-shaped foliage entwines itself around tree trunks.

In many places the outer walls of the houses are completely overgrown with climbing plants and creepers. The dense curtains of wisterias (*Wisteria sinensis*), with their abundance of violet-blue flowers are particularly lovely, as are the star jasmines (*Trachelospermum jasminoides*) with their abundance of small star-like flowers.

Funchal's great variety of climbers often produces dramatic contrasts in colour. The flaming red patches of the golden shower (*Pyrostegia venusta*) or the orangy-yellow flowers of the *Thunbergia gregori* which blossom at the same time as the vermilion-coloured South African *Tecomaria capensis* clash with the purple, bell-shaped flowers of

In the park at Monte.

the lovely "morning glory" (*Ipomoea acuminata*).

The *Allamanda cathartica* is particularly striking for the large, yellow, funnel-shaped flowers it produces. Equally magnificent is the bougainvillea (*Bougainvillea spectabilis*) which provides a uniquely colourful spectacle in spring. Then the rubbish strewn riverbeds dissecting Funchal are transformed from eyesores to features of beauty by the bowers of purple flowers which contrive to cover them.

In the front gardens and on the patios and balconies of the town a rich variety of ornamental plants can be seen. As well as the lush oleander bushes (*Nerium oleander*), there are anthuriums (*Anthurium* hybrids), clivias (*Clivia miniata*), agaves (*Agave americana*), yuccas (*Yucca gloriosa*), cannas (*Canna indica*) and white-flowered lily (*Lilium longiflorum*).

The agapanthus (*Agapanthus praecox*), which originates from South Africa, produces clusters of steely-blue flowers at the end of long stalks. The bird-of-paradise flower or strelitzia (*Strelitzia reginae*) is aptly-named as it is reminiscent both in shape and colour of an exotic bird with its bluish-purple and red flowers. The various orchids captivate with their pleasant scent and the graceful flowers.

Giant ladyslippers (*Paphiopedilum*), orchids in a great variety of colours, and cattleyas, introduced from America, are commonly cultivated in flower tubs and can often be seen on the steps leading up to house entrances. Cymbidiums are also very popular as ornamental garden plants, especially as they are in bloom for many months of the year. These lovely pastel-coloured flowers – in a variety of shades – with their wax-like leaves are sold on the street flower stalls along with the popular birds-of-paradise. On request, visitors can have them carefully packed in boxes to take home with them (customs regulations permitting, of course).

***Quintas* and Parks:** Visitors who wish to get to know more of the different varieties of orchids and other ornamen-

THE QUINTAS DAS CRUZES

The word *quinta* actually means estate, but this dictionary definition is somewhat modest for the 18th- and 19th-century mansions characteristic of Madeira. These fine residences, built by well-to-do Englishmen or wealthy Madeirans who had earned large fortunes as tradesmen or ship-owners, were grand in the extreme.

It wasn't just the architecture of the buildings, though, which reflected the wealth and prestige of their owners. A great deal of time and money was lavished on the extensive grounds that surrounded the mansions. Teams of expert gardeners were employed to tend their exotic species of plants. To ensure the owners' absolute seclusion and privacy, the properties were surrounded by impressively solid walls of stone. Access could only be gained through their formidable wrought-iron gates.

At one time there were a few dozen such large estates and several hundred of the smaller "summer *quintas*". While many have nowadays fallen victim to property speculation - some were divided up and others demolished - some survived and now serve as public museums or as headquarters of the island's various institutions. They include the Quintas Angústias and Magnólia as well as the three finest examples of properties enlarged for functional use, namely the Quinta do Palheiro Ferreiro (Blandy's Garden), the Botanical Garden and the Quinta das Cruzes.

The last of these, Quinta das Cruzes ("*Quinta* of the Crosses") is situated above the Convent of Santa Clara in the Calçada do Pico. According to local tradition, Captain Zarco, one of the island's founding fathers (*see page 33*), took up residence here. Indeed, the oldest parts of the villa date from the 15th century; alterations and extensions were carried out at the end of the 17th and again - after an earthquake - in the middle of the 18th century. The *quinta* has functioned as Madeira's main museum since 1953. It is open every day except Mondays and holidays; on Sundays it is only open in the morning.

In the so-called Archaeological Park, located in the grounds of the estate, among the sub-tropical plants and trees, is a fascinating collection of stone monuments. The centre of the whole green rectangle is marked by the base of a post. Unimpressive though this object may appear these days, it is of considerable historical significance; it is all that remains of Funchal's pillory (removed from its site near the town hall in 1835), where for three centuries the town's transgressors were forced to suffer the ignominy of a public lashing or exposed to public scorn.

Just to the south at the central roundel is the memorial stone of the master builder of the Cathedral in Funchal, Pedro Eanes. A short distance away on a small patch of lawn are the most famous objects on display, namely two window frames overgrown with ivy. Dating from 1517, they are especially fine examples of the Manueline style of architecture (*see page 35*), prevalent at the time of the great explorers. The sea-faring motifs which characterised this style embellished even sacred buildings.

Also well worth seeing is the Orchid Garden, lying to the west of the area. It can be made out some distance away by its sheltering roof; most of the orchids grown here belong to the *cattleya* family which prefers shady conditions. These orchids are epiphytes, meaning they derive their nutrition from the air and the rain, so although they usually grow on other plants they are not parasites. If you are interested and fortunate enough, the attendants here might slip you some rhizomes (root tubers) which, with a bit of luck and customs officers not objecting, might survive the journey back home.

In the villa itself there is a comprehensive collection of *objets d'art* and furnishings from the 17th-19th centuries providing a glimpse of the everyday life and luxury of the landed Madeiran families. There is ivory work, porcelain and earthenware, silverware, sculptures and paintings, carpets and pieces of embroidery, nativity figurines, old sedan chairs and pieces of furniture. Particularly striking are the cupboards and cabinets made from the old haulage chests that were no longer needed after the decline of the sugar trade. They were richly carved and held together with wrought-iron bands.

tal plants should visit the **Quinta das Cruzes** or the **Quinta de Boa Vista**, a private garden where a large variety of orchids is lovingly cultivated by Mrs Betty Garton, one of the island's leading growers.

A stroll through the **Quinta do Palheiro Ferreiro** (Blandy's Garden) is recommended for those with an interest in the aesthetics and harmony of landscape gardening. This park is 5 miles (8 km) from the centre of Funchal and covers an area of 12 hectares (30 acres). It was laid out in 1790 by a French landscape gardener for the first Conde de Carvalhal.

The lower slopes of the garden are characterised by huge plane trees, Himalayan pines, araucarias, magnolias and cypresses, which were mostly planted when the gardens were laid out. Extensive hedges of oleander, hibiscus and camellia line the colourful borders, which are planted with azaleas, rhododendrons, sage, freesias, belladonna lilies, gladioli and clivias. In the garden's more sheltered positions you will notice South African proteas and spider flowers (*Tibouchina semidecandra*), which have a rich inflorescence of purple to deep violet flowers and originally came from Brazil.

At the southern end of the park you will find a rockery dominated by varieties of succulents. There is also a small chapel, the **Capela São João**, built in the baroque style, standing close to a water lily pond. This pond is surrounded by a type of agapanthus (*Agapanthus praecox*) with steely-blue flowers which originates from Australia.

The French character of these gardens can best be seen in the area of the formal **Jardim de Senhora** where there are hedges of boxtrees cut into the rigid geometrical forms typical of French landscape gardening. The white thorn apple (*Datura candida*), with its large funnel-shaped flowers, can also be found here. The smaller flowerbeds contain many ornamental species which are familiar to West Europeans, such as roses and dahlias.

The small wood at the southern edge

The bright red
Erythrina
Abyssinia.

of the gardens is dominated by laurels, eucalyptus trees and acacias. Only the white bracts of the common calla (*Zantedeschia aethiopica*) stand out in contrast to the mass of green.

Botanical Gardens: Visitors who, on walks through the city, are impressed by the splendid variety of exotic plants on display may want to get to know the names and origins of some of the species or be interested in the vegetables, herbs and other useful plants, or the less spectacular and rare flowers indigenous to the island. In this case a visit to the city's **Botanical Gardens** is strongly recommended. The **Jardim Botânico** was formerly an estate (Quinta de Bom Sucesso), the residence of the well-known Reid family, which was later made over to the state. Its creation fulfilled a wish cherished for a long time by many botanists: to lay out a garden which would be the home of plants from all over the world. It was eventually opened in 1960.

The present garden is systematically divided into sections arranged accord-ing to geographical origin or species. There are tropical trees and shrubs, a herbarium containing spices and medicinal plants, a range of creepers and climbing plants, a great variety of indigenous ferns and flora such as fennel, laurel trees and much, much more. In the garden's smaller greenhouses you will find exhibits of various types of orchids and cacti.

The garden is beautifully laid out in terraces with paths climbing from 660–1,150 ft (200–350 metres) above sea level. They wind between dragon and coral trees, hibiscus shrubs and bird-of-paradise flowers to the original stock of trees in the upper part of the garden. Here there are a number of *miradouros* offering magnificent views of the nearby Ribeira de João Gomes gorge and of Funchal itself.

For visitors who would like to know more about the flora of Madeira the guide *Flores de Madeira* by L.O. Franquinho and A. Da Costa, which contains about 600 plates, is one of the best authorities on the subject.

The royal strelitzia, Madeira's flower.

Tours on Madeira

4 km / 2.5 miles

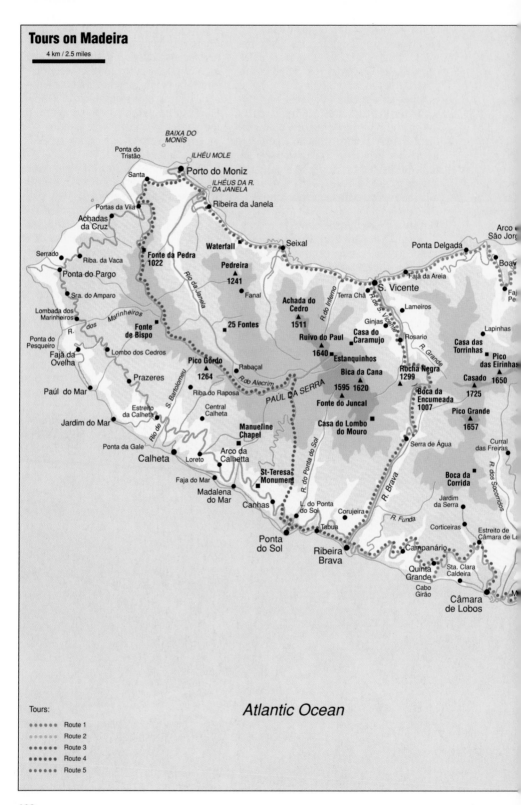

BAIXA DO MONÍS

Ponta do Tristão

ILHÉU MOLE

Porto do Moniz

Santa

ILHÉUS DA R. DA JANELA

Portas da Vila

Ribeira da Janela

Achadas da Cruz

Arco São Jorge

Serrado

Riba. da Vaca

Waterfall

Seixal

Ponta Delgada

Boav

Ponta do Pargo

Fonte da Pedra 1022

Pedreira 1241

Fajã da Areia

Sra. do Amparo

Fanal

S. Vicente

Faj Pe

Lombada dos Marinheiros

R. dos Marinheiros

Terra Chã

Lameiros

Ponta do Pesqueiro

Fonte de Bispo

25 Fontes

Achada do Cedro 1511

Ginjas

Rosario

R. Grande

Lapinhas

Casa das Torrinhas

Fajã da Ovelha

Lombo dos Cedros

Ruivo do Paul 1640

Casa do Caramujo

Pico das Eirinhas

Prazeres

Pico Gôrdo 1264

Rabaçal

R. do Alecrim

Estanquinhos

Rocha Negra 1299

Casado 1650

1725

Paúl do Mar

Bica da Cana 1595 1620

Boca da Encumeada 1007

Jardim do Mar

Riba.do Raposa

PAUL DA SERRA

Fonte do Juncal

Pico Grande 1657

Estreito da Calheta

Central Calheta

Curral das Freiras

Ponta da Gale

Manueline Chapel

Casa do Lombo do Mouro

Serra de Água

Calheta

Loreto

Arco da Calhetta

Faja do Mar

St-Teresa Monument

Boca da Corrida

Madalena do Mar

Jardim da Serra

Canhas

Corujeira

R. Funda

Corticeiras

Estreito de Câmara de L

Ponta do Sol

Tabua

L. do Ponta do Sol

Ribeira Brava

Campanário

Quinta Grande

Sta. Clara Caldeira

Cabo Girão

Câmara de Lobos

M

Atlantic Ocean

Tours:

••••• Route 1
••••• Route 2
••••• Route 3
••••• Route 4
••••• Route 5

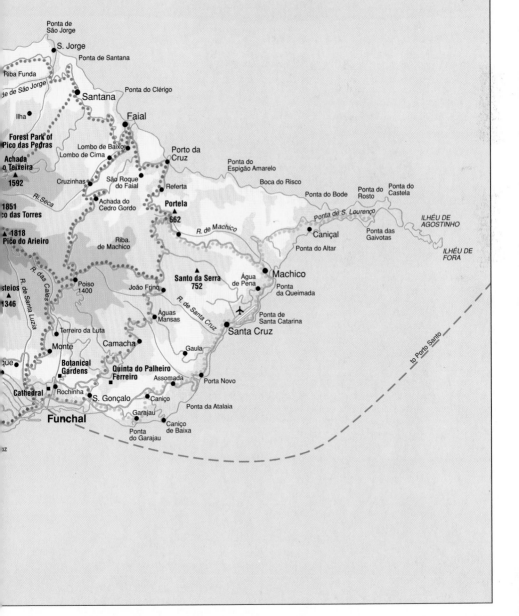

Atlantic Ocean

Ponta de
São Jorge

S. Jorge

Ponta de Santana

Riba Funda

de de São Jorge

Ponta do Clérigo

Santana

Ilha

Faial

Forest Park of
Pico das Pedras

Lombo de Baixo
Lombo de Cima

Porto da
Cruz

Achada
o Teixeira

Ponta do
Espigão Amarelo

Boca do Risco

▲
1592

Cruzinhas

São Roque
do Faial

Referta

Ponta do Bode

Ponta do
Rosto

Ponta do
Castela

Rl. Seca

1851
co das Torres

Achada do
Cedro Gordo

Portela
▲
662

Ponta de S. Lourenço

ILHÉU DE
AGOSTINHO

▲ 1818
Pico do Arieiro

R. de Machico

Caniçal

Ponta das
Gaivotas

ILHÉU DE
FORA

Riba.
de Machico

Ponta do Altar

R. das Calles

Santo da Serra
752

Água
de Pena

Machico

steios
▲
1346

Poiso
1400

João Frino

R. de Santa Cruz

Ponta
da Queimada

R. de Santa Luzia

Águas
Mansas

Ponta de
Santa Catarina

to Porto Santo

Terreiro da Luta

Santa Cruz

Monte

Camacha

Gaula

que

Botanical
Gardens

Quinta do Palheiro
Ferreiro

Assomada

Porta Novo

Cathedral

Rochinha

S. Gonçalo

Caniço

Ponta da Atalaia

Funchal

Garajau

Caniço
de Baixa

Ponta
do Garajau

uz

EXCURSIONS AND TOURS

Visitors who wish to go on excursions in Madeira should take two things into consideration, irrespective of which tour they make. Firstly, distances as they appear on the map can prove to be very deceptive. Places which seem to be a stone's throw away are often more difficult to reach than one might think. Madeira is an extremely rugged and hilly island and travellers should be prepared for long, winding roads full of twists and turns.

This is why making the longer tours by public bus is only advisable for the more adventurous tourist who is prepared for long waits and tiring journeys, although the departure times shown in the timetable (*Madeira by Bus*, available at TURISMO) are generally reliable. Like everywhere else in the world public transport is geared to the needs of the local population who do not think in terms of days out.

The other thing for tourists to consider is that Madeira has four microclimates. This means that light clothing alone, such as a T-shirt and shorts, will be suitable for hardly any of the trips, even on the loveliest summer days. It can get quite cool at higher altitudes and it is often the case that Funchal on the south coast is bathed in glorious sunshine, whereas the northern half of the island huddles under a thick carpet of rain clouds.

This, of course, is all part of the appeal of Madeira. On the longer excursions tourists travel through a rich variety of landscapes full of contrasts and an equally varied range of climates. It is possible to experience all four seasons in one day and in the higher altitudes to look down on seas of clouds. The Madeirans' fanciful claim that the five continents converge on their island is not quite as extravagant as it may sound.

Tour one – round trip of the island: Visitors to Madeira should not miss the chance to make a tour of the whole island. It is best to undertake such a trip at the beginning of the holiday, either by joining an organised tour (many travel agents offer tours with English-speaking guides), by taxi – arranging the price in advance and inviting the driver to lunch – or by rented car. The trip may be tiring but it will be far from disappointing and is worth it in order to get an overall impression of the island. It is best to plan for a whole day and to set off straight after breakfast.

Taking the road leading west out of **Funchal** you will arrive at the traditional fishing village of **Câmara de Lobos**. Remembering that this tour will take the whole day, it is probably best to save sampling the famous *poncha*, a mixture of *aguardente* (a spirit made of sugar cane, honey and lemon juice) for a separate evening visit to the village. As it is not far from Funchal, a walk through the village to get to know something of the life of the fishermen can also be enjoyed another day. For people who are just travelling through, the beach, with its fishing boats and clusters of men playing cards, is worth a short stop.

There is also the small Chapel of **Nossa Senhora da Conceição**. Built in 1420, but later restored, it has many baroque features. Incidentally the outlook from the village could be called the "Churchill perspective". Sir Winston Churchill did some paintings of the village and its views and this is commemorated by a plaque. The two viewpoints, **Pico do Toro** and **Jardim da Serra**, are worth visiting in clear weather if time allows.

The road continues via **Estreito de Câmara de Lobos** through the best vine-growing area of the island. Flowers and vegetables are grown under the vines, providing a living for many families in the area. Not to be missed is the view from **Cabo Girão**. At about 1,800 ft (580 metres) this is the second highest sea cliff in Europe (be warned: it requires a good head for heights).

The road then passes through **Quinta Grande** and **Campanário** before finally reaching **Ribeira Brava**, a good place to take a coffee break. As a concrete hotel at the beginning of the village indicates, a tourist centre is being

The typical woollen hats provide excellent protection against the wind.

developed here, catering for walking holidays in particular. The parish church contains a baptismal font which was a present from King Manuel 1.

A right turn leads into the road which effectively divides Madeira into a west and an east half. This road leads directly to the north coast through the deep, lush green valley of the Ribeira Brava (Wild River) with romantic views of the mountain slopes on either side. The mountains are dotted with small houses and settlements. The fact that their inhabitants have to undertake long marches lasting several hours to reach Ribeira Brava, the nearest important town, is held accountable for the high incidence of illiteracy in this district.

The main road twists and turns its way up a steep hill to the next village, **Serra de Água**, where the island's first hydroelectric power station was built. It then passes the **Pousada dos Vinháticos**, a popular place to stay overnight, especially for walkers. It has the atmosphere of a mountain chalet but with a touch of discreet luxury.

The climb continues to its highest point, the **Encumeada Pass** at 3,300 ft (1,004 metres). If the clouds are not too low, you can enjoy a superb view from here. It stretches as far as São Vicente on the north coast and down the Serra de Água valley to the south. You are also quite likely to learn what a meteorological divide is; if the weather conditions are right, you will see the clouds drifting by below you.

The road now descends past the **Chão dos Louros**, a laurel wood with a picnic site, where a walk in the wood is reputed to bring young lovers luck. It continues through the sleepy village of Rosário and soon arrives in **São Vicente**, a well-kept village with gleaming white walls which has won a preservation prize. To enter the village itself you turn left off the main road. Back on this road there is a small chapel, **São Roque**, which is built into the rock, just before a restaurant with a panorama of the sea. When there is a strong north wind, the view of the roaring Atlantic can be exhilarating. If you are not yet too hungry, you are

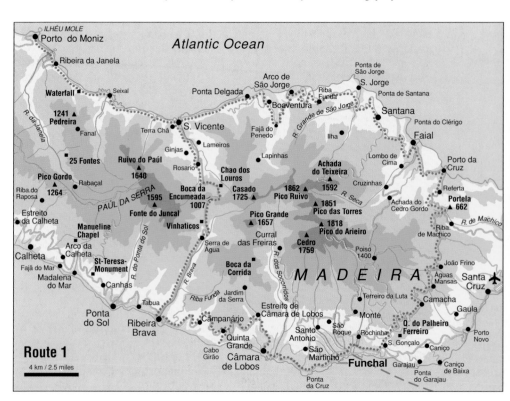

Route 1

4 km / 2.5 miles

recommended to wait until you reach Porto Moniz before having lunch. This is roughly the halfway point on this extensive tour.

A left turn now takes you on to the road which connects São Vicente and Porto Moniz, one of the most beautiful and exciting coastal roads in the world. It demands skilful driving and consideration of other drivers. At many points the road is only wide enough for one car, and drivers should be prepared to reverse frequently in order to let oncoming drivers past. It leads through numerous tunnels and past, sometimes through, waterfalls and small jungles of ferns on the side of the cliff. It is worth stopping at one of the viewpoints along the way to admire the silhouette of the north coast of Madeira.

Because of the harsh climate in the north of the island, the farmers have to protect their gardens from the wind and salt with hedges of heather, giving the landscape a totally different character. In **Porto Moniz** there are a number of restaurants such as the Cachalote and A

Orca, which are designed for tourists, but also a few smaller, more convivial eating places. One of the cheaper ones is the Porto Norte, where the youth of the village like to congregate. After lunch, a short constitutional through the volcanic rocks with their natural, crystal-clear sea-water swimming pools is extremely refreshing.

The road back to São Vicente again demands drivers' full concentration, but it also offers new perspectives of the scenery. Driving past Sao Vicente, the tour continues in the direction of Ponta Delgada and Boaventura. Here the scenery is dominated by orchards and willow tree plantations in fertile valleys. **Boaventura** is the source of most of the raw material for the island's wickerwork. In **São Jorge** there is a baroque church with gilded carvings.

The next place along the way is **Santana**, which is famous for its characteristic architecture. The small cottages (*palheiros*), with their pointed gables and thatched roofs reaching nearly to the ground, are perfect for the

Climax of the round-the-island tour: Porto Moniz.

climate here, staying cool in summer and keeping in the warmth in winter. These cottages are now preserved and carefully maintained for tourists, but a short walk through the village will enable you to see them in their original condition. Santana is surrounded by one of the most beautiful and unspoilt landscapes in Madeira.

From the viewpoint at **Faial** you can see the eastern tip of Madeira, the **Ponta de São Lourenço** peninsula, and, weather permitting, the neighbouring island of Porto Santo. Just past Faial there are two possibilities: to cut the tour short by returning directly to Funchal via **Ribeiro Frio** and **Poiso**, or, if you still have enough time, continuing the round trip to gain an impression of the whole island.

Those undertaking the round trip should continue through **Porto da Cruz** to **Portela** (pay attention to the signposts). Both of these villages are dominated by the **Penha d'Águia**, an enormous, 2,000-ft (600-metre) high, flat-topped rock. In both places you can take a break for refreshments before turning right towards **Santo da Serra**. This is where the wealthiest residents of the island, particularly the rich British, have built their weekend villas. There is also a golf course, which has been extended in recent years.

The road now twists and turns down to Camacha through an area where fruit and vegetables are grown. The small farmhouses scattered along the route give a typical impression of the simple life of the rural population in Madeira. The road just before **Camacha** (*see tour of the east of the island*) is lined with broom shrubs, which were used to make baskets in earlier times. Although Camacha is the centre of the wicker industry, you will notice that it is dominated by apple trees.

There will probably not be sufficient time to visit the display of wickerwork at the wicker warehouse, but the restaurant, O Relógio, attached to the warehouse offers the chance to eat an evening meal here. Otherwise the main road soon takes you back into Funchal, probably arriving at dusk. An increase in the number of houses, many of a newer design than those found in the rural areas and not always in the best of taste, heralds the outskirts of the city.

This trip can also be made anti-clockwise, an option which has the advantage that most other tourists will be travelling in the other direction. What's more, it is more convenient for sampling the *poncha* at Câmara de Lobos when you return.

Tour two – the east of the island: This tour, in the form of a loop around the eastern side of the island, is relatively short. However, it offers so many highlights that it is worth devoting a whole day to it.

The first attraction is the garden at the **Quinta do Palheiro Ferreiro** (Blandy's Garden), which is about 5 miles (9 km) east of Funchal in the direction of Camacha (the small signpost is easy to miss, so if in doubt, ask). The gardens belong to the private residence of the Blandy family and are only open from 9.30 a.m. to 12.30 p.m. Visitors should announce their visit beforehand at Blandy's Travel Agency. Tickets can be bought at the porter's lodge at the entrance. Take your time for a walk around this unique garden; it contains elements of both French and English landscape gardening, and the whole range of Madeiran flora has been assembled here.

The tour continues to **Camacha**, where there is a large display of Madeiran wickerwork at the wicker warehouse attached to the Café Relógio. Visitors can buy or just admire. Camacha is also famous for its performances of folklore which take place in the evening and are worth an extra visit, especially at the weekend.

The country road to **Santo da Serra** is lined with fruit trees and brooms. Santo da Serra is a good place to make a stop. In spite of a micro-climate which is often responsible for bad weather, the air is said to be particularly healthy, and it is still fashionable to own a house here. It is particularly popular at the weekend when people pour into the park to visit its small zoo; the kangaroos are the main attraction. Somewhat of an anomaly in this setting is the holiday camp with houses built in the style of the thatched cottages found at Santana. They were built by INATEL, the Portuguese welfare association for workers. On leaving the village it is important to pay attention to the signposts as the road to Portela is difficult to find.

Portela is worth a short stop for the impressive views it offers (*see* tour one). Again it is important to watch out for the signposts when you take the road down to Machico on the south coast (if you wish to leave out Portela, there is a right turning in Santo da Serra into an old road leading to Machico). The tour continues through Machico to **Caniçal** in order to reach the easternmost point of the island.

The tunnel along this road was not completed until the late 1950s – a fact which explains why the population at the other end of the tunnel is so different from that in the rest of the island. Unfortunately, this has become the *zona franca*, the tax-free zone, where foreign businessmen have put up ugly industrial buildings with fences cutting off the former footpaths.

Not only are the people different here; the climate also undergoes a change. The area around Caniçal and as far as Ponta da São Lourenço has a similar climate to that on the island of Porto Santo. As a result, it is noticeable that the nature of the vegetation is different here, too. Another thing which stands out is the beach at Prainha – it is the only naturally sandy beach to be found on the main island.

It is possible to drive a little further along the peninsula to the point where a futuristic house made of glass and steel stands looking like a setting for a film. Abandoned after a fire and left to rust, it is a sad sight on a rock overlooking the Atlantic rollers. The end of the peninsula can be reached on foot using paths made by goats and cattle. The walk takes about 1½ hours.

On the car park at the end of the road there are sometimes dealers selling the teeth and bones of whales, although there is a strict ban on whaling nowa-

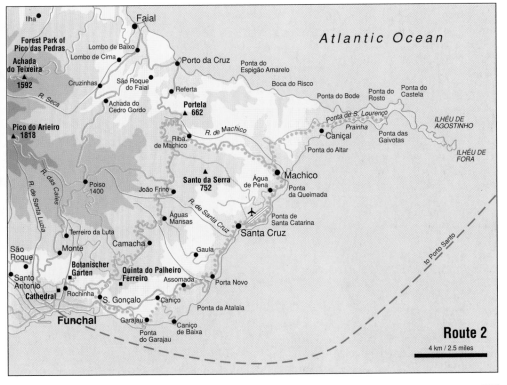

days. Caniçal was once the whaling centre of Madeira, and there is a whaling museum, the **Museu da Baleia**, in the old whaling factory in the village square. In Caniçal you can eat a simple but excellent lunch at a reasonable price. All Madeira's fish specialities are on offer in the many bars and restaurants. One particular local dish, *castanhetas* (small deep-fried fish), at the Amarelo is recommended.

After-lunch coffee is perhaps best taken in **Machico**, where you will need some time to look around this historical fishing port. This is where the discoverers of the island landed and where the tragic love story of Anne d'Arfet and Robert Machin (who, according to legend, landed on Madeira even before Zarco and his men, came to an end – *see page 29)*.

The port's Manueline **Church of Nossa Senhora da Conceição** can be entered through the lovely twin portal, a present from King Manuel I. The small Chapel of Miracles (**Capela dos Milagres**), which is situated at the beach,

is unfortunately now closed to visitors.

Machico has developed into something of a tourist centre, a fact to which the tall building of the Hotel Dom Pedro bears witness.

The route continues along the southern coastal road in the direction of Santa Cruz, past the **Matur Holiday Complex**, which has much the same atmosphere – artificial – as similar leisure complexes on the Canary Islands and around the Mediterranean.

Before driving into Santa Cruz, it is worth turning off at the signpost to have a quick look at the **Beach Club Albatroz**. You may decide to come back to spend a day at this former private *quinta* (**Quinta Dr Américo Durão**) situated directly below the airport (aircraft noise does not disturb). The entrance fee is 500 escudos but this includes lunch at the Albatroz restaurant. The club has direct access to the sea and a cactus garden; it's an ideal place to spend a day bathing and relaxing.

The drive back to Funchal is not very attractive, nor is it very pleasant be-

Rugged and wild: the steep coast at the eastern end of the island.

cause of the heavy traffic. However, a small detour can be made down to Caniço and Garajau (named after the large number of *garajaus*, terns, which nest here). Caniço has an impressive church, fountains and even an aviary in the village square and a number of very good restaurants, popular with the locals and tourists. There is also a modern development with neat front gardens, mainly owned by Germans, a bar which sells German beer, and a lovely seawater swimming pool. A modern development faces a statue of Christ that is similar to but smaller than the statues in Lisbon and Rio de Janeiro.

After leaving Caniço, take care to pay attention to the signposts so as not to miss the coastal road back to Funchal (the first turning after the road leading to Garajau). Again there are fine views of Funchal along this road, and after São Gonçalo it is lined with a series of splendid town villas.

Tour three – up above the clouds: This is a rather unusual mountain tour and cannot be undertaken by bus; a rented car or a taxi are the only options. A long morning or afternoon should allow sufficient time if you do not linger too long in any one place.

The first stage of the tour is **Monte**, the tourist Mecca of days gone by, which can be seen from Funchal. Leaving the haze of Funchal behind, you will see the first of the famous *quinta*s, where the upper classes, particularly British nationals afflicted with tuberculosis, liked to reside at the turn of the century. The hope was that they would benefit from the purer air the elevated site enjoyed. This proved to be a misapprehension, however, as the air up here is very humid.

The station of the short-lived rack-and-pinion railway still exists and is now a car park under the shade of plane trees. A short walk to the baroque Church of **Nossa Senhora do Monte** is not tiring. Emperor Charles I, the last emperor of Austria, was buried here in 1922 (the *quinta* where he lived with his wife, Zita, and family is not open to the public and is slowly becoming dilapi-

The countryside near Machico is much more friendly.

dated, the subject of an inheritance dispute). On 15 August, the day of the patron saint of the island, Nossa Senhora do Monte, the faithful of Madeira climb the 74 steps up to the church on their knees in order to fulfil their vows (*promessa*). At the foot of the steps the Monte toboggans wait to take the better-off tourists back to Funchal. You can return to your transport through the lush green park.

From here the road winds its way up to **Poiso**. The route is lined with acacias and eucalyptus trees, which accounts for the pleasant smell, and higher up it leads into a pine forest. At Poiso there is a major road junction where you turn left in the direction of Pico do Arieiro. At this point you have already reached an altitude of 4,200 ft (1,400 metres). Leaving the pine forest, the road goes through high moorland where only goats and sheep can find enough to eat. In good weather this route is one of the most impressive in Madeira and never fails to surprise.

At 5,900 ft (1,800 metres), **Pico do Arieiro** is the highest point in Madeira which can be reached by car. On a clear day there are magnificent views to all sides of the mountain. Sometimes the layer of clouds is lower than the summit of the mountain and it is possible to get a suntan up here while it is raining or drizzling in Monte and Funchal. Those who are lucky enough to stay overnight at the **Pousada do Pico Arieiro**, a luxurious guesthouse, will be able to go out on to the balcony in the morning and look down on a sea of cotton-wool clouds far below them.

For those who want to get the best out of the place, there is a strenuous but worthwhile walk along a good footpath to **Pico Ruivo**, at 6,110 ft (1,862 metres) the highest peak in Madeira. The walk takes between two and three hours, depending on your level of fitness.

The tour leads back to the road junction at Poiso, going straight on in the direction of Santo da Serra. The area between Poiso and Santo da Serra is an uninhabited, wooded hunting ground, as yet undeveloped, and is ideal country

Preceding pages: the mountain world of the interior. Below, the pilgrimage church of Nossa Senhora do Monte.

for adventurous walkers. After 5 miles (8 km) there is a junction where you turn left. The route to the north in the form of a loop has been described in tours one and two (Santo da Serra, Portela, Porto da Cruz). The second leg, just past Porto da Cruz, leads to the south via **Lombo de Baixo** and **Lombo de Cima**, where the scenery is even more rewarding than hitherto.

Along the way the lush-green, terraced valleys give an impression of the modest and arduous life of farmers in the north of the island. Scattered along the sides of the mountains are *palheiros*, originally thatched cottages but nowadays often with a roof of corrugated iron, which are now used as cowsheds. You may encounter a farmer, so encumbered that he looks more like a moving haystack, taking a huge bundle of freshly-cut grass to his much-prized cow in its shed.

The road leads through woodlands to **Ribeiro Frio**, a protected area with trout hatcheries. This is a good place to stop, breathe in the fresh air and enjoy the

Route 3
2 km / 1.25 miles

sound of the stream. If time and weather allow, there is a pleasant 45-minute *levada* walk to the **Balcãoes**, a viewpoint with a glorious panorama across deep ravines. This walk is particularly recommended for those who want to work up an appetite for the district's fresh trout (*truta*), which can be sampled at Victor's Bar, a cosy restaurant in a log cabin, run by a family of German watchmakers. Unfortunately this area is being developed for tourism and is losing a lot of its unspoilt character.

An alternative to Victor's Bar is the restaurant at Poiso which is open all day and is warmed by a big open fire. Here you can try the typical *açorda* (bread soup with egg and plenty of garlic) or the *espetada* (skewered meat cooked over an open fire). Up here in the cool, invigorating mountains one quickly forgets that Madeira is invariably described in travel brochures as belonging to the sub-tropical zone.

The last stage of the trip takes you back to Funchal via Monte. If by the end of the afternoon the southern side of Madeira is clouded over, careful driving is required and headlights should be switched on.

Tour four – the grand two-day tour: In combination with tour three or tour five this makes a good alternative to the round trip, but can only be recommended in fine weather. It lasts two full days and includes staying overnight at Porto Moniz. It is advisable to book your accommodation in advance, especially if you have a particular guesthouse or hotel in mind.

As far as Ribeira Brava the route is the same as for tour one. At this point a good coastal road continues straight on to Ponta do Sol. For those who wish to follow the tracks of Christopher Columbus, there is a turn-off at Tábua into a narrow road which leads to **Lombada da Ponta**. Here you can visit the former sugar-cane *quinta* belonging to João Esmeraldo as well as the **Capela do Espirito Santo**. Columbus is known to have stayed with the Esmeraldos when he was in Madeira, although it is not known whether he stayed here or in their house in Funchal.

The coastal road continues through tunnels and waterfalls to **Ponta do Sol**. This fishing village, which was once a thriving sugar-cane centre, is in need of extensive renovation and leaves a rather sad impression of unjust neglect on visitors. The village is named after the Sun Bridge, the remains of which can still be seen at the old quay.

The ancestors of the famous 20th-century American writer, John dos Passos, lived here. When he made a pilgrimage to his ancestral home in the 1950s, he described the village as both a paradise and a prison. The house where he stayed has a modest plaque to commemorate his visit.

The road to Porto Moniz is signposted but the turning up to the moorland area of **Paúl da Serra** is difficult to find. If you find the monument to Santa Teresa, the signpost to Paúl da Serra is at the next road to the right. Along this road you can see some of the few thatched sheds left on the island. The road is not in the best of conditions and is lined with a wild tangle of brooms, ferns,

blackberry bushes and, higher up, eucalyptus trees. At about 4,600 ft (1,600 metres) the tree line is reached and from now on moorland dominates the landscape. In places an almost lunar atmosphere prevails.

A sign indicates that you have reached the only plateau on Madeira, Paúl da Serra, which stretches 10½ by 3¾ miles (17 by 6 km). At one time there were ambitious plans to build an airport up here, but these were eventually dropped because of the frequent mists which descend on the plateau and limit visibility to only a few yards. On the right of the road you'll find the **Bica da Cana**, a rest house belonging to the government where picnic tables and benches have been provided.

The road soon comes to the signpost for Rabaçal. It is an adventurous drive down to **Rabaçal,** through a fairy-tale valley covered with moss and lichen offering plenty of idyllic places to picnic – there are even facilities to barbecue. The short walk to the **Risco Waterfall** is signposted. To get to the view-

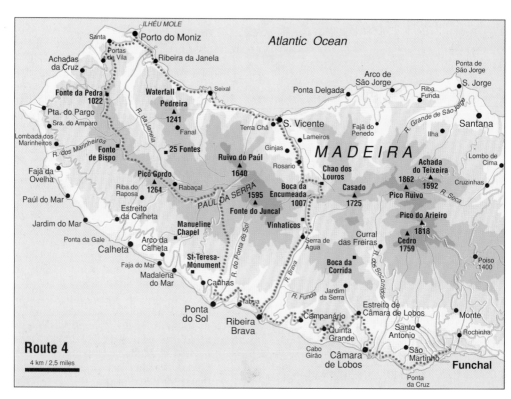

point you have to walk under and through the waterfall, an appealing but dangerous undertaking. There is another walk to the **Vinte-e-cinco fontes** – the 25 springs – which takes longer, about 2 hours there and back.

Back on the main road on the plateau, continue in the direction of Porto Moniz. There are many reasons to stop along the way – to appreciate superb views to the north and the south coast, observe the ever-changing cloud formations and, occasionally, simply because cattle are blocking the way.

The road leads through Santa to **Porto Moniz**, providing a lovely bird's-eye view of the village and the terraced valleys so typical in the north of the island. Staying overnight in Porto Moniz offers the chance to take a closer look at the village. Sadly, the old houses around the small harbour, where whalers used to live, are being pulled down one by one and the centre of the village around the church has plenty of atmosphere but is of no great interest. It is the natural swimming pools cut into the volcanic rock that comprise the main attraction. The entrance fee is low and a visit is safe, healthy and highly recommended. If there is no time for a swim in the evening, an invigorating dip in the morning before leaving Porto Moniz is a good alternative.

Porto Moniz has the only official camp site on the island, and next to it, one of the nicest guesthouses – **Residencial Calhau**. Its rooms – clean and pleasant with balconies directly overlooking the sea – are furbished in the traditional patchwork carpets typical of the area. It is an ideal spot to relax. The roar of the ocean is likely to be the only noise to accompany your dreams. (Room bookings are necessary as the guesthouse has fixed contracts with several travel companies and it can be difficult to secure a room.)

The rest of the route, via São Vicente, Encumeada, Serra de Água, Ribeira Brava, and back to Funchal, is described in reverse in tour one. Incidentally, there is also a public bus which runs between Porto Moniz and Funchal, but using it

A pousada (state-owned hotel) built in traditional style.

means sacrificing the tour of the Paúl da Serra plateau.

Tour five – day trip to Santana: This is an excursion which can be made by public bus and you can plan the day according to your own wishes. However, it requires an early start in the morning. The bus leaves the bus station at the end of Avenida das Comunidades Madeirenses at 7 a.m., winding its way through Monte, Poiso, Cruzinhas and Faial before finally reaching Santana at 9.15 a.m. The adventurous and exciting journey across the island makes the effort of getting up early worthwhile – so long as you are not alarmed by the local women, who make a sign of the cross at every dangerous bend along the way.

In **Santana** itself there is an excellent baker's shop with a café attached to it. Here you can have breakfast and buy provisions for a picnic lunch later in the day. The bus back to Funchal leaves at 5.30 p.m.

Apart from the attractions of Santana itself (*see tour one*), there are two other worthwhile places to head for in the area. The first is the **Queimadas**, which can easily be reached on foot by practised walkers (4½ miles going firstly in the direction of São Jorge and turning left at the supermarket up a narrow, steep road). The Queimadas are gardens complete with government-owned resthouses in the Santana, thatched-cottage style. There are small artificial lakes, a series of streams criss-crossed by bridges and home to colonies of ducks and swans – all contributing to an ideal spot for a romantic stroll.

There are also picnic and barbecue facilities; but no restaurant. The park has a viewpoint from which Porto Santo can be seen in the distance if the weather is good. (Several walking tours also start from the Queimadas, see Walking Tours, page 252.) By the time you return to Santana you may begin to feel the effects of the strenuous walk in your legs. If you should lose your way, the local people are very friendly and always ready to help.

The other goal which can be easily reached from Santana is **Pico Ruivo**. You can either walk to Pico das Pedras (take the turning at the petrol station at the beginning of the village) or go by taxi (4½ miles/7 km). From Pico das Pedras there is a very easy walk up to the 6,110-ft (1,862-metre) high Pico Ruivo, which hardly takes more than 45 minutes. For those who are not used to walking long distances this is a good chance to ascend what is considered to be the highest mountain in Madeira. This walk costs little effort and is rewarded with some of the most breathtaking views on the island.

At the summit there is a mountain chalet where you can buy drinks but you must provide your own picnic. The beautiful scenery and the wonderful silence at the top of the mountain make it easy to forget that you must be back in Santana by 5.30 p.m. to catch the last bus back to Funchal, a journey which takes a good two hours.

The other tours that can be made around Santana take much longer than the two described here and should only be undertaken if you hire a car or stay overnight in Santana.

Right, a traditional Santana house.

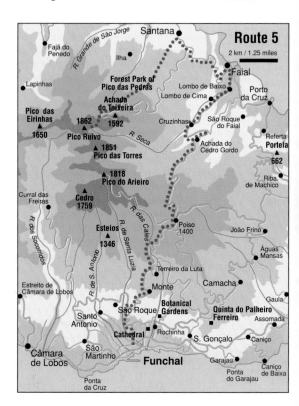

248

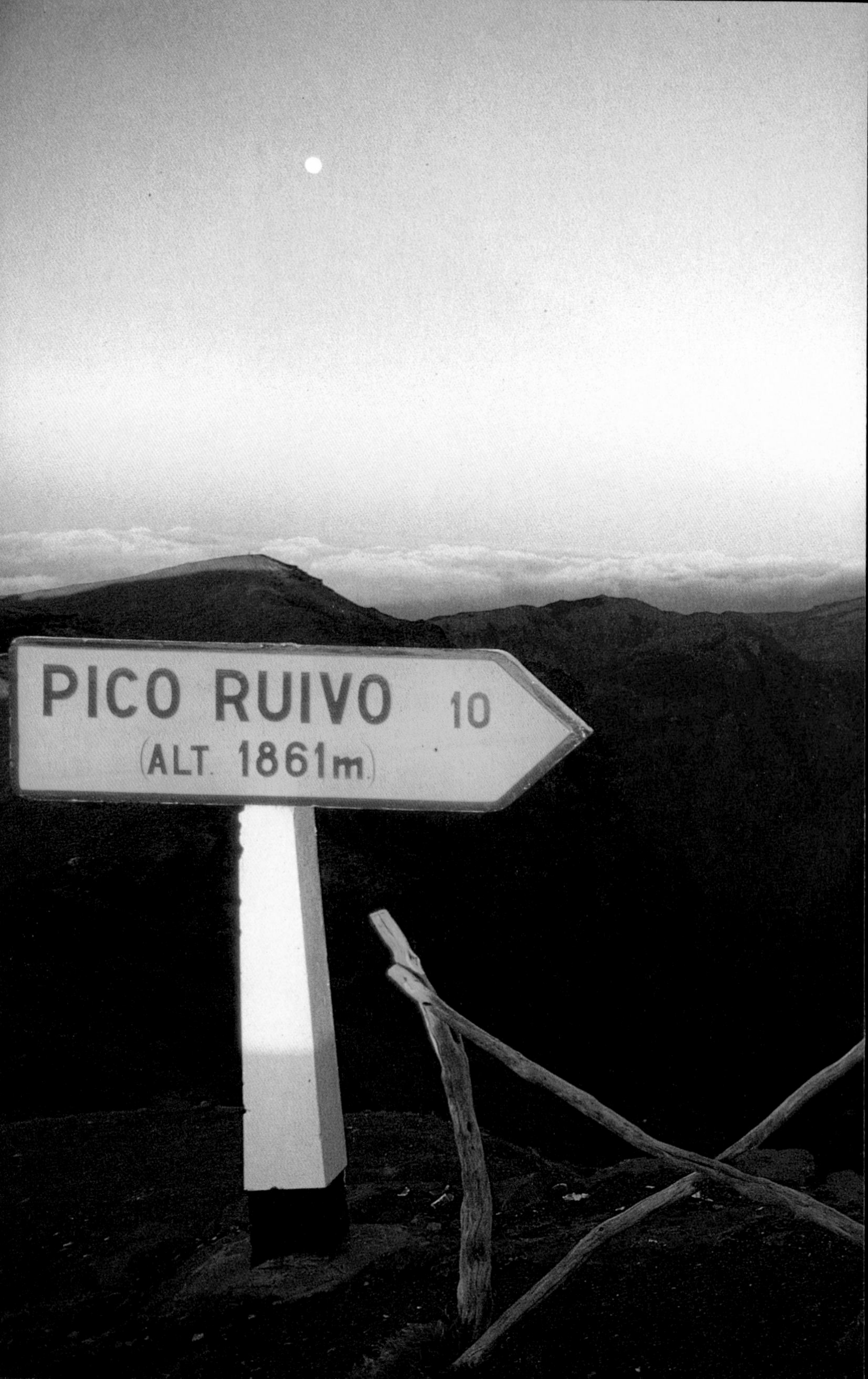
PICO RUIVO 10
(ALT. 1861m)

ISLAND WALKING TOURS

Hardly any other island in the world makes such ideal walking territory as Madeira, with its vast network of footpaths and spectacular scenery. Consequently many reputable ramblers' associations have established bases here and organise a wide variety of tours, both with and without the help of guides. These associations have also played an important part in developing and maintaining the paths.

Most of the walks follow *levadas*, the age-old drainage channels used to carry drinking water and supply the fields and vineyards of Madeira. On these footpaths the walker comes in close contact with the rich and varied nature of the island. For nature lovers who like to be able to recognise and name the great variety of flowers, trees and plants which grow so lushly in this wild and romantic landscape, a guidebook to the flora of Madeira is an indispensable item of equipment. A variety of publications can be bought at bookshops in Funchal or from the tourist information office, Turismo.

As the weather on Madeira is typical island weather, i.e. very unpredictable, some preparation must be made for these tours. All the walks suggested here will take you high up above sea level, and, even in summer, a piece of warm clothing such as a sweater or a cardigan should be taken along. Walkers are often surprised by sudden downfalls of rain, even if the sky was blue and the sun was shining 10 minutes before. This means that a thin plastic mac or cagoule should also be carried.

It is advisable to enquire about weather conditions before setting off. Hotel staff should be able to help you or you can ask at Turismo. Even those who do not speak Portuguese should be able to see what the weather will be like from the chart on the television weather forecast. Even so, don't rely upon it; they don't always prove to be accurate.

A compass is another useful piece of equipment. Although you will be walking on a civilised and populated island, it is easy to lose a sense of direction once you are in the eucalyptus forests. Equally useful is a torch; *levadas* occasionally disappear into tunnels and you won't want to emerge soaked.

It is also important to remember that it gets dark very quickly on Madeira. As in all tropical and sub-tropical regions dusk only lasts about half an hour. Tours should be organised so that you are back at your starting-point before nightfall (note: some of the tours mentioned here rely on transport to complete the homeward leg in the time that has been allocated; check if this is the case before setting out). If you should miscalculate, local people are usually more than willing to help and will probably escort you to the nearest road.

It is recommended that you take food supplies and drinking water or tea on all tours which last more than four hours, as not all these walks have restaurants along the way. It is hardly necessary to mention that sturdy walking shoes with a decent grip should be worn. You need to

Preceding pages: still some way to go to the summit. **Below,** equipment and clothing should account for sudden changes in the weather.

252

be sure-footed, especially in the damp and slippery *levada* tunnels.

Properly equipped and prepared you can set off to enjoy a day in Madeira's glorious scenery.

To Ponta de São Lourenço: The first walking tour mentioned here is not a *levada* walk, but it is excellent for the variety of scenery it offers. It leads to the easternmost point of the island. A warm cardigan or sweater and a plastic mac or cagoule are recommended as there is nowhere to shelter from the rain or wind along the way. As the walk offers opportunities to bathe, you might want to take a swimming costume.

You can take a bus from Machico to the former whaling village of Caniçal. At just over 2,000 ft (630 metres) **Pico Castanho**, a peak just north of Caniçal, is the highest mountain in the district of Machico. This area gained historical significance in 1931, when the slopes of Pico Castanho were the scene of a rebellion against the grain monopoly imposed by the Portuguese government in the so-called "Hunger Law".

Caniçal, in the extreme east of the island, is a typical Madeiran fishing village where trawlers set out for deep-sea fishing, sailing as far as the North African coast in pursuit of their catch. Its name derives from the Portuguese for sedge – *caniços* – which grows so abundantly in this area. This tour goes from Caniçal in an easterly direction to reach Ponta de São Lourenço where the island comes to an end.

The route leads from Caniçal first to Baia d'Abra and then to Cais do Sardinha, all in all a distance of 10½ miles (17 km). Although this is a sandy and dry area, the beauty of the landscape is impressive. The plant life dries out and withers in summer, but in spring and autumn everything is bathed in a rich and splendid green. However, at these times of the year there is often heavy rain.

If you do not want to walk the first 3 miles (5 km) from Caniçal to Baia d'Abra, this part of the tour can be made by taxi. The tarmac road ends at Baia d'Abra, turning into a well-trodden footpath, which should be kept to at all times. Here you will see a sight that is common in most of Europe but rare in Madeira – herds of grazing cattle. In other parts of the island they are generally kept in cramped cowsheds (*palheiros*) and see the light of day only once a week when they are briefly exercised at the end of a rope.

After a short time you will see a rock hollowed out to form an arch over the sea. The footpath now follows the steep shoreline of the north coast past huge boulders of rough and cracked lava rising up like the humps of sea monsters out of the turquoise waters. Unfortunately the footpath is not well signposted but it is well-trodden and easy to follow running directly to the west.

After a while you will see a hill called **Casa do Sardinha**. This is a nature reserve, a biotope for flora and fauna containing a particularly rich variety of birds. There is also a relatively safe footpath down to **Cais do Sardinha**, a quay which, together with the house next to it, was built in 1905. It belongs to a family from Funchal. You might like to take the opportunity to swim in the sea here.

Nearby there is a natural spring with crystal-clear water to quench the thirst on a hot day. To find it, look for a strip of rich green amongst the otherwise pale and dried-out grass; this marks the banks of the stream flowing from the spring. When the tide is out you can walk over to **Prai Nova** (New Beach) from the wooden quay. This beach is situated on the **Ilhéu dos Desembarcadores**. To avoid getting wet feet, you should make sure that you return before the tide comes in.

The tour continues in an easterly direction following a ridge of low hills from which there is a view of the sea on both sides. In the distance looms the island of São Lourenço, easy to recognise because of its lighthouse, which was erected in 1870 and marks the easternmost point of Madeira.

The island, separated from the land by a 180-yard (165-metre) wide channel, can only be reached by boat. There is a small landing stage on its eastern side which is used by the maintenance

staff of the fully automatic lighthouse. Because the island also has a transmitting installation, unauthorised people are not allowed to make use of it.

Early risers who reach this point by 8.30 a.m. may be lucky enough to see the ferry to Porto Santo, *Interpedencia*, which in all but the roughest of weathers passes through the channel between the promontory and Ponta de São Lourenço. The new larger ferry, *Patria*, prefers not to risk this manoeuvre and takes a different route.

To return, take the same path back to the starting point.

On the way, you may find it interesting to make a slight detour to Ponta das Gaivotas to search for the fossils and rock crystals which are contained in the chalk deposits here.

This is one of the few places on Madeira where fossils can be found. The volcanic lava which flowed across the whole island millions of years ago destroyed everything which might have lived here at that time and covered up any evidence of previous life. There have been many hypotheses about these chalk deposits but as yet there has been no satisfactory scientific theory to account for their presence here. The most probable explanation is that they are coral banks which came to the surface a few hundred thousand years ago as a result of changes in the geological stratification.

A satisfactory way to finish the day is to enjoy an evening meal at the Palmeira Restaurant in the little fishing village of Caniçal. Here you can eat excellently cooked *espada* (scabbard), an ugly but very tasty fish, as well as many other types of seafood, all freshly caught from the sea.

Levada Walks – Levada dos Tornos: Visitors who are in Madeira for the first time are sure to hear about the famous *levada* walks sooner or later. In fact many people, especially keen walkers and nature lovers, come to the island specifically for this purpose. The total length of the *levadas* in Madeira can only be estimated, but it is certainly some hundreds of miles. All the main *levadas* have their origins high up in the mountains, coursing down to the fertile valleys in the south of the island, where they are used to irrigate the banana plantations, vineyards and vegetable crops. All of them pass through stunning scenery.

There is no better way to get to know Madeira – its landscape, its nature and its people – than following their routes. For maintenance purposes every *levada* has a narrow path running alongside it, so that, theoretically at least, they can be used to walk the whole length of Madeira from north to south, from the source streams high in the mountains to the cultivated gardens of the *quintas* and the parks on the coast.

Contrary to what some people think, none of the *levada* walks are particularly strenuous because this irrigation system does not involve steep gradients. However, there are other considerations to bear in mind. In places where the *levadas* flow along the tops of very steep slopes overlooking deep valleys walking can become dangerous on the damp and slippery footpaths. Here the walker needs a sure foot and a good head for heights.

One particular advantage of the walk recommended here is that it can be interrupted at any point to return to Funchal. This is because the *levada* follows one of two main roads, the EN 102 or the EN 201, along its whole length. Known as the Levada dos Tornos, it is one of the most important *levadas* in Madeira and was officially opened in 1966. Its water supplies the electric power station at **Fajã da Nogueira** before irrigating the gardens of Funchal and Santa Cruz.

To begin the walk you must take the bus to **Gaula**, which can be easily recognised by its large white church on the main road. Getting off the bus at a stop called Lombo Grande, you will find yourself at a place where a *levada* crosses the main road. Turn left here and follow the *levada* in an upstream direction. At the right time of the year (in late spring), you will witness lovely splashes of yellow broom amongst the pine trees along the way.

A concrete water trough soon appears

Cows are usually confined to their own house, the *palheiro*.

beside the path – a sign that you are following the right route. From here the clay-coloured footpath leads through a characteristic landscape. After a short time the path takes on the character of a narrow village road with women standing at the side doing their washing in stone troughs. If you should wish to photograph these women, it is advisable to ask them first. Madeirans are very friendly people and you are almost certain to get a positive answer, but they like to be asked.

The path continues past camellia and lemon trees. At the right time of the year the oranges will be ripe. The gardens are full of rose bushes and fruit trees and this fertile area is a feast for the eyes. Even when it is high summer in Funchal, the temperatures up here are pleasantly cool and ideal for walking. This is because the route of this *levada* walk keeps to a constant altitude of about 2,000 ft (600 metres).

Eventually you will reach a road paved with cobblestones, where the *levada* flows through a tunnel. Ideally, you should have a torch for this part of the walk, but if for some reason your torch is not working or you have forgotten to bring it, there is a method which will guide you through the dark tunnel without artificial light.

It is a simple trick used by shepherds in Madeira for centuries. It entails cutting a twig to a length of about 20 inches (50 cm) to make a stick. At the beginning of the tunnel you hold one end of the stick against the tunnel wall, adjusting the length so that there is sufficient distance between you and the water. Keeping the end of the stick touching the wall you can now walk through the tunnel without any fear of stepping into the water.

Emerging from the tunnel you can see **Camacha**, the centre of the wicker industry, above you. The footpath follows the *levada* in the direction of the valley. After some time there is a bridge to cross. Looking back from this point you will see a glorious waterfall which plunges down into the valley from about 230 ft (70 metres).

A good excuse for a break.

256

From here on great care needs to be taken as the footpath becomes damp and slippery. Water drops on to the path from a rock face covered in moss, ferns and other plants which enjoy moist conditions. The path then takes you through yet another tunnel. Though only about 160 ft (50 metres) long, this tunnel has the disadvantage of being very low so that you have to double up to pass through it.

Emerging into the daylight you will see a lovely old house with a palm tree in the garden. Here the *levada* disappears into a beautiful rockery full of flowers. This is one of the main attractions along the course of the Levada dos Tornos.

The walk continues along the *levada* crossing an asphalt road and then a sandy track. Here the *levada* leads into private property which cannot be entered. This is a good moment to take a well-earned break and enjoy the magnificent view of the Desertas, a group of offshore islands.

To go round the *quinta*, you follow the road to the left until you reach the end of the wall. There you will see a very steep path leading up to a eucalyptus tree, where there is a fork in the path. The left-hand path leads to a road along which you turn right. After a few minutes the road goes downhill and the Levada dos Tornos soon comes into sight again.

Back on the *levada* footpath you soon find yourself near the *quinta* belonging to the Blandy family, **Palheiro Ferreiro**. The stream then disappears into a tunnel again. Here it is better to use a torch rather than to rely on the stick method of passing through tunnels in order to avoid injury. The ground is very slippery and the rock face has unpleasant, sharp-edged ledges which cannot always be located using a stick. Emerging into the daylight, you will see another *levada* which flows to the south in the direction of Caniço.

The wider of the two *levadas*, the Levada dos Tornos, is covered over in places hereabouts. So at this stage of the tour the path leads on to two roads, the

Washing day at the stream.

EN 102 and, a little later the EN 201. Both these roads offer the chance of taking the bus back to Funchal for those already feeling weary. Those who continue the walk will soon come across a house with red doors which is surrounded by water, part of the **Quinta do Pomar**. There is a magnificent view down to Funchal from here.

To continue the walk along the *levada*, go through a red garden gate next to the chapel. The path leads to the houses of **Romeiros**, the last stage of the tour. There is a view of the church at Monte from here. A little further along the road there is a bus stop where, again, it is possible to catch the bus back to Funchal.

For most people, walking along the *levadas* is a new experience and there are a few "rules of the road" which need to be taken into consideration. Firstly, any gates along the way which need to be opened must be closed again.

Secondly, though it may be tempting to experiment with the sluices which regulate the water flow of the *levadas*, the impulse should be resisted, as any tampering with the ingenious system of of water distribution can lead to minor catastrophes.

At some points you will probably notice that stones have been placed in the *levadas* to form dams. These dams also play their part in regulating the water supply and should on no account be removed. Such misplaced helpfulness would certainly risk incurring the anger of the otherwise friendly farmers. It could mean that their prize banana trees do not get the water which they so urgently need.

Levada do Norte: The second *levada* walk follows the Levada do Norte from **Estreito de Câmara de Lobos** to **Ribeira Brava**.

The starting point for this walk is above the well-known fishing village at Estreito de Câmara de Lobos. The tour leads through fertile vineyards and past fields where vegetables and fruit trees grow. It also takes you through a number of quiet villages varied in character.

To begin the walk take bus number 96 to the stop called Levada do Norte which is just north of Estreito de Câmara de Lobos. When you get off the bus, you will see a small walled house surrounded by water on the left-hand side. This is where the *levada* begins although it is covered with slabs at this point. The walk starts at an altitude of about 1,800 ft (550 metres).

Follow the Levada do Norte in the direction in which it flows. This is an unusual footpath in that along the whole route you never lose sight of the shimmering azure sea some distance below you. As the walk does not take you into any wooded areas, there is no shade to be had along the way. To avoid getting sunstroke it is advisable to take a sun hat or some other form of head-covering with you. Occasionally the *levada* turns inland, following the deep clefts of the valleys. It often flows along a ledge with a steep drop down into the valley, and sometimes across bridges and through channels cut into the rock. However, there is no need to worry: the footpaths are wide and safe and the *levada* can be followed without danger.

Another advantage of this tour is that

Left, banana farmers often sell their produce at the roadside. Right, the land drops a vertical 2,000 metres at Cabo Girão.

it takes you into breathtakingly beautiful valleys which people who keep to the roads of Madeira do not know exist. At two particularly steep points along the way detours must be made. After this the path leads into the valley of the Ribeira da Caixa, a river which in the summer months is reduced to a mere rivulet. It is crossed by a bridge which, rather alarmingly, consists merely of planks; there are no railings. To avoid getting dizzy when crossing it, keep to the middle of the bridge and try not to look down.

Continuing the tour brings you to a house surrounded by water and, a little later, to a road, the EN 101. There is a kilometre stone here (number 5), which provides exact orientation. At this point the *levada* curves southwards and from here you can see the gleaming white chapel of Caldeira.

If you have already made an excursion to Cabo Girão, you will probably recognise the area. Along the way you have to pass through a tunnel which goes under the road used by the tourist coaches en route to the second highest sea cliff in Europe.

When you have passed through the tunnel you reach a climate divide, which may mean that you are met by completely different weather. At the tunnel exit there are a series of steep steps. The *levada* turns to the right eventually leading back to the main road. After crossing this, follow the *levada* on the right-hand-side of the EN 101.

The footpath later takes you into the **Campanário Valley**. It turns to the north here in order to go round the huge cleft in the valley and leads into a pine forest. Walking in a pine forest is a special pleasure – the soft carpet of pine needles is kind to the feet and the trees give off a spicy scent which refreshes the lungs. In this area the *levada* takes you across a number of bridges.

As the EN 101 is nearby, it is possible to finish the walk here and return to Funchal by bus. To get to the road, go down the narrow steps leading down the slope. The church tower of Campanário points the way.

The tour should only be continued by people who do not suffer from vertigo. After a short time you reach a deserted and dilapidated house. There is a *levada* sluice directly next to the road. Here you follow the *levada* in the direction of its flow until, after a few hours, you reach the power station at the Pousada dos Vinháticos, marking the end of this beautiful walk.

Levada do Risco: Two very popular walks begin at Rabaçal. The first is more of a pleasant stroll than a strenuous walk and leads to the breathtaking Risco Waterfalls. The second walk is from Rabaçal to Loreto in the west of the island and is also not particularly difficult.

Rabaçal cannot be reached by public bus, so a taxi or a hired car (only for the first walk) are the only ways of getting there. The route from Funchal crosses part of the Paúl da Serra plateau from where there is a road leading down to the houses of Rabaçal. This road is only wide enough for one car and there are very few passing places on the way. Apart from this, there are some points

Preceding pages: the constantly changing coastline. Left, the waterfalls flow into the *levadas*. Right, blossoms in the mountains near Vinháticos.

where there are sheer drops of a few hundred metres and no barriers between them and the road. Drivers, therefore, must have a strong nerve and should take particular care, especially when negotiating bends.

The houses in Rabaçal belong to the island government and at weekends are usually let out to government employees who wish to go there with their families. As the journey here from Funchal takes several hours, it may be an idea to stop in the village's small and narrow car park for a picnic. There are a number of wooden benches strewn around and drinks can be cooled in the dammed-up spring.

Afterwards, descend the steps in front of the house on the car park and keep to the right. The steps on the left lead down to the 25 Fontes. Although this is only a light stroll you should nonetheless ensure that you are wearing sturdy footwear. The route described is very wet and there are a number of rivulets that have to be crossed. Nevertheless it is a leisurely walk. The sluggish **Levada do Risco** is to the right of the path. It flows through the trees towards the Risco Waterfall, and this is where you want to head as well.

The background noises of such an excursion will be familiar to all *levada* fans. Every step is accompanied by the constant sound of splashing and bubbling water. The *levada* is intermittently joined by small streams cascading down the steep cliffs. Thousands of species of mosses and ferns thrive in this damp environment, and one's gaze is continually diverted by all the luxuriant tones of green. Seen against the light, the spray of the water coming down the cliffs is transformed to all the colours of the rainbow.

You'll also pass bilberry bushes reaching up to the height of your shoulders. If the people who went before you were considerate enough to leave any fruit, you will be surprised to find that these bilberries don't turn the tongue blue, but still have the same aromatic taste as the smaller variety you are probably familiar with at home.

Strolling along a *levada*.

At the end of this path there is a walled observation platform which affords a breathtaking view over a sheer drop. A number of waterfalls cascade down this drop into a deep ravine. At the bottom of the ravine is a lovely lake into which the roaring waterfalls plunge.

Although it has been established that the lake is only a modest 115 ft (35 metres) deep, the Madeirans like to claim that it is bottomless. This exaggeration is easy to forgive when you stand on the platform with its breathtaking view of the narrow ravine below, walled in by a rock face towering hundreds of metres above you. From this angle, it is easy to imagine that you are looking down into bottomless depths.

Everywhere hereabouts water drips off the rock face, which is overgrown with a dense covering of moisture-loving plants. Those who are not bothered about getting wet can go through the tunnel next to the platform. The entrance to the tunnel is nearly always covered by a curtain of water and before entering you should make sure that your camera or video camera cannot get hammered by the cascade.

The tunnel goes round in a semicircle to a veranda with a rock ledge forming a roof on the other side of the waterfall. From here you have an unobstructed view down into the ravine and can admire the awe-inspiring beauty of the lake below. Local people have many stories to recount of desperate people who have put an end to their unhappiness here.

You can, of course, follow the tunnel to the end. However it would be dangerous and inadvisable to continue the walk beyond this point. After the end of the tunnel there are no railings between the path and the sheer drop, and the ground is wet and extremely slippery. The only alternative is to return through the curtain of water.

A plastic mac or a cagoule are essential on this tour as even without rain you may get wet. However, it is well worth the trouble in order to enjoy it to the maximum.

From Rabaçal to Loreto: After this walk, really no more than a short interlude, the full tour continues from Rabaçal to Loreto in the west of the island. This is a tour which presents few difficulties but, as already mentioned, you will need to take a taxi to get to the starting point. You should also ask the taxi driver to pick you up again in Loreto at an arranged time. Otherwise you may find that you have trouble returning to Funchal in time for the evening meal at your hotel.

Rabaçal is situated at an altitude of 3,490 ft (1,064 metres) somewhat below the Paúl da Serra plateau which is between about 3,900–4,750 ft (1,200–1,450 metres) high. The starting point is the small government building next to the car park in Rabaçal. Here you will see a signpost to the **Levada das 25 Fontes** (the 25 springs). Following this signpost, go down some steps and after a short time you should come to a bridge which crosses the *levada*. A little further on you will reach a lush green meadow, an inviting place to stop and have a picnic.

In front of you there is a *levada* tunnel

Flowers bloom everywhere.

which was cut through the rock in the last century. The stick method of navigation is only of limited use in this instance. A torch is more advisable in order to reach the other end in safety and without injury.

The passage through the tunnel does not take long and after about 10 minutes you come out at the southern end. In this short distance you have also passed under a climate divide, which means that you may emerge into completely different weather. Nearby there are various facilities, such as a small wooden shelter, benches and drinking water, making it another convenient place to take a break. Anyone who is planning to camp should know that this is the last place along the way where one is allowed to erect a tent.

The route continues over a small and ancient stone bridge and along the *levada*. Take care not to take the turning to the left by mistake.

After a short time the footpath crosses two pipelines, which supply the electric power station at Calheta, and continues to the next *levada*, the **Rocha Vermelha**. Follow this *levada* along a track as far as the next junction where you must keep to the right. There is a fork in the path a little further along and here you take the left-hand path which leads to a paved village road. On this road you soon come to a *levada* which transports the turbine water from the electric power station down to the valley.

The tour continues past some stables and comes to the **Levada Calheta – Ponta do Pargo**. Follow this *levada* to the left in the direction of flow as far as a new bridge which crosses the Ribeira do Atouguia. Continuing along the *levada*, you eventually come to a wooden bridge across the Ribeira das Faias. A little further along the path is a steep paved road which leads on to a main road, the EN 101.

If you wish to continue the walk, you pass through a 16-ft (5-metre) long tunnel and eventually come to another stone bridge and a reservoir. At the reservoir, turn left in the direction of Loreto. After a few hundred yards there is a very steep

How green is my valley. A view from Encumeada.

road which leads to Loreto where, hopefully, your pre-arranged transport will be waiting to take you back to your accommodation.

From Pico do Arieiro to Pico Ruivo: If you wish to get some fresh mountain air, there is a short 2½-mile (4-km) walk from Pico do Arieiro to Pico Ruivo. This is an easy walk and in spite of altitudes between 5,250–6,110 ft (1,600–1,862 metres) mountaineering equipment is not required. However, it can be quite cold at this height with strong winds, so be sure to take some warm clothing.

Cars can be driven up as far as Pico do Arieiro, where there is a small café. Here you can pause to stock up on energy for the walk and admire the awe-inspiring view. There is also a mountain hotel nearby which is especially popular with walkers.

The footpath to Pico Ruivo, well-protected by railings, begins directly behind the snack bar. The signpost shows the way clearly. The steepest parts of the footpath are protected by wire cable. After a short time you come to a picnic site and a little further on there is an observation platform.

At **Pico do Gato** the footpath is similar to a *levada* in that it also takes you through a tunnel. After the tunnel, the path continues to some steps, at the end of which you should turn left. There is another tunnel to go through at this point. Continuing to the left, you should eventually arrive at Pico Ruivo. Here, providing the cloud level is not too low, you should be able to enjoy a magnificent view of the north coast. Even if the weather is overcast, looking down on a thick sea of fluffy white clouds can be impressive.

On Pico Ruivo there is a resthouse where you can take a well-earned break from your walk. To the right is a goat fence with a path running alongside it which leads down to Santana. The path to the left leads up to the highest summit on the island. If you have organised your tour properly, your car or a taxi will be waiting for you down in Santana; alternatively, you can return to Funchal by public bus.

The crowning end to a tour: Reid's Hotel.

PORTO SANTO: BATHING RESORT

Madeirans often refer to the inhabitants of the neighbouring island, Porto Santo, as *profetas* – prophets. The people of Porto Santo do not seem to object to this nickname; the local rock band has even adopted it.

The origins of the name are surrounded by myths going back to the 16th century. Some stories cite a man who prophesied the future at public gatherings on the beach. Another story features an eccentric 16th-century farmer called Fernão Bravo and his 17-year-old niece Filipa, who believed themselves to be messengers of God. Sceptical islanders became convinced of their claim when Fernão turned on them and enumerated their most secret sins.

In all countries people earmark one part of the population as the butt of their jokes, and the *profetas* have a reputation among Madeirans for their slowness and lethargy. It is this supposed lethargy which serves as a target for many Madeiran anecdotes and jokes. Even in allegedly scientific treatises the people of Porto Santo are depicted as workshy. It is true, however, that the inhabitants can often be seen sitting at street corners for hours on end, languidly brushing away the flies and watching the world go by. The island, which measures 3¾ by 7 miles (6 by 11 km) and is situated 41 nautical miles from Madeira, has a population of 5,000.

Tourists who come to the island expecting a holiday full of action and high life will inevitably be disappointed. It is far too quiet for that. On the other hand, this is precisely what appeals to many visitors that come here. Some have been returning to the island for 20 years or more and are anxious that it should remain exactly as it is.

Certainly, it has changed little over the last 600 years. Although Porto Santo was the first in the Madeiran group of islands to be discovered, it was soon neglected in favour of the larger, more hospitable island. Mr T. Edward Bowdich, a visitor to Porto Santo in the autumn of 1823, was astonished by its lack of development and low profile: "During the three days I resided there I could never discover that the governor had more than one king's servant under his command... he (distinguished by being clothed in tattered remnants of various uniforms) opened the gates, hoisted the flag, beat the drum at sunrise and sunset, swept the yard, helped in the kitchen, and waited at table when the governor had company."

Bowdich went on to describe the governor's humble home: "[It] looked like that of the lawyer in a small village in England; it was very neat, of one storey, and contained but two sitting-rooms... a row of cannons (some of which had fallen from their carriages, whilst the others, from their monstrous touch-holes and rusty condition) were emblems of peace rather than war, and fit subjects for a society of antiquaries."

Headline news: The world spotlight did, however, eventually fall on Porto Santo – in 1990. The island was the scene of a catastrophic oil leak, an ecological disaster which was reported on television and newspapers throughout the world. Thanks to the rescue operation, which was carried out with the help and perseverance of the local population, the largest part of the oil lost by the leaking Spanish tanker has been cleared away and there is now little evidence of what happened. The balance of nature on the island, however, will need some years yet to recover from that part – in the main unseen – which remains.

There are still 5½ inviting miles (9 km) of gently curved beach to enjoy. The golden sand lapped by the turquoise water of the Atlantic Ocean is much praised and little used. The climate here is described as dry and stable. In summer the landscape is a patchwork of yellows, ochres and browns. Older travel guides usually describe the island as the "brown island", an epithet that was later changed to the golden-brown island. Nowadays the tourist office, with an ear for more saleable epithets, has dubbed it the *Ilha Dourada* – the gilded island.

Recent years, however, have witnessed reafforestation of the island, especially with cedars and Aleppo pines, in an attempt to stop the natural desolation of the island and to increase rainfall. A rain shower in winter can mean that the island suddenly takes on a rich green colour overnight.

There have been a number of attempts to develop the island as a tourist centre. Two ugly concrete hotel blocks, situated on the beach, some miles from the main town, bear witness to this. The Hotel Novo Mondo was recently given yet another facelift in the hope of attracting more tourists, but it remains empty. The explanations for this stagnation range from the chronic lack of fresh water, to speculation about economic difficulties and bureaucracy. Whatever the reason, in the main holiday season the majority of the visitors are Madeirans who have their own houses on the island.

Not much remains of the island's indigenous vegetation. All attempts to find the legendary Dragon's Blood Tree or juniper trees and heather end in vain. Agricultural production on the island is also limited. The soil is not very fertile and produces meagre crops of melons, figs and pumpkins in fields sheltered by dry-stone walls. More successful are the grapes which grow along the south coast. Most of these are cultivated for eating but a small part of the harvest is used to produce the Vinho de Porto Santo, a heavy red wine with a reddish-brown colour. It has a pleasant taste and tempts many first-time samplers to drink a glass too many. The wine is available in small quantities of varying quality. It can be bought in some bars, for example, the Marques Restaurant in Vila Baleira or in the Estrela do Norte and the Torres in Camacha.

A matter of survival: The people of Porto Santo only have a limited interest in fishing. Most of the fresh fish which can be found on the island is imported from Madeira, as is nearly all the food. For this reason the small market situated on the edge of Vila Baleira is seldom worth a visit.

In the history of Porto Santo its people have nearly always been faced with

Preceding pages: there are still empty beaches on Porto Santo. **Below,** everyone goes to church on Sunday morning.

some form of hardship. They have suffered from invasions by pirates from Morocco, Algeria, France and England, from drought and famine, and, in more recent times, from recessions in the tourist trade which have badly hit the island. The inhabitants have taken all this with a stoical composure and it is just this which has such a calming effect on the tourists who come looking for peace and quiet. The unhurried atmosphere of putting off till tomorrow what can be done today infects visitors as soon as they set foot on the island.

Vila Baleira: Visitors are usually very grateful to reach Vila Baleira after being tossed about on the rough waves of the Atlantic for 1½ hours. The *Patria*, a modern catamaran, which is owned by the government and was bought with the help of European Community subsidies in 1990, can carry up to 400 passengers from Madeira to Porto Santo. Nobody is quite sure where, were the catamaran ever full, so many people would eat or sleep.

In earlier times the arrival of the ferry from Madeira was a festive event, but the modern catamaran is greeted with respect rather than joy. Concern for the safe arrival of the boat is paramount; when the sea is too rough for it to sail islanders may wait for several days for essential provisions.

Vila Baleira can easily be reached on foot from the harbour, although there are taxis and a public bus available (costs of transport are somewhat higher than in Madeira, as is the case for most other things). A more romantic way of travelling is by horse and carriage, also available at the harbour (the few houses at the beach near the harbour can hardly be called a village).

There are few buildings of interest on Porto Santo, and these are all at the centre of the village, the square around the Town Hall which is planted with palm trees – **Largo do Pelourinho**. One of the most interesting is the parish church – **Nossa Senhora da Piedade** – which has recently been restored. On the outer wall is a picture on painted tiles which stands out against the gleaming white of the walls. On the southern side of the church are the remains of the original Gothic chapel, one of the first places of worship to be built on the archipelago.

Porto Santo was, in fact, discovered two years before Madeira in 1418. The term "discover" is, however, somewhat misleading. Porto Santo (Sacred Harbour) was already known to sailors in the 14th century and often provided them with refuge from the rough Atlantic. It is recorded on 14th-century sea charts under the same name.

Next to the church a narrow street leads to the **Casa de Colombo**. This recently restored house is worth a visit. The museum guide is unusually competent and visitors should profit from her knowledge of the sailor and discoverer, whose life is shrouded in mystery. Exhibitions are planned for the museum and the small amphitheatre in the courtyard is going to be used for concerts. The museum is closed on Tuesdays and Thursdays.

It seems to be a fact that Columbus lived on the island for a period and it is

Things must be done in the correct order: first church...

certainly true that he married Felipa Moniz Perestrelo, the daughter of Bartolomeu Perestrelo, who was appointed the first Governor of Porto Santo by Henry the Navigator. However, it is less certain that they married on Porto Santo and the story that his son, Diego, was born on the island is also without historical confirmation.

The dates, which are derived from different historical sources do not fit together. It seems probable that the Genoese sailor came to the island some 15 years before his spectacular voyage of discovery in 1492 (1479 and 1480 are the years which seem most probable). He is said to have studied maps and charts in secret on the island in order to develop his hypotheses about lands lying across the sea. His involvement in the sugar trade was probably a cover-up for these activities, and many volumes have been filled with speculation about this. Authors have made a sport out of producing new theories and ideas (*see pages 41–42, Columbus and Madeira*); studying this material is one way of

passing a rare rainy day on Porto Santo. The museum has a small Columbus library for this purpose.

After taking in the island's history visitors can take a well-earned break at the Baiana Café next to the museum. Here you can soak up the slow and gentle pulse of life on the Ilha Dourada. You may also get to know Heather Krohn, one of the most interesting and perhaps most eccentric personalities on the island. Heather, an English woman of indefinite age who came to Porto Santo in the 1970s, is a journalist, colour psychologist, yoga teacher and estate agent. She sometimes invites the visitors whom she takes a liking to to her windmill, the cornerless rooms of which she has converted into a comfortable home with her husband Raleigh.

Here she shows her visitors the so-called Columbus beans. These beans, washed up on the beaches of Porto Santo, are said to have helped Columbus in his studies of the ocean currents and ultimately to have shown him the route for his voyage to America. Heather has a

...then the bar.

wealth of knowledge about Porto Santo and may ask for a small donation for the stray cats and dogs of the island.

Heather is not the only source of information for visitors. On the eastern side of Largo do Pelourinho is the **Tourist Information Office** housed in the **Delegação do Governo Regional** building. On workdays two friendly women provide information on the island in English, French and a little German. They will give you photocopies of useful information about the bus service, air and sea transport, hotels, guesthouses and private boarding houses. They apologise for the modesty of the printed material, but are more than willing to help visitors in any other way. It is Porto Santo's ambition to change its role as Madeira's poor cousin and become a tourist centre in its own right.

There is a small arts and crafts display with a variety of interesting exhibits. Unfortunately hardly any of them are regularly available at **Bazar Colombo**, the only souvenir shop in Vila Baleira. Potential buyers are told that there has

been a shortage of the lovely figures made out of palm leaves since Dona Bemvinda, their creator, started working at the school; apparently she now has no time for her craft. The only things readily available are the very nice and very useful Porto Santo hats. Even the cobbler, who makes lovely clay figures and sandstone sculptures, works at the camping site now and can only be persuaded to produce his works if you contact him personally and give him an order in advance.

In the street leading off from the main square, a continuation of Avenida da Henrique Vieira e Castro, are two of the island's three banks and the post office. There are as yet no cash dispensers on the island. The third bank is in Rua João Gonçalves Zarco (the first street on the right at the beginning of the village), which could be described as the main business street on the island. As well as the **ferry agency** and a decent supermarket there are rows of shops selling all manner of things. Without doubt the showpiece is the bakery – *paderia* – at the other end of the street, the only one on Porto Santo. It is well worth waiting in the queue to sample its range of delicious Porto Santo cakes and pastries and the milky coffee served at the bar.

There are branches of the two **travel agencies**, Star and Blandy, in the street which runs parallel to the beach (it can hardly be called a promenade). Here you can book a boat trip around the island for 1,400 escudos per person. In principle these trips take place on Thursdays and Saturdays. In principle because there has to be a minimum of four persons on the trip to make it pay, and this is not always the case. During the summer months the chances of the boats setting out are better. It is best to enquire at the pavilion where the buses stop or at the Transmadeira office (opposite the pavilion).

Tour of the island: For those who wish to explore the island without joining an organised tour there are two firms where you can hire cars, Moinho Rent-a-Car (13, Rua Dr Nuno Silvestre Teixeira) and Atlantic (Avenida Vieira e Castro). The alternatives are to travel by rusty

Heather from England knows the island like the back of her hand.

public bus or, for the more adventurous, to rent a bicycle. All the bicycles available have seen better days and so it is advisable to arrange an hourly or daily price in advance. Journeys by taxi take between one and two hours depending on the route, and fixed prices of up to 3,500 escudos can be expected (the price in 1990).

Whichever means of transport you choose, a trip through the landscape of the "Ilha Dourada" made rugged by erosion should not be missed. Keen photographers will be grateful for every stop along the way. The standard tour takes you through **Portela** and **Serra de Fora**, where sulphurous yellow and ochre are the dominant colours, to **Serra de Dentro**, which is the part of the island with the most water and was formerly the agricultural centre. The terraced hillsides bear witness to the arduous attempts to make a meagre living from the arid soil here. Nowadays they are deserted and serve only as subjects for photographers. The remains of abandoned farmhouses provide an op-

portunity to study the characteristic architecture of the island. Apart from a few grazing cattle, goats and sheep, the area is uninhabited and shrouded in an almost eerie silence.

As you will notice on this tour, attempts are being made to store rain water in reservoirs in some of the smaller eroded valleys. Together with reafforestation, these measures are intended to increase the fertility of the island and thus improve the chances for agriculture.

The tour continues to **Camacha**, a village whose only claim to fame is its delicious barbecued chicken. The only thing of much interest in the village is the traditional windmill which is open for visitors.

Drinking the very palatable fresh water from the spring at **Fonte da Areia** is said to guarantee eternal youth. The water rises out of the sandstone formed into bizarre sculptures by erosion. It is worth making a day trip here with a picnic basket (take the bus to Camacha and then walk). There is a small bar with

Home from the market.

covered benches and chairs where you can enjoy the view of the rough and rugged north coast. There is a footpath leading down to the sea, a wonderful place to fish or just relax and enjoy the roar of the waves.

The tour continues to **Pico do Castelo**, where, at an altitude of 1,440 ft (438 metres), there is a view of the whole island. Pico do Castelo used to serve as a hiding place for the inhabitants of the island when it suffered one of its frequent invasions by pirates. From here you have a good view of the most advanced part of the island's infrastructure, Porto Santo Airport, a 9,850-ft (3,000-metre) long runway running in a north-south direction down the middle of the island. In the airport building, where the organisation is still fairly makeshift, there is a model of the intended airport complex. However, this is still awaiting completion in the near or distant future. Porto Santo will then be able to receive the large charter planes which it so urgently needs to develop the tourist industry on the island. At present there is a daily shuttle service between Porto Santo and Madeira. The flights are four times a day and last 20 minutes. The small planes of the LAR airline are a help for those visitors who suffer from seasickness and are prepared to pay about double the price of the sea crossing.

The next stage of the tour takes you to **Pico das Flores** in the east, passing **Campo de Cima** and **Campo de Baixo** as well as a few windmills and perhaps the occasional donkey, the typical form of transport in earlier days, along the way. Pico das Flores offers a panorama from the west to the east of the island. From here you can see the results of the reafforestation of the island, and, on a clear day, you will be able to see the outline of Madeira in the distance.

Eventually you arrive at the easternmost point of the island. **Ponta da Calheta**, where the sandy beach ends and the coast is dominated by intriguing rock formations. There are two makeshift restaurants here which serve mainly fish dishes (Toca do Pescador and Pôr

Windmills are disappearing fast.

do Sol), where you can have an evening meal and watch the sun set. After this there is a rather long walk back to the starting point. If you have arranged with a taxi driver to wait for you or to pick you up from here, it is advisable to agree on a price in advance.

The other mountain peaks – *picos* – on the island are ideal for exploring on walking tours. The highest is **Pico do Facho** at an altitude of 1,696 ft (517 metres). One walking tour which should not be missed is to see the fossilised rocks at **Morenos**.

The *ilhéus*, the offshore islands, are also interesting because of their grottoes and rock formations, many of which have poetic names such as the *Pedra do Sol* (Rock of the sun) on Ilhéu de Fora, or the *Aranjas* (Oranges), which are orange-shaped calcareous formations on Ilhéu de Cima. The islands can be reached by boat. For more information about this you should enquire at Turismo or at the Moinho Rent-a-Car office.

The island's sand is said to have curative properties.

Those people who are more interested in cultural history than the quiet atmosphere of a small island will inevitably be disappointed on Porto Santo. There are a few chapels which are usually closed, such as the **Nossa Senhora da Graça**, where, according to legend, the Virgin Mary appeared. It is a popular chapel for weddings and on the 14 and 15 August the important Feast of the Assumption is celebrated here. The **Chapel of São Pedro** on the gentle slopes of Pico Ana Ferreira opens its doors on St Peter's Day, the 29 July. The **Espirito Santo Chapel** is now the seat of the local council. Masses are held on Saturdays and Sundays, and tourists relaxing at the Hotel Porto Santo swimming pool will catch their sounds drifting across on the wind.

The island is adorned with a total of three monuments. One is a bust of Columbus at the end of the old quay, looking boldly across the Atlantic to the southeast. On Pico do Castelo there is a sculpture of the father of the reafforestation plans. In Alameda do Infante there is the official Discoverers' Memorial, which has earned the nick-

name the "soap stone" amongst locals. Abstract sculpture does not seem to enjoy great popularity on Porto Santo.

Visitors gain the impression that there is all the time in the world on Porto Santo and there is never any reason to rush. Time seems to have passed leaving no trace. It has become a precious commodity in the rest of Europe, but here the supplies seem to be inexhaustible. There are many words to describe the welcome which the inhabitants offer to their guests: friendly, modest, peaceful, helpful, unspoilt and simple are just some of them. Nothing in their behaviour reminds one of the troubled history of the island. This history begins with three murders in the families of governors of the island; in each case the victim was the wife of the governor. The islanders were also the victims of frequent invasions by pirates.

The facial features of the inhabitants give some clues about their origins. Sometimes you find yourself looking into watery blue eyes in a finely chiselled face framed by blonde curls. At other times, eyes that are a sparkling dark brown, a reminder of Arab ancestors. There is much evidence of the Arabic inheritance on the island. The dome-like roofs of the traditional houses, supported by a single tree trunk, and the clay plasterwork resemble the Arabic architecture of North Africa.

Culinary legacies of such settlement have sadly all but died out. Cous-cous, brought here by women who were abducted to North Africa from the island and later allowed to return, can no longer be found on menus. Many other traditional dishes are also no longer cooked. One exception to this is *bolo do caco*, a kind of round flat loaf which was originally baked on clay tiles. Occasionally *biscoitos* are available at the baker's or the supermarket. These are a kind of hard, dry, salty biscuit of indefinable taste.

Accommodation and restaurants: The most common dishes on Porto Santo nowadays are *frango* (barbecued chicken) as well as *espetada* (meat cooked on a skewer), also popular in Madeira, and grilled fish freshly caught from the sea. If you are lucky, you will be able to sample a traditional fish soup in east Calheta. The Mare Sol restaurant at the beach at Campo do Baixo and the Arsénios in Vila Baleira serve international cuisine. The Forno Restaurant in Avenida Henrique Vieira e Castro specialises in grilled food. For those who prefer Italian food a hand-painted sign opposite the Hotel Santo Porto points to a pizza restaurant.

The **Hotel Santo Porto** is rightly said to be the best hotel on the island. It is a four-star hotel which it deserves to be, taking into consideration the meagre resources of the island. It is the heart of tourist life, and everything which tourists may need is available here, including surfboards, diving equipment, pedaloes and tennis courts.

All tourists find their way to this hotel sooner or later. It happens to be situated in the loveliest and sunniest location, directly next to the beach. The **Praia Dourada** is the only other place which can compete with this. For people who cannot afford the hotel, there are several alternatives – the Palmeira, Central and Zarco guesthouses being the best. There is also a camp site, a cheap place with an excellent snack bar on the Vila Baleira beach. The only drawback is the lack of shade on the site.

Private accommodation can be arranged at the Tourist Information Office. In the main holiday season visitors to Porto Santo are recommended to book in advance.

The little night life on the island takes place almost exclusively at the Hotel Porto Santo, which organises folklore evenings and barbecues. Recently, however, three discotheques have opened – the Challenger, Big Boy and Ventanias. The last of these is run by two young German women. There are a number of bars for people who are just looking for a quiet drink (if in doubt, ask a taxi driver). Two of these are at the beach.

The tourist industry on the island can hardly be called fully developed as yet. This does not seem to bother the people of Porto Santo very much, but they are proud of the healing powers attributed to the sand on their beaches. It is not unusual to see locals lying buried from head to toe, patiently waiting for the sands to work their magic.

These claims are not completely bogus. More than a few visitors who have suffered from the humid climate prevailing on Madeira have made a speedy recovery on coming here. Skin complaints also improve, and stomach, liver and intestinal problems are said to benefit from the island's mineral water. (Incidentally, if you buy a bottle of Porto Santo mineral water, you will search in vain for an exact chemical analysis of the water on the label. What's more it can be difficult to find – the people of Porto Santo do not seem to be as convinced of the beneficial properties of their water as the people of Madeira, where most of it is sold.)

The tap water on the island is desalinated sea water and is not suitable for drinking or for making tea or coffee. It is therefore recommended to keep well stocked up with mineral water or water from one of the fresh water springs. In fact, there is a good natural source opposite the camping site just outside the mineral water factory.

Future prospects: The highly praised healing properties of the island and its attractive beaches have led local politicians to make bold plans for its future development. Their intention is to increase the present modest number of beds to times the current total. A riding centre and a golf course are being built. To meet the rising requirements a sewage works has already been completed. Alternative sources of energy in the form of wind-powered generators are beginning to compete with traditional windmills. And, of course, the travel industry's favourite project – the extension of the airport – should not go unmentioned in this context.

You do not need to be a *profeta* to predict that one of Europe's last unspoilt holiday areas will eventually become a fully developed tourist resort with all the usual infrastructure. Anyone who values peace and quiet while on holiday would be wise to get to Porto Santo before it does.

Tilling the soil is hard work.

DESERTAS & CO.

The Desertas – the desert islands – lie south-east of Madeira, only 19 nautical miles away from Funchal. Sometimes, however, when you look out of your hotel window, they seem to have come closer, almost near enough to touch. For Madeirans this is a warning of bad weather to come; then the southwest wind, which causes this illusion of nearness, is sure to bring rain and stormy seas with it.

The islands possess many moods. As one early traveller, W. H. Koebel, noted, "viewed from the mountain tops, their glamour is of an elusive order… they would seem to hang high aloft, poised between sea and sky." As the picture postcards testify they are at their most beautiful in the late afternoon when the last rays of the setting sun bathe them in colours ranging from grey-blue to pink and mother-of-pearl. Although they are uninhabited, the three islands – **Ilhéu Chão**, which is flat and round like a cake, **Deserta Grande** and **Bugio** – are steeped in colourful legends.

The islands are very inhospitable for man and only one creature feels very much at home here – a ferocious and highly poisonous black spider (*lycosa ingens*), the largest in the archipelago. The meagre vegetation can barely survive in the arid soil and there is no fresh water apart from the little which manages to seep through the vaulted grottoes. For this reason there have never been any communities on the islands. All attempts at settlement ended in failure and all visits have inevitably been of a short nature. There is, however, a legend that tells of a community of goatherds who successfully defended the islands against 80 British pirates in 1564; the battle is said to have ended in a bloodbath.

The role of the Desertas in European history is limited. The native *orseille* plant was at one time much in demand as a dye derived from it was prized in England and Flanders, and at the turn of

The Desertas are uninhabited.

the century a Monacan prince wrote a report about successful rabbit hunts (rabbits were introduced to the islands by man). The islands' high point, however, occurred in World War I when a German submarine made use of their waters to hide in while they planned the torpedoing of the French battleship *Surprise*.

The islands' shores provide the richest interest here. It is probably thanks to the inhospitality of the islands that a small colony of monk seals (*monachus monachus*) still exists here. These seals were threatened with extinction because the fishermen – who traditionally saw them as enemies – culled them to prevent depletion of their fish stocks. The seal population became so diminished that animal protectionists took up their cause internationally and now they are a protected species.

The waters of the Desertas have always contained plenty of fish. The islands were originally private property belonging to the Hintons, a well-known British family who used them for occasional hunting trips, before coming under the supervision of the state. In 1988 a biological observation station was set up on the islands. Its tasks include keeping a count of the pairs of monk seals and their young and training a close eye on the biological and ecological balance of the Desertas.

Further efforts to protect the environment here have met with equal success. In 1990 part of the 7-mile (12-km) long and 1-mile (2-km) wide Deserta Grande became a nature reserve. Now this biotope for rare species can only be visited with a special permit, for example for research purposes, and the rest of the island can only be visited to within 10 metres of the shoreline. These strict measures are intended to put a stop to the over-exploitation of the island.

In 1982 the Regional Government passed a law creating the Natural Park of Madeira whose aim is the protection of the environment and the animal world including the underwater nature park of **Garajau** and the remaining laurel woods on Madeira itself.

However, sport fishing (not profes-sional) is still allowed in the waters around the Desertas, providing it is within the context of day excursions, and visitors can still take part in boat trips to the islands. On the crossing, they may, if they are lucky, be able to observe dolphins or turtles sunbathing on the surface of the sea.

These trips are a good opportunity to experience the eerie quality of these islands which have remained unchanged for millions of years. The only sound likely to break the silence is the curious laughing call of the Atlantic shearwater – the *cagara*. The Desertas are a paradise for birds. It is not difficult to imagine Miss Marple, Agatha Christie's amateur detective and ornithologist, on the look-out for shearwaters or soft-plumaged petrels.

The only people on the island are two biologists, who take it in turns (14-day shifts) to keep an eye on the seals. They can sometimes be seen on the black sands and may inquire about any water supplies the visiting boat parties can spare. Occasionally sailors lose their

Only conservationists and scientists are allowed to land on this haven for rare species.

way and land on the beaches here and once President Soares paid a visit to this last corner of the Portuguese Republic. There is nothing else here apart from the caves and weird rock formations and an endless rust-brown wilderness.

Even more remote: Totally untouched and out of bounds to all lesser mortals are the "wild" islands, the **Selvagens**, another unpopulated Portuguese group of islands to the south of Madeira. Although they lie geographically closer to the Canary Islands, 103 miles (165 km) from the island of Tenerife, they nevertheless come under the political control of the autonomous regional government of Madeira, from which they are separated by 177 miles (285 km) of water. They consist of the main island of **Selvagem Grande** (0.95 sq. miles/2.46 sq. km) and **Selvagem Pequena** (0.23 sq. miles/0.16 sq. km) as well as a number of small island reefs.

It was only in 1971 that these islands ceased to be the private property of the Madeiran banking family Rocha Machado. Since 1976 sentries have been

stationed on this distant Portuguese outpost. They are relieved every two weeks.

There are scientific expeditions to the islands and biology students are occasionally granted permission to study their rich flora and fauna. The first research was carried out in 1963 by the founder of Funchal's natural science museum, the German Günther Maul (the results of his work can be be seen in the museum). It is the islands' wealth of fauna that persuaded the government to make them a nature reserve.

Just like the Desertas, the Selvagens are breeding grounds for shearwaters, a bird whose young graced the dining tables of Madeiran and Canarian fishermen and their families until not so long ago. Some 20,000 birds were caught here every year and salted and dried before being taken back to Madeira. But fishing and harvesting of the islands' plants for dyes were always kept under fairly strict control. Even today the "wild" islands, with their spectacular array of indigenous fauna, look much the same as they must have done millions of years ago.

But the scientific work that has been carried out has not unravelled all the secrets of the Desertas: they remain shrouded in mystery and steeped in stories concerning the lost treasure of the legendary Captain Kidd.

The last serious expedition to find the said treasure was mounted in the 1950s, after numerous previous attempts had been doomed to failure. Between 1848 and 1851 the English corvette *Rattler* was dispatched to the islands no less than four times with the blessing of the British Crown. His particular mission was to locate the treasure of Lima Cathedral, which, according to reports of an escaped mariner, the famous pirate had hidden here.

In the early 1920s the British Antarctic explorer Sir Ernest Shackleton (1874–1922) intended to continue the search on his way back from the South Pole. But he died at the Pole, taking the secret of the sunken treasure and all information concerning its whereabouts to his icy grave. The treasure still waits to be raised today…

Left, seagulls dive for food. **Right**, the storm petrel is almost extinct.

THE GRAND FINALE

The luckiest visitors to Madeira are those who manage to get a grandstand seat on one of the cruise ships which drop anchor in the amphitheatre of Funchal Bay on New Year's Eve. Of all Madeira's festivals and holidays the New Year is celebrated with particular gusto and panache. Everything centres on Funchal and people come from all over the island to join in.

The evening culminates in some 350,000 lamps being switched on all round the bay and a magnificent firework display. This is not the loud and gaudy flashing and blinking of neon signs typical of places like Las Vegas but rather a set of illuminations created by artists. There is no hint of vulgarity.

Preparations for the New Year celebrations always begin on 8 December. The streets are garlanded in leaves and straw flowers; houses are repaired and newly whitewashed; sweets – notably honey and almond cakes – are prepared by the women; and special liqueurs made according to age-old recipes are brewed by the men. The trees and roofs of the houses are elaborately decorated with lights, as well as aluminium frameworks and trellises made specially for the firework displays.

It isn't just an occasion for the locals. Every year between 10 and 15 cruise ships jostle for the best places in the bay to anchor. Flags from all countries of the world can be seen fluttering in the warm evening wind. The legendary British cruise ship *Canberra* is one of the regular visitors to this annual spectacle, as are the two famous German liners *Europa* and *Berlin*. Most of the others sail under Russian, Spanish or Norwegian flags.

Transatlantic liners have even been known to interrupt their long voyages across the ocean, change their courses at short notice and head for Madeira to surprise their passengers with a New Year's Eve celebration of a lifetime.

Over 5,000 cruise passengers board

Cruise ships and yachts descend on Funchal's harbour...

these ships to escape the cold winters in their home countries and enjoy the warm summer temperatures further south. Arriving in Madeira on New Year's Eve, most of them – at this time of the year, by and large wealthy visitors – leave their ships to take advantage of the opportunity to make their last shopping expedition of the year on dry land. These people are an important economic factor in balancing the books of the Madeiran tourist industry.

By 11 p.m. that night the whole of Funchal and its suburbs on the slopes surrounding the bay are bathed in bright light. It is customary for each household to switch on all the lights and throw open the doors and windows. Then, when the clocks strike midnight, rockets are fired into the starry sky from a total of 45 launching ramps. They signal the start of an extravagant but tasteful inferno in which the Madeirans once again prove themselves to be pyrotechnical maestros.

...for the New Year's Eve firework display.

At the last stroke of midnight, on the eastern tip of the semi-circle of Funchal Bay the illuminated numbers of the old year change to the figures of the new year, seeming, as one onlooker remarked, like "a symbol of mystery, marking a death, a birth, and heavy with unknown destiny." All at once an incredible cacophony engulfs the whole bay and seems to make the moment between the two years stand still.

There are deafening shots fired from cannons, a loud chorus of "ahs!" and "ohs!" from the people watching the spectacle, the horns of all the cars in the town seem to go off at once, and the ships in the bay join in this ear-piercing concert by sounding their sirens.

This is the grand finale to a fantastic opera on a magnificent stage. Everybody is invited to join in and play his part in the ending of the year.

The trials and tribulations of the old year seem to be forgotten. This joyful spectacle invokes luck, happiness and success for the Madeirans and their guests and, as at the end of every year, wishes:

Happy New Year!

TRAVEL TIPS

GETTING THERE

BY AIR

Don't take too much notice of the horror stories about the most dangerous airport in the world; pilots who fly into Santa Cruz's Santa Catarina airport are specially trained to cope with the problems, and at the first sign of a contrary wind the airport is immediately closed (unfortunately this happens rather frequently). In the 1990s the airport is being upgraded and extended with money from the European Community.

The Portuguese national airline, TAP, has a virtual monopoly on scheduled services in and out of Madeira, linking Funchal with Lisbon. It also has flights to London, Paris, Lyon, Madrid, Geneva, Zurich and Frankfurt.

The cheapest and often the quickest flights to Madeira will be charter flights, which take roughly four hours from Northern Europe. Consult your travel agent or local newspapers for details; for some reason, particularly cheap charter flights leave from Brussels.

Madeira's link with the largest airport on the neighbouring island of Porto Santo is maintained by the small airline LAR. In addition, many of the charter and scheduled services will make a stopover in Porto Santo to refuel. The airline SATA has a regular service to the Azores.

Santa Catarina airport has a duty-free shop, a bureau de change, a tourist information office and several car-hire agencies. A taxi to Funchal costs around 2,500 escudos. The bus is much cheaper and stops right outside the airport, but the timetable is rather indecipherable. Wait patiently, and admire the view until the next bus comes. Package tourists will have their own prearranged transport from the airport.

BY SEA

Surprising though it may seem, there are no regular passenger ferry services to Madeira, and the freight-carrying ships from Lisbon no longer take passengers. However, Funchal harbour is a famous anchorage for cruise ships such as the *Queen Elizabeth II*, the *Royal Princess*, the *Black Prince*, the *Eurosun* and the *Cunard Princess*. Some of these will take passengers who don't want to stay on board for the complete cruise: therefore it is possible – if you know a good travel agent – to rendezvous with one or other of them at its departure ports on mainland Europe and arrive on Madeira in style.

TRAVEL ESSENTIALS

MONEY MATTERS

The Portuguese unit of currency is the escudo, with 100 centavos to an escudo. It's much better to wait until you are on Madeira to exchange money. Keep in mind that as a rule, it's best to exchange as much as possible at one time as the commission fee for each transaction is relatively high everywhere, regardless of how much is exchanged. In addition to banks and hotels, money can also be exchanged at STAR (Avenida Arriaga 23) and the tourist information centre TURISMO (Avenida Arriaga 16), in which you'll find change offices affiliated with various banks. It is also possible to exchange money at the airport during regular business hours.

The 1,000 escudo note exists in two different styles and is what you will most frequently find yourself using. Besides this, there are 10,000 and 5,000 escudo notes and 100, 50, 20, 10, 5, 2, and 1 escudo coins. The 1 escudo coin is also minted in a variety of styles. Occasionally you'll also come across 50 centavo coins; these correspond to half an escudo. Over the past years the rate of inflation has levelled off at around 9 percent.

Credit cards are accepted in many restaurants and in upmarket shops. With a Eurocheque card you can withdraw money from your regular account at four different cash machines. These machines can be found in the hotel zone at the hotel complex Eden-Mar and diagonally across from the cathedral in the Banco Nacional Ultramarino building (Avenida Arriaga 2) in Funchal. Money can also be taken out from your Post Office Savings Account upon the presentation of your savings book, account and identification card at the main post office (Avenida Zarco), as well as in every post office located in the main areas in Madeira.

CUSTOMS

Customary restrictions apply to luxury goods. Duty-free items include 300 cigarettes, 150 cigarillos, 75 cigars or 400 gm of tobacco. You are permitted up to 3 litres of spirits with an alcoholic content of up to 22 percent. If the alcoholic content exceeds this, you are allowed to bring in only 1.5 litres. Coffee is limited to 1 kilo, tea 200 gm, perfume 75 gm and *eau de toilette* 0.3175 litre. You must be at least 17 years of age in order to take these items into the country. Officially, the importation of fresh foodstuffs and potted plants is not allowed. Animals weighing over 5 kilos are charged as freight.

HEALTH

Special vaccinations apply only to animals. In order to avoid getting ill while travelling, allow yourself enough time to get acclimatised; don't rush full steam ahead, especially during the most humid months. Your thirst is best quenched with mineral water held at room temperature, rather than with other ice-cold beverages; give your stomach enough time to get used to the foreign cuisine, which is generously spiced with garlic. Tap water is drinkable, but this is frequently not the case with *levada* water.

The sun's rays are extremely intensive due to the moderate temperatures and frequent, light breezes that play over the islands; it therefore pays to be careful, and a sun hat, especially on Porto Santo, is a wise precaution.

WHAT TO WEAR

Regardless of when you are travelling, it is seldom extremely hot and never very cold. Therefore it's best to bring an assortment of "between-season" clothes. When going on a tour be sure to take along a change of clothing or at least something to throw over your shoulders. In the evening temperatures can drop considerably. An especially important item you won't want to be without is a pair of comfortable, rubber-soled shoes. You'll be glad you brought them along in Funchal, where walking is done either on pavement composed typically of round, basalt pebbles or on slick cobblestones, not to mention going up and down steep hills! For the mountains you'll need a pair of sturdy hiking boots, to keep you from slipping on patches of loosely packed volcanic earth; rain gear; a sun hat; knife and fork; a pair of scissors and a torch.

GETTING ACQUAINTED

GOVERNMENT

The archipelago of Madeira is called RAM, Regiao Autónoma da Madeira, and under the Portuguese constitution has been granted the right of self-determination. Because of this, Madeira exerts extensive political, administrative and financial autonomy. The regional parliament, composed of 50 elected members, has the power to make decisions regarding legislative issues – in so far as they concern the islands – and, above all, decisions relating to the regional budget.

The governing party is the PSD, the Social-Democratic Party. The chief administrator is Alberto Joao Jardim, a charismatic figure who has assured the victory of his party for years. The executive branch is made up of the president, vice-president and six secretaries, each with various responsibilities and concerns.

The Portuguese central government is represented in Madeira by a "Minister of the Republic"; the regional government dispatches five parliamentary representatives to Lisbon. On Porto Santo the regional government is represented by a single delegate.

Vilas (small towns) have their own *conselhos* or town councils which exert only a limited authority corresponding to their geographical area. Porto Santo has its own council. Things are liable to become quite turbulent when political factions hostile to the government, e.g. the PS (Socialist Party) or the Communist Party dominate these secondary governmental organs. At the municipal elections in 1989 the Socialists allied – albeit unsuccessfully – with the conservative CDS party against the present, all-powerful governing party.

ECONOMY

Madeira's economy is to a large degree dependent on tourism. However flowers, embroidery, basketry, Madeira wine and bananas are exported. Some 500,000 tourists visit the archipelago annually. There are plans to increase the number of available beds to 20,000 in the 1990s.

Primarily vegetables, wine grapes, bananas, willow trees and sugar cane are cultivated on the islands. Subtropical fruits such as passion fruit, avocados and anona thrive, but are not exported. Fish and livestock are destined for domestic consumption. Twenty-two percent of the population is involved in agriculture, 34 percent in industry and 44 percent in services.

The minimum income is a ridiculous 30,000 escudos per month. By comparison, regional prices are so shockingly high that as a rule, one income alone is not sufficient. Prices are generally higher here than in Portugal, and debts owed to the mainland are overwhelming.

Despite the revolution in 1974, Madeira was not quite able to escape the bonds of its previous feudal structure. The reality of this predicament in the country cannot be discerned from official statistics, but can easily be seen with one's own eyes...

POPULATION

With approximately 270,000 inhabitants spread out over 286 sq. miles (741 sq. km) Madeira is extremely densely populated. This fact is easy to establish just by taking a walk through the centre of Funchal. Conditions are a bit better on Porto Santo where only 103 people inhabit a single square kilometre.

The Desertas (three islands) and the Selvagens (two islands as well as several other small reef islands) are uninhabited – if you don't count the people attending the biological observation stations – and also belong to the archipelago.

GEOGRAPHY

The islands all share volcanic origins. You'll find yourself at the top of an enormous mountain range which rises up from 13,100 ft (4,000 metres) beneath the sea. The total land area of the entire archipelago is exactly 303.58 sq. miles (795.98 sq. km) with the geographical characteristics of each island quite distinct from one another. In stark contrast to mountainous and emerald-green Madeira, where the highest point, Pico Ruivo, is 6,100 ft (1,861 metres) above sea-level, is the gently rolling, almost barren landscape of the remaining islands. Porto Santo's highest mountain, Pico do Gacho, is 1,700 ft (517 metres) high.

On Madeira, the main island, there are no sandy beaches to speak of. Almost everywhere the coastline is characterised by steep cliffs which provide space only in a few areas for tiny fishing ports. The small beaches are composed of basalt scree. If you're looking for fine sand, you'll find it along Porto Santo's 5 mile stretch (9 km) of beach.

It is also worth mentioning that here on Madeira the rest of the "Laura Silva" the laurel woods, has been preserved, encouraging theories regarding continental displacement. Many areas in the archipelago are protected natural reserves attracting naturalists and film crews from all over the world.

CLIMATE

The climate in Madeira is consistent and warm; the annual average temperature varies between 16° and 22°C (61° and 72°F),

THE COLOUR OF LIFE.

A holiday may last just a week or so, but the memories of those happy, colourful days will last forever, because together you and Kodak Ektachrome films will capture, as large as life, the wondrous sights, the breathtaking scenery and the magical moments. For you to relive over and over again.

The Kodak Ektachrome range of slide films offers a choice of light source, speed and colour rendition and features extremely fine grain, very high sharpness and high resolving power.

Take home the real colour of life with Kodak Ektachrome films.

LIKE THIS?

OR LIKE THIS?

A KODAK FUN PANORAMIC CAMERA
BROADENS YOUR VIEW

The holiday you and your camera have been looking forward to all year; and a stunning panoramic view appears. "Fabulous", you think to yourself, "must take that one".

Unfortunately, your lens is just not wide enough. And three-in-a-row is a poor substitute.

That's when you take out your pocket-size, 'single use' Kodak Fun Panoramic Camera. A film and a camera, all in one, and it works miracles. You won't need to focus, you don't need special lenses. Just aim, click

and... it's all yours. The total picture.

You take twelve panoramic pictures with one Kodak Fun Panoramic Camera. Then put the camera in for developing and printing.

Each print is 25 by 9 centimetres. Excellent depth of field. True Kodak Gold colours.

The Kodak Fun Panoramic Camera itself goes back to the factory, to be recycled. So that others too can capture one of those spectacular phoooooooooootoooooooooooooos.

with water temperatures between 16° and 20°C (61° and 68°F). In spite of this, the image of "the island of eternal springtime" is misleading. It rains a lot, particularly from October to March, and it is rare during the summer months to find days completely without clouds. If you're looking for sunshine, your best bet is in the capital city Funchal. The humidity here is bearable; at other places on the main island it often reaches over 80 percent! At the turn of the century the allegedly excellent air encouraged the tubercular nobility to travel to the high altitudes of Monte and Santo da Serra in hopes of being cured.

There are various micro-climates that can be distinguished in Madeira. A semi-arid trade wind climate reigns along the southern coast and on Porto Santo, where there's altogether more sunshine during the course of an entire year. Theoretically, you can expect holiday weather the whole year round although you can never be 100 percent sure of what you'll encounter while you're there. In any case, you can rest assured that the weather will be better than what you've just left. Downpours during the winter can be quite drenching, but as a rule they don't last very long.

TIME ZONE

The time in Madeira corresponds to Greenwich Mean Time (GMT), which is one hour behind Central European Time (CET).

ELECTRICITY

The electricity supply is AC 220 volts. During heavy winter rainfalls there are sometimes blackouts, and during the summer the water supply will be occasionally cut off. However, all good hotels have reserve tanks at their disposals.

CULTURE & CUSTOMS

Great importance is attached to proper etiquette and everywhere you go the British influence is evident. Take into consideration what you would while travelling in any other Latin country, keeping in mind that the Portuguese are emotionally more reserved. Amongst friends the "social kiss" is customary – one on the left cheek, one on the right – but not between men. Generally, men shake hands, particularly in business situations. Topless sunbathing is frowned upon, though at large Lido Beach it is tolerated.

Hotels each have their own particular etiquette. In Funchal the emphasis is on being well-dressed; the image you present is important. Getting invited to somebody's house carries much greater social significance than in our part of the world and usually happens only within the context of the family. Most social contacts take place in cafés; no island native stays happily at home for long. In accordance with this, the concept of home decor is commonly totally different from what we're used to.

BUSINESS HOURS

You'll find banks just about everywhere you go and they all have the same exchange rates. Business hours are from 8.30 a.m.-3 p.m. The small bank **Totta e Açores**, located in the Savoy Hotel on the Avenida Infante, is also opened on Saturdays from 9 a.m.–12.30 p.m. In larger towns and on Porto Santo you'll find bank branches too. Most businesses are open weekdays from 9 a.m.-1 p.m. and from 3 p.m.–7 p.m. and Saturdays from 9 a.m.–1 p.m. Shopping hours on Saturdays are extended before Christmas. All shopping centres are open from 10 a.m.–10 p.m, large supermarkets until 8.30 p.m. or 9 p.m. Both the Hipermercado and the supermarket Lido-Sol (you'll find them on the tourist strip above Lido) keep their doors open until 10 p.m! Office hours generally correspond to those in most of Europe.

HOLIDAYS

National holidays fall on 1 and 25 January, 25 April, 1 May, 10 June, 15 August, 5 October, 1 November and 1, 8 and 25 December. Further holidays are specifically tied to various areas, for example 21 August in Funchal. No one works during sliding holidays, e.g. on Fat Tuesday, Ash Wednesday, Palm Sunday, Good Friday, Easter Sunday and the Feast of Corpus Christi.

In Madeira there are numerous and joyously celebrated festivities whereby, of course, you have to distinguish between those primarily organised for the sake of tourists and those deeply rooted in religion which take place in villages. The **New Year's Eve firework display**, with its sea of lights in the city of Funchal and boat cruises in the harbour, is famous.

February is the month for **Carnival**, with parades styled on those in Brazil.

In April the **Festival of Flowers** takes place, also in the form of a parade.

A **Music Festival** is organised in June, and in August it is often impossible to find a free hotel room because of the international **Madeira Wine Rally**.

In September, the month of the grape harvest, there's good reason to celebrate the **Wine Festival** treading the grapes and tasting different wines.

Musical Bands rendezvous in Ribeira Brava in October to be followed soon after by **Christmas** festivities.

In addition to all these, further festivals are celebrated by the larger hotels. Unfortunately, to find out the exact dates of these events you must scan the daily newspapers or enquire at your hotel reception.

The most important religious holiday takes place on 15 August in Monte in honour of the **Patron Saint of Madeira.**

Country festivals include the **Sheep Shearing Festival** in June, the **Apple Festival** in September (Ponta do Pargo) and October (Camacha), and the **Chestnut Festival** in November (Curral das Freiras). The **Folklore Festival** in Santana is usually organised in July. For further information and the exact dates of festivals determined on the basis of the lunar calendar, enquire at TURISMO.

FESTIVAL PROGRAMME

JANUARY

5: *Santo Amaro*, at Santa Cruz.
20: *S. Sebastião*, at Caniçal, Câmara de Lobos.

FEBRUARY

3: **S. Brás**, Arco da Calheta.
On the two Thursdays before Carnival: *Festa dos Compadres Carnival*, at Santana and other locations throughout the island.

APRIL

Middle to end of April: *Festa da Flôr* (Flower Festival), Funchal.

APRIL/MAY

Moveable feast: *Esperito Santo* (Whitsuntide), Camacha.
13 May: *Nossa Senhora de Fátima*, in Funchal.

JUNE/JULY/AUGUST

International Sport and Games Competitions: bridge, car rallies, swimming, tennis, cycling; held in Funchal.

JUNE

Festival of Classical Music, Funchal.
13: *Santo António*, Santo da Serra, Santo António.
24: *S. João*, at S. João, S. Martinho, Camara de Lobos, Lombada, Ponta do Sol, Fajã da Ovelha etc.
29: *S. Pedro*, at Câmara de Lobos, Ponta do Pargo, Ribeira Brava
End of June: *Festa das Tosquias* (Sheep-Shearing Festival), at Santana, Paúl da Serra.

JULY

Moveable feasts: *Festa do Senhor*, Santa Cruz.
Santa Maria Madalena, Porto Moniz, Madalena do Mar.
22: *Santa Ana*, Santana.
26: *"24 Horas a Bailar"*, at Santana.
Weekends, middle to end of July: *Folklore Festival "24-hour dance"*, Santana.
Feira Agro-Pecuária (Agricultural Fair and Festival), Porto Moniz.

AUGUST

1st Sunday: *Nossa Senhora do Monte* (Madeira's patron saint), Monte.
14/15: *S. Laurenço*, Camacha.
Last Sunday: *S. Francisco Xavier*, Calheta.
Festa do Santissimo Sacramento, Machico.
Nossa Senhora do Livramento, Curral das Freiras.

SEPTEMBER

1st Sunday: *Nossa Senhora dos Remédios*, Quinta Grande.
Nossa Senhora da Piedadet, Caniçal.
3rd Sunday: *Festa do Vinho Madeira* (Wine Festival), Estreito de Câmara de Lobos, Funchal.
Middle to end month: *Festa do Pêro* (Apple Festival), Ponta do Pargo.

OCTOBER

1st Sunday: *Festa do Rosàrio*, S. Vicente.
8/9: *Nossa Sehnora do Livramento*, Ponta do Sol.
A Sunday at end of month: *Festa do Senhor dos Milagres*, Machico.
Festival de Bandas, Ribeira Brava.
Festa da Macã, Camacha.

NOVEMBER

1: *Festa da Castanha* (Chestnut Festival), Curral das Freiras.
Moveable feast: *S. Martinho*, S. Martinho, etc.
30: *Santo André Avelino*, Canhas.

DECEMBER

8: *Nossa Senhora da Conceiçao*,Ribeira Brava, Câmara de Lobos, Machico.
31: *New Year's Eve* (Firework Display), Funchal.

COMMUNICATIONS

POSTAL SERVICES

There are post offices – *correios* – all over the islands of Madeira and Porto Santo, but as a tourist you'll probably fare best in the **Main Post Office** on Avenida do Zarco. Here you'll find English-speaking postal employees and convenient business hours (8.30 a.m.–8 p.m). You can even make a telephone call right up until 10 p.m! The main post office is open on Saturdays from 9 a.m.–12.30 p.m. and is closed all day Sunday. When sending letters, don't be fazed by the little glue pots; just watch what the natives do and follow suit!

TELEPHONE, TELEX & TELEFAX

In the opening pages of all local telephone directories you'll find a list of international dialling codes, as well as emergency numbers. Rather than trying to make a long distance call from a coin-operated telephone (the success rate is generally very low), use the small *credifone* cards instead. Telephone booths that accept these cards are marked and not difficult to find. Cards are available at the post office and at some kiosks. Night rates for long-distance calls unfortunately don't go into effect until midnight and stop at 8 a.m. The previously mentioned main post office has telex and telefax services.

MEDIA

Naturally, it's important for holiday-makers interested in hiking to get a weather report. Local radio stations are planning to broadcast a special report furnishing this particular information.

BOOKS & MAGAZINES

The usual travel guides and brochures can be found in TURISMO in a variety of foreign languages. However, many of them are fairly outdated. For walkers, a good book to buy is John and Pat Underwood's "hiking guide" *Landscapes of Madeira*. There is also a series of quite good publications covering flowers found on Madeira, each volume with a different emphasis. Maps are handed out free of charge as is also the tourist English-language magazine *Madeira Island Bulletin*, and the brochure *Hello Madeira*, put out in four different languages. These publications are issued monthly. The bus schedule "Madeira By Bus" is kept up-to-date and can be purchased at TURISMO for 100 escudos. Most of the aforementioned literature can also be found at the reception areas of good hotels and at various kiosks. Photographers are best off consulting with TURISMO's Public Relations Department (Promoçao), located right next-door to the tourist office on Avenida Arriaga 18.

NEWSPAPERS

There are two local daily newspapers: the *Diário de Notícias do Funchal* and the *Jornal da Madeira*. If you can understand the language at all, it's worth purchasing one of these in order to get information concerning current events which is not always available at TURISMO. The two weekly newspapers on the island are *Eco do Funchal* and *O Parcial*. All Portuguese newspapers published on the continent are also available, as are English newspapers (with only a day's delay).

TELEVISION

The sole regional television channel presents good films in the original (with subtitles) particularly on Wednesdays, Fridays and Saturdays. These are usually good English and American productions. The five-star hotels (the Casino Park Hotel and the Carleton) have acquired satellite discs. As a rule, cinema films are not synchronised.

RADIO

Local radio stations broadcast excellent music programmes and are already planning a radio service for tourists beginning in the 1990s. BBC World Service can be received on shortwave at the following times (GMT):

8 a.m.	to	4.15 p.m.	17705 kHz
8 a.m.	to	8.30 p.m.	15070 kHz
4 p.m.	to	11.15 p.m.	12095 kHz
6 a.m.	to	9.15 a.m.	9410 kHz
6 p.m.	to	11.15 p.m.	9410 kHz

EMERGENCIES

DOCTORS & CHEMISTS

You'll find plenty of chemists even in smaller towns and on Porto Santo. There is always one which is open around the clock; on every chemist's door you'll find the current schedule posted. There are many medications that should be available only with a prescription but which you can often get without one. In theory, over-the-counter sale of these medicines is illegal.

Portuguesa, Rua Joao Tavira. Tel: 20028
Mendes, Rua Joao de Deus. Tel: 35244
Santa Maria, Rua Boa Viagem 20. Tel: 21384
Confiança, L. Phelps 19. Tel: 22528
Carmo, L. Phelps 8. Tel: 23788
Morna, Rua Dr Fernao Ornelas 23. Tel: 22600
Avenida, Rua do Alube 51–55. Tel: 20709
Central, Rua do Bettencourt. Tel: 20439
Nacional, Rua dos Ferreios 60. Tel: 23510
Luso Britanica, Rua dos Netos 68–70. Tel: 22529
Chafariz, L. Chafariz 13. Tel: 20759
Almeida, Rua Joao Tavira 39. Tel: 23366
Honorato, Rua da Carreira 62. Tel: 23297
Dois Amigos, Rua Câmara Pestana 10. Tel: 25547
Inglesa, Rua Câmara Pestana 23–25. Tel: 20158.

MEDICAL FACILITIES

In an emergency, many hotels will arrange for their respective hotel doctors to come, but this can turn out to be quite expensive. As a rule, the payment for a consultation with a doctor must be made immediately. Ask for a receipt which you can then present to your own health insurance company back home. Generally, you won't have any trouble getting reimbursed. If you really want to be sure to do everything absolutely correctly, before going to the doctor pay a visit to the **DRSP, Centro de Saúde de Bom Jesus**, Rua da Hortas 67, tel: 29161. Open: 9.30 a.m.–noon and 2 p.m.–4 p.m.. Here you can obtain a medical insurance booklet valid everywhere in Portugal.

In extremely urgent emergencies go directly to one of the hospitals or private clinics (outside Funchal, go to one of the Centros de Saúde). For more minor aches and pains the **Centro Médico da Sé**, located directly next to the cathedral, can be recommended. English is spoken here.

Ambulance can be called by dialling 41115.

General emergencies: Emergency number 20000. A total of 115 hospitals and clinics are linked in to this number.

Hospital Cruz de Carvalho, Avenida Luís de Camôes. Tel: 42111.

Clínica da Carreira, Rua Câmara Pestana 24. Tel: 21001.

Clínica de Santa Catarina, Rua 5 de Outobro 115. Tel: 20127.

Cruz Vermelha, Largo Severiano Ferraz. Tel: 20000.

Centro Médico da Sé, Rua dos Murças 42. Tel: 30127.

Centro de Saúde Machico, Queimada, Água de Pena. Tel: 96121.

Centro de Saúde Porto Santo, Estrada do Penedo. Tel: 982211.

Animal clinic: VET-Funchal, Calçada da Cabouqueira 61. Tel: 44883.

Getting Around

INFORMATION

Tourist information is available at the tourist information centres TURISMOS. The central office is easy to find on Avenida Arriaga 16. Tel: 25658. There are other branch offices in Câmara de Lobos, Machico and at the airport Santa Catarina. On Porto Santo the TURISMO regional office is located on Delegação do Governo. Tel: 982361. The centre is open 9 a.m.–8 p.m. and on Sundays and holidays 9 a.m.–6 p.m; on 25 December, 1 January and Easter Sunday it is closed. Smaller TURISMO branch offices are open only during regular working days.

The representative of the **Portuguese Chamber of Commerce** (ACIF) is located in Edifício D. Henrique on Avenida do Infante. Tel: 30137.

The **Automobile Club** can be reached through Club Sports da Madeira, Avenida Arriaga 43. Tel: 37313.

DOMESTIC FLIGHTS

Inter-island flight traffic bound for Porto Santo is regulated by the small airline company LAR. They offer four flights per day; usually two in the morning and two in the evening. You can book a flight at all travel agencies, as well as at TAP, the national Portuguese airlines office.

BY BOAT

Crossing with the fast ferry is less expensive than flying and takes about 1½ hours. The boat makes the trip once a day with the exception of Tuesdays. Two freighter ships, the *Madeirense* and the *Vila Baleira*, carry cars across but no passengers. However, there is some leeway regarding this rule and with a little talking you may be able to get yourself on board. For more information contact TRANSMADEIRA, Rua dos Tanoeiros 8-10. Tel: 32085, or enquire directly at the harbour.

During the summer the government-owned yacht *Pirata Azul* makes irregular voyages out to the Desertas: commencing in 1990, the yacht *Tamisa* will be making the trip weekly. Further information is available at appropriate agencies in the yacht harbour. (For more information pertaining to boat excursions along the southern coast, refer to the *Sport* section.)

BY BUS

City bus traffic is managed by the enterprise Horários do Funchal. The bright orange buses are easy to spot; you can board at any of the bus stops in Funchal. (When you want to get off all you need to do is raise your arm slightly!) If you plan to use the bus service frequently, you're best off purchasing a tourist pass. These are valid during your entire holiday stay on all routes. (Passes are available at business pavilions in the Funchal bus station along the Avenida do Mar.) It's best to buy single tickets before you board as they are more expensive when bought on the bus. Small cancellation machines are located in every bus.

All the rest of the country bus lines are operated by other companies and depart from the bus station. On these lines, tickets are purchased after boarding (the person who sells them will eventually come round). It's highly recommended that you obtain a copy of the bus schedule *Madeira By Bus* from TURISMO (Zentrale), and if you need further assistance, consult with the personnel at the information desk. The locations of bus stops depicted on the general map are prone to frequent change, so don't hesitate to ask once again at the bus station itself just to make sure. You just have to say the name of your destination accompanied by baffled gestures and someone is sure to come to your rescue.

The following are a few examples of bus routes: Buses to the **Botanical Garden** leave approximately every half hour from 7.30 a.m.–10.30 p.m. Departures for **Monte** are about every 15 minutes from 4 a.m.–12.45 a.m. It has recently become possible to travel to **Porto Moniz** via Ribeira Brava and S. Vincente, leaving at 9 a.m. and arriving at 12

p.m. The return journey along the west coast begins at 4 p.m, depositing you at 8 p.m. back in Funchal (this extremely exhausting trip which allows only for a brief stay in Porto Moniz). Theoretically you can hop aboard a bus at any of the stations it stops at between major destinations, the only difficulty being at places where no schedules are posted. In this case, you either have to try to estimate when a bus is most likely to come by, or ask advice from the locals. In general, you can rely on the schedule given.

BY CAR

The best way to get to know Madeira is by rented car. Keep in mind, however, that this pleasure is rather expensive on both Madeira and Porto Santo. A rented car costs about 5,000 escudos per day plus tax. In general, there is no mileage limit. If you rent a car for 7 days the price will come down a bit. You have to be 21 or older and should have at least one year of driving experience. Credit cards are accepted. At some car rental agencies you can hire a chauffeur along with the vehicle.

Car Rental Agencies:
Atlantic, Estrada Monumental 239. Tel: 22880

Atlas, Av. Infante (Shell service station). Tel: 23100

Avis, Largo António Nobre 164. Tel: 63495

Budget, Estrada Monumental (Hotel Duas Torres). Tel: 25619

Europcar, Estrada Monumental 306. Tel: 28116

Hertz, Rua Ivens 12. Tel: 26026

In addition to these international car rental agencies, there are a number of local enterprises; your hotel reception can put you in touch with them, or if you're feeling brave, take a look through the yellow pages in the local telephone book. Motorcycle fans can also find contacts here, but generally speaking, due to the dangerous nature of most streets this form of transportation is uncommon. Enquire about Mini-Mokes and Jeeps.

On Porto Santo a good place to try is *Moinho*, Rua Dr Nuno Silvestre Teixeira 13. Tel: 982403. Here you can also find Mini-Mokes for 6,000 escudos per day, or 40,000 escudos for an entire week.

Taxis are relatively inexpensive. Fares are fixed, but if your journey is to be on the long side, it pays to discuss the price in advance. In case of a misunderstanding, ask for the price list every taxi driver is obliged to have handy. On this list the fare from the airport to the Funchal city centre is given as 2,160 escudos, for instance. For shorter rides the fare is calculated on a 120 escudos base rate plus 6 escudos per 328 ft (100 metres). A complete tour around the island costs 10,000 escudos. After 10 p.m. you're required to pay an additional charge of 20 percent.

DRIVING TIPS

Madeira may be a paradise for rally drivers, but it can be quite harrowing for average drivers. The people of Madeiria have a distinctly anarchic driving style which includes a relaxed attitude towards fastening seatbelts and drink driving. Despite this, accidents are rare, probably due to the fact that no one is concerned with asserting their right of way to the bitter end and drivers pay more attention to actual patterns of traffic than to road signs. Drive carefully and be considerate. It's not unusual to hear someone honk approaching a sharp curve or have them overtake you in a daredevil manoeuvre. Officially, cars in Madeira are driven on the right-hand side of the road.

WHERE TO STAY

HOTELS & PENSIONS

The inhabitants of Madeira are proud to be associated with a quality holiday destination. High quality service always comes first and, indeed, the personnel in most hotels is extensive. Hotels falling into the middle category sport 3 or more often, 4 stars. Depending on the level of comfort, the price for a double room ranges between 7,000 and 11,000 escudos. Hotels in this category usually boast pools (often located on sun roofs), rooms with balconies and bathrooms, as well as other customary facilities such as bars, restaurants and television rooms. Receptions often prove themselves to be veritable mines of information and can put you in touch with or direct you to who or what you are seeking. A "very British" air still wafts through many hotels and it seems difficult to imagine operating things any differently. Luxury hotels offer double rooms ranging in price from 15,000 to 38,600 escudos. If you're looking to find good value for your money, pensions are your only choice. However, they usually don't have much to offer in the way of comfort, are located in busy city centres and charge at least 4,000 escudos for a double room.

The number of stars following the names of hotels and pensions indicate the quality of the accommodation.

Price Range:
The comfortable, very British oriented **Savoy** (☆☆☆☆☆) charges from 17,000–20,000 escudos for a double room, and from 12,000–20,000 for a single.

At the **Carleton** (☆☆☆☆☆), formerly the Sheraton Hotel, rates for a double room range between 18,800–36,800 escudos, singles between 12,400–21,400 escudos.

At the new **Baia Azul** (☆☆☆☆) a double room costs between 9,000–19,000 escudos, a single room from 8,100–13,500 escudos.

The architecturally attractive **Monte Carlo** (☆☆☆) offers double rooms from 5,000–7,500 escudos, singles from 3,500–4,750 escudos.

In the city centre **Pension Monte Rosa** has double rooms at 4,400 escudos and single rooms for 3,300 escudos.

At the **Pousada do Pico do Arieiro** a double room costs 9,700 escudos, a single 8,400 escudos.

FUNCHAL

Top Hotels

Reid's (☆☆☆☆☆), Estrada Monumental. Tel: 23000/23011. 158 rooms.

Savoy (☆☆☆☆☆), Avenida do Infante. Tel: 22031. 353 rooms.

Carleton (☆☆☆☆☆), Largo António Nobre. Tel: 31031. 371 rooms.

Casino Park Hotel (☆☆☆☆☆), Rua Imperatriz D. Amélia. Tel: 33111. 368 rooms.

Madeira Palácio (☆☆☆☆☆)Estrada Monumental. Tel: 300001. 260 rooms.

The **Reid's** and **Savoy** are the most British hotels of all; at Reid's, don't forget to bring along a tie, as men aren't allowed in the bar without one. The **Carleton** maintains the old Sheraton standard, the **Casino Park Hotel** offers its guests noble but not always cozy Niemeyer architecture. The **Madeira Palácio** is lovely hotel with an international atmosphere, located outside of Funchal.

☆☆☆☆ Hotels

Girassol, Estrada Monumental. Tel: 31051. 133 rooms.

Quinta do Sol, Rua Dr. Pita 6. Tel: 31151. 116 rooms.

Raga, Estrada Monumental. Tel: 33001. 159 rooms.

Vila Ramos, Azinhaga da Casa Branca 7. Tel: 31181. 116 rooms.

São Joao, Rua das Maravilhas 74. Tel: 46111/23/4/35. 208 rooms.

Baia Azul, Estrada Monumental. Tel: 29 197. 215 rooms.

Windsor, Rua das Hortas. Tel: 33081. 67 rooms.

Santa Isabel, Avenida do Infante. Tel: 23111. 69 rooms.

Eden Mar, Rua do Gorgulho 2. Tel: 62222. 105 rooms.

Of the hotels listed, the **Vila Ramos** is perhaps well worth singling out on account of its particularly tasteful atmosphere and tranquil setting. The **Baia Azul** and **Eden Mar**, two new hotels, are post-modern in style with elegant interiors. The **Windsor** is located right in the middle of the city and is therefore quite convenient for both people on business and passionate city-dwellers.

Apartment Hotels

Alto Lido (☆☆☆☆), Estrada Monumental. Tel: 29197. 115 rooms.

Apartamentos do Mar (☆☆☆☆), Estrada Monumental. Tel: 31001/6. 140 rooms.

Navio Azul (☆☆☆☆), Estrada Monumental 240. Tel: 26031. 43 rooms.

Duas Torres (☆☆☆), Estrada Monumental 239. Tel: 30061. 266 rooms.

Gorgulho (☆☆☆), Rua do Gorgulho 1. Tel: 30111/4. 226 rooms.

Florassol (☆☆☆), Estrada Monumental 306. Tel: 33121. 250 rooms.

Buganvilia (☆☆☆), Caminho Velho da Ajuda. Tel: 31015. 212 rooms.

Mimosa (☆☆☆), Casa Branca, Caminho Velho da Ajuda. Tel: 31021. 200 rooms.

Lido Sol (☆☆☆), Estrada Monumental 318. Tel: 29006. 88 rooms.

Santa Luzia (☆☆☆), Rua Pedro José de Ornelas 33 B. Tel: 23045. 38 rooms.

Casa Branca (☆☆☆), Caminho Velho da Ajuda. Tel: 30043/4. 74 rooms.

Belo Sol (☆☆☆), Caminho Velho da Ajuda. Tel: 62332. 128 rooms.

Machico Atlantis (☆☆☆☆☆) former Holiday Inn, Água de Pena-Machico, 9200 Machico. Tel: 962811. 290 rooms.

Dom Pedro (☆☆☆☆), Vila de Machico, 9200 Machico. Tel: 962751. 218 rooms.

Machico (☆☆☆), Pracete do 25 Abril, 9200

THE KODAK GOLD GUIDE TO BETTER PICTURES.

Good photography is not difficult. Use these practical hints and Kodak Gold II Film: then notice the improvement.

Move in close. Get close enough to capture only the important elements.

Frame your Pictures. Look out for natural frames such as archways or tree branches to add an interesting foreground. Frames help create a sensation of depth and direct attention into the picture.

One centre of interest. Ensure you have one focus of interest and avoid distracting features that can confuse the viewer.

Use leading lines. Leading lines direct attention to your subject i.e. — a stream, a fence, a pathway; or the less obvious such as light beams or shadows.

Maintain activity. Pictures are more appealing if the subject is involved in some natural action.

Keep within the flash range. Ensure subject is within flash range for your camera (generally 4 metres). With groups make sure everyone is the same distance from the camera to receive the same amount of light.

Check the light direction. People tend to squint in bright direct light. Light from the side creates highlights and shadows that reveal texture and help to show the shapes of the subject. If shooting into direct sunlight fill-in flash can be effective to light the subject from the front.

CHOOSING YOUR KODAK GOLD II FILM.

Choosing the correct speed of colour print film for the type of photographs you will be taking is essential to achieve the best colourful results.

Basically the more intricate your needs in terms of capturing speed or low-light situations the higher speed film you require.

Kodak Gold II 100. Use in bright outdoor light or indoors with electronic flash. Fine grain, ideal for enlargements and close-ups. Ideal for beaches, snow scenes and posed shots.

Kodak Gold II 200. A multipurpose film for general lighting conditions and slow to moderate action. Recommended for automatic 35mm cameras. Ideal for walks, bike rides and parties.

Kodak Gold II 400. Provides the best colour accuracy as well as the richest, most saturated colours of any 400 speed film. Outstanding flash-taking capabilities for low-light and fast-action situations; excellent exposure latitude. Ideal for outdoor or well-lit indoor sports, stage shows or sunsets.

INSIGHT GUIDES

COLORSET NUMBERS

You'll find the colorset number on the spine of each Insight Guide.

Machico. Tel: 963511/12. 6 rooms.

Parque Santo da Serra (☆☆), Casais Próximos-Santo da Serra, 9200 Machico. Tel: 55136. 8 rooms.

Caniço Roca Mar (☆☆☆☆), Caniço de Baixo, 9125 Caniço. Tel: 933334. 37 rooms.

Galomar (☆☆☆☆), Caniço de Baixo, 9125 Caniço. Tel: 932410. 36 rooms.

Alpino Atlántico (☆☆☆☆), Caniço de Baixo, 9125 Caniço. Tel: 932443. 30 rooms.

Pensao Residencial a Lareira, Sítio da Vargem, 9125 Caniço. Tel: 932494. 18 rooms.

Dom Pedro Garajau (☆☆☆), Garajau-Caniço, 9125 Caniço. Tel: 932421. 282 rooms.

Pensions
Penha de França (☆☆☆☆), Rua Penha de França 2. Tel: 29080/7/8/9. 35 rooms.

Monte Rosa (☆☆☆☆), Rua Joao Tavira. Tel: 29091/4. 39 rooms.

Sirius (☆☆☆), Rua das Hortas 31-37. Tel: 26117. 23 rooms.

Monumental (☆☆☆), Estrada Monumental 306. Tel: 26117. 44 rooms.

Astória (☆☆), Rua Joao Gago 10-30. Tel: 23820. 16 rooms.

The aforementioned pensions comprise only a small selection of available pensions; when in doubt, consult with a TURISMO agent. Although it's not cheap, the **Penha de França** is highly recommended for its architecture. **Monte Rosa** and **Sirius** are city pensions; the latter is especially neat and clean. The pension **Monumental** is an alternative on the tourist strip and the **Astória**, located in the shadow of the cathedral, makes a good base.

PORTO MONIZ

Porto Moniz Calhau (☆☆☆☆), Vila-Porto Moniz, 9270 Porto Moniz. Tel: 852104. 15 rooms. The Pension Calhau has really earned its four stars!

Orca (☆☆☆), Sítio das Pogas-Porto Moniz, 9270 Porto Moniz. Tel: 852359. 12 rooms.

Santana O Colmo (☆☆☆), Sítio do Serrado, 9800 Santana. Tel: 57478. 8 rooms. This pension is relatively new and presents itself rather coolly. Don't expect the atmosphere you'd find in the little Santana houses. It is, however, a good starting point for hikes along the northern coast. If you'd prefer an alternative, enquire in the village.

RIBEIRA BRAVA

Brava Mar (☆☆☆), Vila da Ribeira Brava, 9350 Ribeira Brava. Tel: 952220/24/28. 51 rooms.

Hotel Porto Santo (☆☆☆☆), Ribeiro Cochinho, 9400 Porto Santo. Tel: 982381. 93 rooms.

Praia Dourada (☆☆☆), Rua Dr. Pedro Lomelino, 9400 Porto Santo. Tel: 982315. 35 rooms.

Palmeiras (☆☆), Vila Baleira, 9400 Porto Santo. Tel: 982212. 25 rooms.

Central (☆☆☆), Rua Colonel Abel Magno Vasconcelos, 9400 Porto Santo. Tel: 982226. 12 rooms.

SPECIAL ACCOMMODATION

For those who appreciate the offbeat and prefer to escape the bustling tourist centres, the following accommodations are recommended.

Pousada dos Vinháticos, Serra d'Ãgua, 9350 Ribeira Brava. Tel: 952344. 14 rooms.

Pousada do Pico do Arieiro, Pico do Arieiro, 9800 Santana. Tel: 48188. 22 rooms.

Estalagem da Montanha (☆☆☆☆), Sítio das Neves – S. Conçalo, 9000 Funchal. Tel: 20500. 10 rooms.

For tourists travelling with a backpack and tent there are only two campgrounds to choose from. One of these is located on **Porto Santo**, the other in **Porto Moniz**, along the northwestern edge of Madeira. Pitching a tent spontaneously in some out-of-the-way place is tolerated as it is still done only rarely.

Visitors sporting backpacks but without tents are best off enquiring at the TURISMO agency regarding the previously mentioned list of private quarters available. Those in doubt about the type of accommodation they want could begin by contacting **Vila Toca**, Senhor Manuel de Sousa, Rua dos Ilhéus 63, Funchal. Tel: 29581. (English is spoken here.) A double room costs about 2,500 escudos, a single room 1,500 escudos.

All **pensions located in smaller towns** – and this applies to both Madeira and Porto Santo – are quite reasonably priced and generally have rooms available from the TURISMO office. On Porto Santo you can obtain addresses of privately run accommodation.

The government-managed mountain huts, **Casas do Abrigo**, are usually not very accessible to tourists. Theoretically, you have to apply for one in writing long before your projected date of arrival and even then the chances of getting into one are pretty slim. If you still want to try your luck, get in contact with the **Presidência, Governo Regional**, Quinta Vigía, Avenida do Infante. Tel: 20042. The mountain huts located on Pico Ruivo present an emergency solution for undemanding guests, though these should also be booked in advance.

CONFERENCES

Conference facilities can be found at the Casino Park Hotel and the Carleton. As of late these two hotels have really made an effort to attract "conference tourists". Information regarding off-shore banking and the free trade zone is available from the representative of the Portuguese Chamber of Commerce ACIF, Edifício Dom Henrique, Avenida do Infante. Tel: 30137.

FOOD DIGEST

CUISINE

On Madeira you can still eat well and relatively inexpensively. The island's national dish is *espetada*, ox meat roasted on the spit. Traditionally the meat should be grilled on a laurel spit, but today most restaurants serve it on an iron one suspended over the table. *Carne vinho d'alhos* is a speciality made from pork and available mainly at Christmas time; pieces of meat are marinated in wine and garlic before being fried in pork drippings. In the fish department you'll find *espada*, or swordfish, prepared in one of at least a hundred different ways, just about everywhere on the island. *Espada á Madeira* is served with bananas. *Atum*, usually offered as tuna fish steak, is always fresh and tasty. Fresh fish include *pargo* (brace), *garoupa* (bass) and a special delicacy – not necessarily corresponding to everyones' taste buds – *lapas*, which are limpets. Most other fish is imported from the mainland; Madeira itself has no shellfish to offer.

Naturally, specialities of continental Portuguese cuisine are also available, for instance *bacalhau* (dried cod) in all its many variations and *cozido à Portuguêsa*, a kind of butcher's platter. Typical side dishes include *milho frito* (cornmeal croquettes), sweet potatoes and occasionally *inhame* (yams). *Bolo do caco* is a well-known bread made of sweet potatoes and backed in a stone oven. From a wide range of desserts, puddings – especially maracuja pudding – are well worth mentioning. *Bolo de mel*, actually a Christmas cake, is served all year round and is a much appreciated gift to take when you go visiting. It stays good for about a year and is roughly similar to gingerbread.

And, of course, there's no way of escaping Madeira wine. Many restaurants serve customers a complimentary glass. In the country, cocktails originally thought to be medicinal, are popular. *Poncha*, a famous/infamous mixture of sugar cane schnapps, honey and lemon juice, is said to be a speedy remedy for a cold. The excellent table wines are imported from Portugal and are therefore not inexpensive. The island's own beer called *Coral* is light and delicious.

Because the working population of Funchal tends to eat out in restaurants for the midday meal, there are numerous opportunities in the city centre to find a reasonably priced *almoço*. On average, the daily special will cost you about 500 escudos and snacks are even cheaper. In restaurants falling into the middle category, you can have a meal for between 700–1,200 escudos. Prices in haute cuisine restaurants offering national and international specialities start at about 2,000 escudos.

RESTAURANTS

As there are about 300 restaurants and 200 bars (most of which serve at least snacks) on the island of Madeira, you won't have to worry about finding something to eat. The best tip is to follow your own nose. In any case, you can be sure of a delicious – if expensive – meal in any of the speciality restaurants housed in five-star hotels, frequented also by the high society diners of Madeira.

OLD FUNCHAL

If you're looking for an extra-special dining experience in or outside Funchal, try the **Estrela do Mar** where the owner himself prepares international delicacies, including lobster, at guests' tables. Keep in mind that this is not the place to go if you're trying to stick to a budget.

Right next-door in the Zona Velha in the old part of the city on Largo do Corpo Santo is **A Romana**, an establishment that prides itself on its prominent guest list.

If you happen to find yourself in the old section of the city late at night, pay a visit to **Banana's**, located directly opposite A Romana. This simple, earthy restaurant with very pleasing prices remains open as long as its guests stay awake.

A hot insider tip, the **Bar Jacquet**, is also located in the old part of the city, directly next to the market (Rua de Santa Maria 5).

Here customers just about come to blows for a place to sit down, gladly accept the fact that they're going to have to wait awhile and as if that weren't enough, happily put up with a variety of good-natured impertinences from the boss.

In addition to creating mouth-watering fish specialities, his mother cooks up delicious oregano chips. Fastidious guests are better off keeping their eyes on their plates; prices do not exactly correspond to the exceedingly simple decor.

On the Avenida do Mar (actually named Avenida dos Comunidades Madeirenses) you'll find the **Caravela**, one of few restaurants commanding a panoramic view. Prices here range between the middle and upper categories, but are well justified due to the lovely view.

CITY CENTRE

Among the many restaurants located in the city centre the following are recommended: the **Apolo** (situated next to the cathedral); the self-service **Pátio** (on account of its lovely inner courtyard) entered either from the Avenida Zarco or Rua da Carreira; **Xaramba** (if you're hankering for a piece of pizza), located in Rua da Carreira 67, as well as at the yacht harbour and in the old part of the city); the **Golden Gate** on Avenida Arriaga 25 and **O Celeiro**, perhaps best suited for an evening meal (middle price range, Rua dos Aranhas 22). If your taste tends towards simpler fare, try the **Lido Surf** (right next-door to O Celeiro) or the **Londres** (located at Rua da Carriera 64) where many Funchal natives spend their lunch hours.

If you're in a hurry you can grab a quick bite to eat while standing at the **Penha d'Águia**, located directly behind the cathedral, or at **Comempé**, situated in the Bazar do Povo Shopping Centre. In the latter you can even order sausage with mustard!

The **Fim do Século** (Rua da Carriera) is brand-new and especially favoured by lovers with a liking for imitation turn-of-the-century flair. If you're heading in the direction of the tourist zone, the snack bar **Santa Catarina (Avenida do Infante 22)** serves quite good, lighter meals; be sure and try their delicious fruit juices. Across from the Savoy is the restaurant **A Rampa**, specialising in Italian cuisine.

IN THE TOURIST ZONE

Four restaurants especially worth mentioning in the tourist zone are the **Moby Dick**, **Sol e Mar**, **Toca do Polvo** and **Doca do Cavacas**. The latter two are middle-range fish restaurants with lots of atmosphere. The most delicious fish is served at **Gavinas**, but it is on the expensive side. You can get a reasonably priced midday meal on the **Esplanade of the Lido Swimming Pool** without even changing out of your bathing suit! (The restaurant is also open to non-swimming visitors.) In the higher class areas around the Savoy and Carleton hotels you can eat well and expensively at the **Casa do Reis** and **Casa Velha** (both located on Rua da Imperatriz D. Amélia).

If Chinese food is more your style, try the **Hong Kong** (in the Olimpo Shopping Centre), for vegetarian fare visit the **Alpendre do Pátio** (a natural foods restaurant located in the previously mentioned Pátio in the city centre) and for salad specialities go to the **Saladerie** (Centro Comercial Navio Azul).

If you're looking for the perfect midday meal complete with everything you could ever imagine, reserve a table at the **Quinta Magnólia**. Reservations here are mandatory and can be made one to two days in advance (tel: 64013). For around 2,000 escudos – not including beverages – you'll be spoiled in fine style by students of the hotel management school.

OUTSIDE FUNCHAL

Outside Funchal you can get a good, substantial meal at **Casa do Abrigo do Poiso** with its cosy fireplace, regional specialities and reasonable prices. **Victor's Bar** in Ribeiro Frio specialises in trout and has the atmosphere of a log cabin. Or how about the **Coral** in Câmara de Lobos, where you also might want to pay a visit to the simple bar on the beach. Other restaurants worth noting include the **O Boieiro**, located on the main street to Caniço (Sítio das Figueirinhas), **A Rede** (in the municipality of Santa Cruz, Lojas Ventur, Rua 5 V), **O Galo** (Caniço de Baixo), **Guiseppe Verdi,** known for its homemade pasta (Caniço), **Albatroz** with its wonderful ambience (in the beach club Albatroz, Santa Cruz, Sítio da Terça), **Stop** in S. Gonçalo where the speciality is grilled chicken (Sítion da Igreja) and **Churrasceria Montanha** (S. Gonçalo, Sítion das Neves), where in addition to the fantastic view there is music and dancing – at a corresponding price, naturally.

ESPETADA RESTAURANTS

Some of the aforementioned restaurants entertain diners with music. **A Seta**, an enormous *espetada* restaurant at Estrada do Livramento 80, has been doing this for years. Apropos *espetada*, the most down-to-earth restaurants serving all kinds of meat dishes are to be found in Estreito de Câmara do Lobos. Once you've made it into this vicinity, just let your nose be your guide!

The **Casino Park Hotel** offers **shows** – regularly and irregularly – during mealtimes. Don't worry about wearing a tie; Reid's is the only place where it's obligatory.

Take-away-services have recently become quite popular. The restaurant **A Faca**, located in the residential area Bairro da Nazaré, Avenida do Colégio Militar 6-8, is especially speedy and good. So far there aren't any McDonald's on Madeira...

COFFEE CULTURE

The **Coffee and Tea House Pluma** is especially romantic. It's a family-run business in the garden of a little quinta situated directly opposite the Hotel Dom João, Rua das Maravilhas 13b. Since most social contacts are cultivated over a *bica* (espresso), it's important to be familiar with a few cafés open during the day where you can partake in normal Funchal city life. Usually men meet at the **Café Funchal**, located just next to the cathedral, while older women frequent the **Apolo** for their afternoon *bicas*. Art and politics students have a preference for the **Pátio**; at the beginning of the century this was the main meeting place in Funchal. The **Golden Gate** with its aura of nostalgia is pleasant, though a bank has now taken over the ground floor. It is now principally visited by the government employees and prominent politicians working just across the street. To top the list is the **Theater-Café**, its clientele composed mainly of people involved with art and culture, or who are just a little bit off the wall.

THINGS TO DO

Many different agencies offer a variety of tours. Don't be surprised if you find yourself in a "multiple-language" bus. This situation may well contribute to a better understanding of people in general, but it is at the expense of understanding the commentary on the island. Hiking tours, especially *Levada* hikes, are organised.

Madeira is a great place for walking, and a number of English tour operators run special walking holidays. Most operators offer a range of programmes catering for different levels of ability. The companies include:

Castaways, Travel House, 2/10 Cross Road, Tadworth, Surrey. Tel: 0737 812255.

Classic Collection Holidays, 9 Liverpool Terrace, Worthing, West Sussex. Tel: 0903 823088. This company also specialises in botanical holidays in Madeira.

Exodus Expeditions, 9 Weir Road, London SW12. Tel: 081-675 5550.

Prestige Holidays, 14 Market Place, Ringwood, Hants. Tel: 0425 480400.

Ramblers Holidays, Box 43, Welwyn Garden City, Herts. Tel: 0707 331133.

For wine buffs, a company called **Fourwinds Holidays** (Bearland House, Longsmith Street, Gloucester; tel:0425 27880) specialises in wine holidays in Madeira.

For those wanting to arrange organised excursions *in situ*, there are plenty of travel agents in Funchal.

PARKS & NATURE RESERVES

The Botanical Garden and Bird Park, Caminho do Meio. Tel: 26035. Open: daily 8.30 a.m.–6 p.m.

The **Quinta Magnólia** (park, swimming pool, restaurant and bar operated by the school for hotel management), Rua Dr Pita, Funchal. Tel: 64013. Open: daily 8.30 a.m.–6 p.m.

The **Quinta do Palheiro Ferreiro** (Blandy's Garden), located 6 miles (9 km) outside Funchal in the direction of Camacha. Further information is available at Blandy's Travel Agency. Tel: 20161. Open: workdays 9.30 a.m.–12.30 p.m.

The **Santo da Serra Park** in Santo da Serra. Open: daily.

The **Ribeiro Frio Nature Park**, always open.

The **Santa Catarina Park** in Funchal, Avenida do Infante, constantly accessible.

The **Quinta Vigia Park** (presidential palace), Avenida do Infante, is open workdays 9 a.m.–5 p.m; it is necessary to inform the guard before entering.

The **Archaeology Park of the Quinta das Cruzes**, Calçado do Pico 1. Open: Tuesday–Sunday 10 a.m.–6 p.m.

The City Park, Avenida Arriaga, across from the theatre. Open: constantly.

A small **Nature Park** boasting native plants has recently been established along the north coast in **S. Vincente**.

A brand-new **Recreational Park** offering just about everything you can imagine is planned to open in the 1990s on the street leading towards **Monte**.

ENTERTAINMENT

Animation and entertainment for tourists and special groups are not very well developed on Madeira; people are only just beginning to consider the possibilities. Hotels organise their own events, parties and **fashion shows**, and there are **Folklore Evenings** offered nearly everywhere you go.

CHILDREN

Traditionally Madeira is an island better suited for middle-aged and older tourists than for children. There are no generous sandy beaches for kids to play on and for younger children the few places where it is possible to bathe can prove dangerous. Because of this, activities for youngsters are pretty much limited to splashing around in the swimming pool. The large hotels will supply babysitters for 500–800 escudos per hour. If the kids need a good romp, take them to either Santa Catarina Park in Funchal, Avenida do Infante, or to the Quinta Magnólia, Rua Dr Pita, Funchal. Madeirans are extremely fond of children.

CULTURE PLUS

ARCHITECTURE

CHURCHES, CHAPELS & MONASTERIES

The chief site are **Funchal Cathedral**, the **Colégio Church**, the **Santa Clara Monastery**, the **Santa Clara Chapel** and the **Corpo Santo Chapel**. Agents at the TURISMO office will point out the exact location of these churches on the city map. None of them maintains regular visiting hours or offers tours.

Outside the city of Funchal the **Church of Santa Cruz** and the **Church of Monte** are worth seeing, though only culture buffs are likely to think they merit special journeys. They contain some real jewels in terms of religious architecture.

FORTRESSES & BUILDINGS OF CIVIL ARCHITECTURE

Generally speaking, the following edifices can only be surveyed from the outside: the **São Lourenço, Pico** and **São Tiago** castles, the **Government Palace**, the **Quinta Vigia** and the **Old Customs House**, and the **Alfândega Velha** which is currently home to the regional parliament. Most of these buildings house public offices and are only accessible to people involved with them.

MEMORIALS

There are only a small handful of memorials worth mentioning and these can be discovered while taking a walk through Funchal. The large **Zarco Statue** on Avenida do Zarco and the statue of **Nossa Senhora da Paz** in Terreiro da Luta, above Monte, are two you might want to take a look at. The **Quinta Nossa Senhora da Conceiçao** in Monte is only open on weekdays; relevant signs are hanging across from the little bar which belongs to the memorial, in the direction of Barbosas.

MUSEUMS

Museu de Arte Sacra (Museum of Sacred Art), Rua do Bispo 21, Funchal. Open: Tuesday–Saturday 10 a.m.–12.30 p.m. and 2.30 p.m.–5.30 p.m, Sunday 10 a.m.–12.30 p.m.

Casa-Museu Frederico de Freitas (Museum of Decorative Art), Calçada de Santa Clara, Funchal. Open: Tuesday–Saturday 10 a.m.–12.30 p.m. and 2 p.m.–6 p.m.

Museu Quinta das Cruzes (Museum of Decorative Art), Calçado do Pico 1, Funchal. Open: Tuesday–Sunday 10 a.m.–12.30 p.m. and 2 p.m.–6 p.m.

Museu Henrique e Francisco Franco (museum of 20th-century painting), Rua do Bom Jesus 13. Open: workdays 9 a.m.–12.30 p.m. and 2 p.m.–5.30 p.m.

Museu Municipal (aquarium and museum of natural science), Rua da Mouraria 31, Funchal. Open: Tuesday–Friday 10 a.m.–8 p.m; Saturday, Sunday and holidays noon–6p.m.

Museu Photographia Vicentes (Museum of Photography), Rua da Carreira 43. Open: Tuesday–Friday 2 p.m.–6 p.m.

Museu da Cidade do Funchal (Museum of the City of Funchal), Praça do Município (the city hall). Open: workdays 9 a.m.–12.30 p.m. and 2 p.m.–5.30 p.m.

Museu de História Natural (Museum of Natural History), Caminho do Meio, Quinta do Bom Sucesso (in the botanical Garden). Open: daily 9.30 a.m.–12.30 p.m. and 2 p.m.–5.30 p.m.

Museu da Madeira Wine Company, Adegas São Francisco (the museum of wine), Avenida Arriaga 28. Open: Monday–Friday 10.30 a.m.–3.30 p.m. (Tours are also offered.)

Museu Biblioteca Barbeito (An exhibition of the history of Madeira and of Columbus), Avenida Arriaga 48. Open: workdays 10 a.m.–1 p.m. and 3 p.m.–7 p.m, Saturday 10 a.m.–1 p.m.

Museu do Vinho (The Wine Institute), Rua 5 de Outobro 78. Open: workdays 9.30 a.m.–noon and 2 p.m.–5 p.m.

Museu do Bombeiro (The Fire Brigade Museum), Estrada Luso-Brasileiro. Open: Sunday 9 a.m.–1 p.m.

The IBTAM Museum (The Institute for Handicrafts), Rua Visconde Anadia 44. Open: workdays 9 a.m.–12.30 p.m. and 2 p.m.–5.30 p.m.

All these museums are located in Funchal. So far there is only one museum outside of Funchal, the **Whale Museum** in Caniçal.

GALLERIES

There is a permanent **Exhibition of Contemporary Art** at the **Quinta Magnólia**; other art galleries are rare. The TURISMO **Gallery**, Avenida Arriaga 18, and the little **Machico TURISMO Gallery**, Ribeirinho, Edificio Paz both present temporary exhibitions. The private art gallery **Funchália** is located in the Lido Shopping Centre (in the hotel complex Eden Mar).

BOOKSHOPS & LIBRARIES

There are two book shops which offer a selection of foreign language literature: the **English Bookshop**, Rua da Carreira 43 (Pátio) and the **Livaria Esperança**, on Rua dos Ferreiros 119. The best library is the **Direçao Regional Assuntos Culturais** (DRAC) in Rua dos Ferreiros.

Public libraries include the **Calouste Gulbenkian**, located in the Praça Município and Avenida Arriaga (by the Theater-Café), the library in the **Palácio São Pedro**, Rua da Mouraria 31 (historical archives), as well as a few smaller branches situated throughout various parts of the city. Two new, little libraries, are the **Sala de Leitura "American Culture Corner"** (America) and the **Sala de Leitura e Biblioteca de Simon Bolivar** (Venezuela), both housed in the TURISMO office. The **Barbeito** library, on Avenida Arriaga 48, is also new. Here a selection of books about Columbus is at your disposal.

MOVIES & THEATRE

Of all the local cinemas two in particular are recommended: the **Cine Casino**, which is a part of the casino complex (Avenida do Infante), and the **Cine Deck** in the Centro Comercial Navio Azul. Occasionally special films are shown in the small cinema at the Dom João Shopping Centre, Caminho Dom João 27.

Unfortunately concerts, theatre and ballet performances are extremely rare. If they do take place, they are usually held in conjunction with festivals and are not publicised sufficiently. Don't hesitate to ask for information at TURISMO if, due to a deficiency of Portuguese, you can't decipher the daily newspapers.

SHOPPING

SOUVENIRS

If you want to get a good overall impression of the handicrafts produced on the island, pay a visit first to the **Casa do Turista**, where you'll find a large selection of native arts and crafts elegantly displayed.

Among the loveliest souvenirs available are different kinds of embroidered goods. But beauty has its price, and it's best to purchase the finest needelwork directly from the various embroidery factories.

If you're interested in acquiring some samples of basketry, your best bet is in Camacha, although there are also a few outlets in Funchal, for example **Sousa & Gonçalves**, located in Rua do Castanheiro 47.

You can find Madeiran wine just about everywhere you look! If you'd like to taste a little before buying, stop first at **Madeira-Wine**, **Barbeitos** or **Oliveiras**.

Boots made of goat hide, woollen hats, caps and all kinds of other folkloric items are sold on the streets and in the usual tourist shops, as is also the delicious *bolo de mel*.

The best place to buy flowers is at the market, but they can be purchased some at the airport. Officially you are not allowed to transport fresh fruit and *tremoços* (lupin seeds) out of the country.

FASHION

Madeirans are quite fashion-conscious, and clothes are competitively priced. A quick – or longer – look in the Benetton and Stefanel shops may prove worth your while.

You'll also find quite a large selection of attractive shoes at good prices. You can purchase footwear by Charles Jourdan and Christian Dior for about £40 at **Helio**. Good quality Portuguese shoes are stocked at **Cloé**, **Godiva** and **Artecouro**, all of which are located both in the city centre and in the larger shopping centres. The latter company also manufactures other leather goods, though these sell for only slightly less there than they do elsewhere. Younger visitors may want to take a look at Hera shoe fashions, available at **Mattas** (Rua dos Ferreiros). If your feet are not particularly choosy, there are cheap shoes to be had everywhere.

NIGHTLIFE

PUBS

If you're looking for a place in which to relax and have a drink after dinner you'll find a fair number of pubs to choose from. The problem is that there aren't very many good ones. Recommended for the young and young-at-heart is **Berilights** (located on the corner of Estrada Monumental and Rua do Gorgulho), offering good music and peppy decor. If you'd rather gander at the Funchal yuppie population in all its multi-generational glory, try the **Salsa Latina**, Rua da Imperatriz D. Amélia. An excellent local band (sometimes guests too), does its best to keep the atmosphere pulsing.

Pubs still maintaining a British character include **Joe's Bar** and the **Pombo Mariola**. The drinks here are quite good. **Number Two**, Rua do Favila, right next to the Carleton, is the most well-known bar with the reputation of being a good place to pick up a friend.

Last but not least, if you can't decide exactly where to go, head over to the pubs and restaurants in the **Funchal Yacht Harbour** where there's always something going on. Don't expect to find much excitement in the east in Caniço, Santa Cruz or Machico, although there are attractive pubs in many smaller town centres. Better-known is the pub next to the restaurant **A Rede** in Garajau and the **Boite des Hotel Atlantis**.

NIGHTCLUBS

The belief that Madeira doesn't have any nightlife to speak of is pure prejudice. The nightclubs and bars in the **Casino Park** and **Carleton** hotels are quite attractive and the **Galáxia**, located in the Savoy, is also pleasant, if a trifle conservative. At the Casino Park Hotel guests are offered a well-rounded **Show Programme** and **Cabaret**, and you can get rid of the money burning a hole in your pocket right next-door in the **Casino da Madeira** with a game of bingo or blackjack.

The rather more louche clubs are generally marked with a red light. If you want to just take a look around, your best bet is in the **Zona Velha**, in the old part of Funchal. Here a few places you might want to check out: **Mambo**, Rampa D. Manuel, **Porto Rico**, Rua das Hortas, **Jaguar**, Rua 5 de Outobro, **Royal**, Rua 31 de Janeiro, and **Kalifa**, Rua Conde Canavial.

DISCOS

If a night at a good disco is more your style, try the **Art Rock** (generally a younger clientele), Caminho Velho da Ajuda; the **Pombo Mariola**, Rua Carvalho Araújo; **Rock's** or **Vespas**, both located on the same street as Pombo Mariola. The natives tend to congregate in the **Jet Set**, Rua da Alfândega; **Reflex**, Travessa da Praça, and in the **Duas Torres** hotel disco on Estrada Monumental.

FADO & JAZZ

If you've got your heart set on a night of *fado*, pay a visit to **Marcelino**, Travessa das Torres. Keep in mind that although *fado* is closely associated with Portugal, it has relatively little to do with Madeira. Right next-door you'll find the **Jazz-Club**. With a little luck you can show up right on time for a good jam session.

SPORTS

GOLF

The golf course with the most beautiful view of the sea is situated in Santo da Serra, Quinta do Lago, 9100 Santa Cruz; tel: 55321 and 55139. Up until now golfers have had to content themselves with 9 holes, but plans for a total of 27 have already been completed. Don't forget to bring along your handicap certificate; lessons to improve your strokes are also available. If you didn't bring your clubs along, you have the option of either renting or buying a set. Plans for a golf course on Porto Santo have not yet been realised.

RIDING

If you're interested in horse riding, get in touch with the Hotel Estrelícia, Caminho Velho da Ajuda; tel: 30131. They will also organise your transportation to the riding club (Hipismo). Plans to open a riding centre on Porto Santo are also on the drawing board. (For further information contact the TURISMO office there.)

TENNIS

Because tennis has become akin to a national sport on Madeira, tennis courts are numerous. All the larger hotels have their own and can also put you into contact with tennis teachers, if you so desire. In Quinta Magnólia, Rua Dr Pita, the setting is quite lovely and the court fees are especially reasonable. Don't forget to check in punctually at the little gatekeeper's house at the entrance. This advice also applies in regard to the squash courts.

WATERSPORTS

Madeira offers a wide variety of watersports, including swimming, diving, windsurfing, sailing, as well as deep-sea fishing.

SWIMMING

Many large hotels, including the Savoy, Carleton and Aparthotel Do Mar, boast swimming pools with beach access. As a rule, entrance fees are rather steep (between about 500–2,000 escudos). Public swimming pools charging more reasonable entrance fees (from 150–250 escudos) are:

Lido, Rua do Gorgulho. This is the largest swimming pool on Madeira with room for more than 3,000 visitors! Lounge chairs and sun umbrellas cost extra and must be paid for at the cashier's. Those who only want to soak up the sun while having a drink or two must pay 40 escudos to get in.

Quinta Magnólia, Rua Dr Pita. This heated swimming pool is set in the middle of a lovely park. It is frequently visited by school classes and is especially suitable for families with children.

Club Naval do Funchal, Estrada Monumental. It is not necessary for tourist to be members here; for a minimal entrance fee you can use their access to the beach as well as the club rooms. Various watersport activities are also available.

Club de Turismo, Estrada Monumental. This club cultivates an exclusive image. The only way to reach the beach is by lift!

Barreirinha, located behind the old part of the city (the S. Tiago Castle). This is an antiquated swimming pool in the old area of the city which is almost exclusively frequented by the natives.

Beach-Club Albatroz, Santa Cruz, Sítio da Terça. A tranquil, seldom visited private club located on the property of a quinta.

Galo, in Caniço de Baixo (next to the Galomar). Access to the beach is via a path through the cliffs. Here it's easy to spend the entire day just hanging out.

Children and senior citizens might feel more comfortable at the **Dom Pedro Garajau Indoor Swimming Pool** in Garajau, or the **Olympia Swimming Pool at the Matur holiday resort.**

The natural **Sea Water Swimming Pools** at **Port Moniz**, located on the northwest tip of Madeira, are especially beautiful and, it's said, beneficial for your health.

If you're not averse to stony beaches, you'll find a string of them in the small towns on the southern coast, from Ponta da Sol to Machico. And for those who refuse to deprive themselves of the feel of sand between their toes, don't forget the **small, sandy beach Prainha in Caniçal**, as well as the **large sandy beach on Porto Santo**.

All the swimming pools mentioned here are open 9 a.m.–6 p.m; during the summer hours are somewhat extended.

DIVING

Manta Rainer Madeira Diving Club: There are diving bases in Galomar in Caniço de Baixo. Tel: 932410 (private: 932010) and at the Carleton Hotel in Funchal. From here you can join up with a group heading off to explore the underwater national parks. Diving equipment, cutters and a decompression chamber are at your disposal; diving courses are also available.

Atalaia, in Roca Mar, Caniço do Baixo. Tel: 933334. Here diving equipment and courses are offered. If it's more convenient, you can get in touch with this club through the Hotel Pedro in Machico.

Urs Moser Diving Center, Porto Santo. Tel: 98216. (Open: from the beginning of May until the end of October). You can hire all your diving equipment and boat. Courses are also offered. There are excursions for beginners, as well as for those with many years of experience.

WINDSURFING

The only windsurfing school is located on Porto Santo (Alugabarc on the beach at Porto Santo). You can rent surfboards from just about all good hotels, including Hotel Porto Santo, Reid's, the Casino Park Hotel, the Carleton and the Savoy.

SAILING

If you are interested in sailing, the two sailing yachts *Albatroz* and *Mont Carmel*, both moored in the yacht harbour at Funchal, are available. Enquire directly on board or at any of the small agencies located in the yacht harbour. To date, it has not been possible to hire sailing boats without crews.

DEEP-SEA FISHING

Get in touch with either of the following two operations: Turipesca; tel: 31063 and 42468 (hours: 9.30 a.m.–4.30 p.m. daily), or Amigos do Mar; tel: 24390 (departures contingent on registration). Both are situated in the yacht harbour in Funchal. It is also possible to arrange for other, less-involved excursions and special requests are considered.

EXERCISING & FITNESS TRAILS

Nearly all larger hotels offer exercise programmes. The fitness centre in the Casino Park Hotel, under the artistic and professional management of Sian Lesley, is in particular worth recommending. (Here you can also indulge in a sauna, massage, whirlpool bath, etc.)

There is a fitness trail in Quinta Magnólia.

A new recreational centre called Relax, offering mini-bowling, billiards and gambling machines has just opened its doors across from the Hotel Madeira Palácio Complex Piornais.

SPECTATOR SPORTS

Hardly any sport is not played with enthusiasm in Madeira, but soccer remains an all-time favourite. (There are three teams which participate in the Portuguese National League!)

For further information, sports fans should enquire directly at the Direçao Regional dos Desportos, Rua da Carreira 43 (Pátio); tel: 33561/62. Here you'll get information regarding both places to watch and places to participate in sports, as well as details of international tournaments (tennis, swimming, cycling, bridge, rallies, etc). They can also put you in contact with any of the numerous sports clubs. Hotels organise internal and international championships too.

LANGUAGE

PRONUNCIATION

If you go to Portugal thinking you'll be able to make yourself understood in Spanish, you're in for a big surprise. They may be able to understand you, but you won't be able to understand a word they say back, since in Portuguese the vowel sounds are frequently flattened out or completely swallowed. And, as if that weren't enough to make things difficult, "s" (except when it comes at the beginning of a word) is pronounced "shh". All this tends to give you the impression that what you're hearing is a Slavic rather than a Latin language! "E", when it falls at the end of a word, is scarcely audible and "o" is often pronounced as "u".

So don't be alarmed if, when you are paying for something, you're asked for "shkudsh"; what's meant here are plain old *escudos*. When saying *Bom dia* (Good day), the "om" is slightly nasalised. After midday *bom dia* is transformed into *Boa tarde*, pronounced "boatart" (Good afternoon).

The following are a few pronunciation examples which indicate special cases:

Se faz favor (please), pronounced "se fash favor". A "z" at the end of a word is pronounced "sh".

A simple "r" is rolled only once and not several times, as is common in other Latin languages. The double "rr", found in *carro* (car) for example, is "rolled"; an "o" found at the end of a word is spoken as "u", therefore *carro* is pronounced "carru".

Generally speaking a "c" when it precedes a, o and u is pronounced "k", for instance in the word *a Conta* (the bill). This holds true unless it is accompanied by a cedilla, as in *açucar* (sugar), which is pronounced "assukar". If the "ç" falls in front of an e or i, it is pronounced as "s", for example *çedo* (early) is pronounced "sedu". The "j" of *jardim* (garden) is soft and corresponds to the "g" in the English word genie.

The odd plural endings "ães" and "ôes", like the Portuguese ending "cão", are spoken like a nasalised "tion".

Don't forget that *obrigado* means thank you. (The original feminine form *obrigada* has gradually been phased out over time.)

USEFUL WORDS & PHRASES

Please
por favor/Faz

Thank you
obrigado/a

Yes/no
sim/não

Excuse me
desculpe/com licença

Waiter, please…
faz favor… Garçom!

How much is it?
Quanto custa isto?

Where are the restrooms?
Onde é a casa de banho?

Can you tell me…?
Pode-me dizer…?

where/when/why
onde/quando/porquê

Can you please help me?
Ajude-me, por favor.

I'm lost
Perdi-me.

What does that mean? I don't understand.
O que significa isto? Não compreendo [Não entendo].

Where is the… consulate?
Onde fica o consulado…?

Place names	Pronunciation
Achada da Serra	Ashada d'a séra
Calheta	Caljéta
Caniçal	Canissal

Câmara de Lobos	Camara de Lobsh
Estanquinhos	Eshtangkingush
Funchal	Fungshal
Jardim de Serra	Sharding d'a Séra
Jardim Municipal	Sharding Municipál
Palheiro	Paljéru
Paúl da Serra	Powl d'a Séra
Pico dos Barcelos	Piku dush Barcelush
Portela	Portéla
Porto Moniz	Portu Monish
Porto Santo	Portu Santu
Pico do Arieiro	Piku du Ariéru
Ribeiro Frio	Ribéru Fríu
Santa Cruz	Santa Crush
São Lourenço	Sang Lorenssu
Seixal	Sé-ishal
Vinháticos	Vinhatikush

For information regarding Portuguese lessons enquire at hotels or in the language school Academia de Linguas da Madeira, Rua Ribeirinho de Baixo 33. Tel: 31069.

FURTHER READING

GENERAL

If you can read Portuguese or Spanish (the former is not at all difficult to decipher if you have a good working knowledge of Latin and Spanish), take a look in the library or at the retail outlet of the DRAC, Direçao Regional Assuntos Culturais, Rua dos Ferreiros 165. Both places possess an assortment of literature pertaining to Madeira.

USEFUL ADDRESSES

National Tourist Office
Secretaria Regional do Turismo
Avenida Arriaga 18
9000 Funchal

France
Avenida Infante 58
9000 Funchal
Tel: 25514

Great Britain
Avenida de Zarco 2, CP417
9000 Funchal
Tel: 21221

Holland
Rua Alfandega 1, 2nd Floor
9000 Funchal
Tel: 238310

Italy
Rua Bom Jesus
Escritorio 14, 1st Floor D
9000 Funchal
Tel: 23890

Spain
Rua Dr Juvenal 13a
9000 Funchal
Tel: 20076

USA
Avenida Luis Carmes
Edificio Infante/BI/B/AP/B/4
9000 Funchal

TOUR OPERATORS

Alternatives, Montpelier Travel Ltd
17 Montpelier Street
London SW7
Tel: 071-584 1050

Arrow Tours
40 West Street
Drogheda, County Louth
Ireland
Tel: 041-31177

Blackheath Wine Trails
13 Blackheath Village
London SE3
Tel: 081-463 0012

Cadogan Travel Ltd
9/10 Portland Street
Southampton
Tel: 0703 332661

Caravela Tours
38/44 Gillingham Street
London SW1
Tel: 071-630 9223

Castaways
Travel House, 2/10 Cross Road
Tadworth, Surrey
Tel: 0737 812255

Classic Collection Holidays
9 Liverpool Terrace
Worthing, West Sussex
Tel: 0903 823088

City Travel Service
116 City Road
London EC1
Tel: 071-251 6389

Destination Portugal
Madeira House, 37 Corn Street
Witney, Oxon
Tel: 0993 773269

Exodus Expeditions
9 Weir Road
London SW12
Tel: 081-6735 550

Fourwinds Holidays
Bearland House, Longsmith Street
Gloucester
Tel: 0425 27880

Holiday Islands Ltd
125 East Barnet Road
New Barnet, Herts
Tel: 081-441 4064

John Hill Travel (S&L) Ltd
Herbel House, 25 High Street
Belfast
Tel: 0232 232331

Latitude Forty Enterprises Ltd
13 Beauchamp Place
London SW3
Tel: 071-581 3140

Martyn Holidays
390 London Road
Isleworth, Middlesex
Tel: 081-847 5855

Portuguese Options
26 Tottenham Street
London W1
Tel: 071-436 3246

Prestige Holidays
14 Market Place
Ringwood, Hants
Tel: 0425 480400

Southfields Travel Limited
241 Wimbledon Park Road
Southfields, London SW18
Tel: 081-874 9019

Transair (Midlands) Ltd
216 Alcester Road, Drake's Cross
Wythall, Birmingham
Tel: 0564 82626

ART/PHOTO CREDITS

Photography by

Page 73, 83, 99, 103, 108/109, 135, 177, 234, 242/243, 254, 255, 262/263, 269, 270/271, 273, 275	**Archives Leonore Ander**
28, 30, 36/37	**Tony Arruza**
39	**British Museum London**
56, 193	**Casa Museu Frederico de Freitas**
35, 57, 59	**Dieter Clarius**
142, 143, 144/145, 156/157, 159, 161, 285	**Deimer/Monachus**
158	**Deimer/Schomer**
283	**Martina Emonts**
55	**Empresa Publica dos Jornais, Noticas e Capital**
52	**Foul Anchor Archives**
22, 72, 100, 102, 148, 167, 252/253, 282	**Thomas Grimm/Abacus**
98, 99, 101, 102, 103, 104, 105, 126/127, 231, 264, 266	**Günther Heubl**
154/155, 164, 163, 165, 288	**Monachus/FAW**
29	**Museu Nacional de Arte Antiga, Lissabon**
65	**National Maritime Museum Greenwich**
48/49	**New York Public Library**
3, 14/15, 16/17, 18/19, 20/21, 24/25, 67, 79, 81, 95, 98, 106/107, 110/111, 112, 113, 114, 118, 120, 121, 128/129, 130, 133, 140, 151, 153, 175, 176, 178/179, 181, 182, 187, 190, 191, 196, 197, 198/199, 207, 208, 224, 225, 228, 229, 251, 256, 268	**Gerhard H. Oberzill**
64	**Photographia Museu Vicentes, Funchal**
26/27, 32, 33, 38, 40, 42, 43, 53, 58, 66, 68, 76, 77, 78, 80, 82, 84, 85, 87, 88, 93, 96/97, 115, 116, 117, 122/123, 124/125, 131, 132, 134, 136/137, 138, 141, 146/147, 150, 152, 162, 168/169, 171, 172, 173, 174, 175, 182, 184/185, 188/189, 192, 194, 195, 200, 209, 210, 211, 212, 213, 214, 216, 218, 219, 220, 221, 222/223, 226, 227, 236, 237, 240, 241, 244/245, 246, 248, 258, 260, 261, 265, 266, 267, 274, 276, 277, 278, 279, 281, 286	**G.P. Reichelt**
31	**Victor Miguel Sousa**
44, 45, 46/47	**Scholastic Magazines Inc.**
287	**Turismo Funchal**
9, 34, 70, 71, 86, 91, 95, 149, 180, 230	**Bill Wassman**
61	**Weidenfels Archives/British Library**
50, 51	**Wilmington Society of the Fine Arts**
Maps	**Berndtson & Berndtson**
Illustrations	**Klaus Geisler**
Visual Consultant	**V. Barl**

INDEX

A

B

C